Building Sustainable Urban Settlements

Urban Management Series

Series Editor: Nick Hall

Titles in the Urban Management Series:

Building Sustainable Urban Settlements:
Approaches and Case Studies in the Developing World
Edited by Sam Romaya and Carole Rakodi

Communicating for Development:
Experience from the Urban Environment
Edited by Catalina Gandelsonas

Governing Cities: New Institutional Forms in
Developing Countries and Transitional Economies
Edited by Meine Pieter van Dijk, Marike Noordhoek and Emiel Wegelin

Planning in Cities:
Sustainability and Growth in the Developing World
Edited by Roger Zetter and Rodney White

Building Sustainable Urban Settlements
Approaches and Case Studies in the Developing World

Edited by

Sam Romaya and Carole Rakodi

PUBLISHING

Published by ITDG Publishing
103–105 Southampton Row, London WC1B 4HL, UK
www.itdgpublishing.org.uk

First published in 2002

ISBN 1 85339 541 2

A catalogue record for this book is available from the British Library.

ITDG Publishing is the publishing arm of the Intermediate
Technology Development Group.
Our mission is to build the skills and capacity of people in developing
countries through the dissemination of information in all forms,
enabling them to improve the quality of their lives and
that of future generations.

Index by Indexing Specialists (UK) Ltd, Hove, East Sussex
Typeset by J&L Composition, Filey, North Yorkshire
Printed in Great Britain
by bell & Bain Ltd., Glasgow

Contents

Foreword

WORKING TOWARDS PRACTICAL MEASURES FOR IMPLEMENTING THE HABITAT AGENDA IN THE 21ST CENTURY

The importance of learning lessons for practical sustainable development is generally underestimated. Making such information available for others to use is of critical importance in helping people to realize their own goals and aspirations for development. Only in this way will development become sustainable. People themselves are the drivers of change and indeed the drivers of the very fundamentals of development.

Learning from the experience of the practice of others is a theme that is being helped by this book, the outcome of the Inter-Schools Conference held in Cardiff in 1998. At the time I introduced some thinking on the issue of better dissemination of research findings. I believe much has been learnt in the intervening period and we are now better equipped to make more relevant information about development available to practitioners. This series of books is one example of that process.

The role of the Department for International Development (DFID) in disseminating a view on development started with the UK White Paper on International Development 'Eliminating World Poverty – A Challenge for the 21st Century'. Much has also been done collaboratively with UN-HABITAT, the Commonwealth and others in taking the issues of sustainable urban development forward in practical terms.

For the greater part of my 30 year professional career I have been a field operator, with the task of helping people realize their responsibilities and their ambitions in the realm of rapid urbanization and fast growing urban areas, the subject of the Cardiff conference. To take an example, there is the challenge, typically from local authorities, of setting out in the field new urban areas for say 1000 low income families – perhaps 5000 or more people – in perhaps a twelve month period. So, how to go about it? There are the 'conventional' techniques for assessing the practicalities of where best to offer the opportunity for urban expansion: survey techniques to understand the existing settlement, why it is where it is, and who lives there, the dynamics of its constituent parts; a socio-economic understanding of its growth patterns; the topography of the setting and surroundings offering the constraints and opportunities for expansion; together with the associated land tenure implications. In other words, all the ingredients to produce a sieve map of spatial concerns. Some of these are typically fairly lengthy procedures which often means they do not get done, or are not properly assessed, which can lead to inadequacies of operations.

Some of these procedures are vital; others are of a lower priority. Some are pointlessly time consuming, for example, the Cadastral procedures, which in some legal situations are necessary to achieve the full land tenure rights which would in turn provide a plot holder with recognized collateral for bank loans, may in part be overcome, and yes, there are methods for financial institutions to follow which can recognize a pooling of the tenure rights to give access to loans.

But, and this is a big but, do community leaders, activists and local bodies on the ground and in other new areas know this? And if not, how should they go about finding out about it? How do they know what it is that they don't know? Answering this conundrum is indeed the source of the power of knowledge. In many ways, this is the dilemma posed by the Habitat Agenda. Who is it for? And are they really benefiting through it?

I have a belief that finding out relevant information in the field is as difficult as it has ever been. And this when we have an information explosion on our hands – information is more and more available, and much of it is brilliant and useful (some perhaps is less relevant to a field operator). And yet it is people themselves that require information to help their own development. Helping people become practitioners is our greatest challenge, yet one which we can assist.

We are talking about driving 'by the seat of our pants'. But driving is nevertheless what I am attempting to do. So, a reminder about the Habitat Agenda. How does one go about finding out what it is about? There is the official documentation – The Istanbul Declaration, The Habitat Agenda, and The Global Plan of Action, not to mention the National Plans of Action, the Best Practices Programme and the Global Urban Indicators Programme – but it is tough reading and bewildering to try to find out what it means in practice.

The then-named United Nations Centre for Human Settlements (UNCHS), now UN-HABITAT, staged the Habitat II Global Conference or 'Cities Summit' at Istanbul in June 1996, and holds the primary responsibility for its dissemination. But it is individual nations that are responsible for its implementation, and that in turn means the people on the ground – the local governments, community leaders and neighbourhood activists.

What is interesting is how the Habitat Agenda has informed the leading joint world programmes such as the Urban Management Programme. The Sustainable Cities Programme forms the basis for the Global Urban Observatory – a combination of the original Global Urban Indicators Programme and the Best Practices and Local Leadership Programme. In this respect the issue of learning from the experience of others with a view to enabling the definition and articulation of requirements for development, both locally and on the larger scale, has become central to a theme of transfer of knowledge locally. This will be aided by dissemination techniques such as the 'tool boxes' required for effective transfer of knowledge in the field, coordinating and cross referencing what we already know, and thus providing the framework for what is yet to be known. This will provide a basis for examining place-specific knowledge learning, and places for people's access to knowledge and local level training for sustainable urban development.

For me this book is an essential first step on the path towards a greater understanding of the practical measures for implementing the Habitat Agenda locally. The more such practice can be shared amongst the people of the world, the better the world will become.

Michael Mutter
Department for International Development

The Urban Management Series

Nick Hall

The Urban Management Series focuses on the impacts of demographic and economic change in developing countries. The series offers a platform for practical, in-depth analysis of the complex institutional, economic and social issues that have to be addressed in an increasingly urban and globalized world. One of the UN's Millennium Development Targets calls for significant improvement in the lives of at least 100 million slum-dwellers by 2020, but this is a very modest target.

By 2025 it is estimated that two-thirds of the poor in Latin America, and a third to almost half the poor in Africa and Asia, will live in cities or towns. An estimated 600 million people currently live in life and health threatening homes and neighbourhoods. The urban poor face different issues and livelihood choices in comparison to the rural poor. The reduction of urban poverty requires appropriate policies and approaches. The livelihoods and rights of the poor must be at the centre of any strategy to reduce poverty and develop an inclusive society. This is equally true in urban areas.

Cities and towns, and the industrial and commercial activities located in them, are a positive force for national economic growth. This is why cities are popular: where you find the mass of bees is where to look for honey. Urban areas provide consumer markets and services for agricultural producers. They are also gateways to larger national, regional and international markets. But the opportunities from urban development have not been maximized by poor people. Their rights are curtailed and they are often excluded from accessing secure land, shelter, services, employment and social welfare due to the discriminatory practices of government, the private sector and civil society.

This series of books addresses the many challenges facing urban management professionals. First and foremost, they aim to improve understanding of the impact of urbanization on the livelihoods and living conditions of poor people. With better understanding, the institutional and political conditions for poor people to participate and benefit from the urban development process may be improved. New knowledge from research and dialogue should show how best to involve the private sector and civil society in mobilizing the necessary resources for inclusive and sustainable development; how to mitigate the impact that poor environments and natural hazards have on the poor; how to enhance the economic synergy between rural and urban economies; and how to strengthen efforts by the international community to coordinate support for a positive urbanization process.

Building Sustainable Urban Settlements recognizes that questioning the balance between economic growth and environmental goals is not a new debate. The contribution of this volume is to review some of the issues from the point of view not just of government policy makers and industrial operators, but also of low-income residents who live in close proximity to industrial and other enterprises, in their neighbourhoods or homes, and for whom the livelihood benefits of this proximity generally outweigh the adverse effects on their living environments. This is not to say that regulation is not needed, but that it needs to be sensitive to the importance of location in livelihoods.

The discussions collected here demonstrate that it is possible, given sound analysis, an appreciation of the needs and views of poor residents, as well as other urban actors and political commitment, to produce and maintain physical patterns of urban development that contribute to more environmentally sustainable resource consumption and waste management; provide a conducive environment for economic, social and cultural activities; and result in safe and healthy living and work environments for all residents.

Acknowledgements

The chapters published in this volume are a selection of the papers presented at the 15th Inter-Schools Conference on Development held in Cardiff from 29–31 March, 1998. They have been revised and updated for this publication.

The editors and the publishers are grateful to the Department for International Development (DFID) for making the publication of this book possible. They would also like to make it clear that the views expressed in the book are those of the individual contributors and are not necessarily the views of DFID nor of the editors.

In addition, the support of the Department of City and Regional Planning, Cardiff University, is duly acknowledged.

The publishers would like to thank Jeremy Horner/Panos Pictures for permission to use the cover photograph.

Figures

Boxes

Tables

Acronyms and abbreviations

AAK	Architectural Association of Kenya
ASCEND	Association for Settlement and Commercial Enterprise for National Development, Jamaica
CAPROM	Centro de Apoio e Promoção ao Migrante (Centre for the Support and Promotion of Migrants), Brazil
CBO	community-based organization
CEDEP	Centro de Evangelização e Educação Popular (Centre for Popular Education and Evangelism), Brazil
CEV	Comisión Especial de Vivienda (Special Housing Commission), Costa Rica
CIDCO	City and Industrial Development Corporation, Navi Mumbai (New Bombay), India
CODESA	Corporación Costarricense de Desarrollo (Costa Rican Development Corporation)
COFOPRI	La Comisión de Formalización de la Propiedad Informal (commission to regularize informal property), Peru
DANIDA	Danish International Development Assistance
DDA	Delhi Development Authority, India
DFID	Department for International Development, UK
EIA	environmental impact assessment
EIED	Environmental Impact Evaluation Division of the OEPP, Thailand
EIS	environmental impact statement
EPDP	Environment Protection Department Punjab, Pakistan
FCV	Frente Costarricense de Vivienda, Costa Rica
FDV	Frente Democrático de Vivienda, Costa Rica
FTZ	Free Trade Zone, China
GONGO	government-oriented NGO
HBE	home-based enterprise
IMF	International Monetary Fund
INVU	Instituto Nacional de Vivienda y Urbanismo (National Institute of Housing and Planning), Costa Rica
ITDG	Intermediate Technology Development Group, UK

MCN	Municipal Council of Nakuru, Kenya
MHUD	Ministry of Housing and Urban Development, Iran
MIVAH	Ministry of Housing and Human Settlements, Costa Rica
MLGNH	Ministry of Local Government and National Housing, Zimbabwe
MOSTE	Ministry of Science, Technology and Environment, Thailand
NEDP	National Economic Development Plan, Iran
NEQA	National Environmental Quality Act, Thailand
NGO	non-governmental organization
OEPP	Office of Environmental Policy and Planning, Thailand
ONEB	Office of National Environmental Board, Thailand
PI&MDD	Punjab Industries and Minerals Development Department, Pakistan
PLN	Partido Liberación Nacional, Costa Rica
PROFAC	Proyecto de Fortalecimiento de la Autogestión Comunitaria (Project for the Strengthening of Community Self-Management), Costa Rica
PRSP	Poverty Reduction Strategy Programme
RGP	Rincón Grande de Pavas, Costa Rica
SMEPB	Shanghai Municipal Environmental Protection Bureau, China
SMG	Shanghai Municipal Government, China
TERC	Technical Expert Review Committee, Thailand
ULO	Urban Land Organization, Iran
UNCHS	United Nations Centre for Human Settlements (now UN-HABITAT)
UN-HABITAT	United Nations Human Settlements Programme (formerly UNCHS)
ZEIS	Zonas Especiais de Interesse Social (special social and economic zones), Brazil

Introduction

Carole Rakodi and Sam Romaya

In this introduction, some of the concepts and issues central to the discussions in this collection are introduced, and the ways in which these themes are addressed by the following chapters are outlined. This is done by reflecting on the title of the volume, first examining what is meant by *sustainability*; second reflecting on whether the concept of a *sustainable urban settlement* is valid; and third by suggesting some of the implications of our focus on *building urban settlements*.

SUSTAINABILITY

Sustainability means that which can be maintained or perpetuated, something capable of being upheld or defended. It is derived from *tenire*, to hold, and has come to the fore in the context of concerns about resource depletion, environmental degradation and loss of biodiversity. It attributes value to ecological systems and environmental resources, either for their own sake or because of the dependence on them of human existence. In its strongest form, based on a belief that natural capital should be preserved intact, it leads to advocacy of a halt to further economic growth and population reduction, in the belief that current population has already, or will soon have, exceeded the carrying capacity of the earth, and that no technological 'fixes' that can be envisaged will be sufficient to avert environmental crisis. However, less ecocentric versions of environmental sustainability recognize that the implied perpetuation of social and economic inequities is unjustifiable and that, in any case, a significant proportion of the population in poor countries (and their cities) have consumption levels so low that they contribute little to the depletion of non-renewable resources and the generation of waste, including greenhouse gases. They also recognize that market forces will continue to provide incentives for resource exploitation, but that processes of technological change can contribute to less wasteful and environmentally destructive forms of resource use (see also Dodds, 2001).

Acknowledgement that the rights of poor people and countries should have priority over those of non-human life, and also that concerns over environmental deterioration are justified, underpins the concept of sustainable development, defined famously in the Brundtland Report and embodying three principles in dialectical tension: economic development, social justice and ecological responsibility (Gleeson and Low, 2000). Satterthwaite has developed this concept to apply to cities (Satterthwaite, 1997a):

Meeting the needs of the present . . .

■ Economic needs – *includ[ing] access to an adequate livelihood . . . also economic security when . . . unable to secure a livelihood . . .*

■ Social, cultural, environmental and health needs – *includ[ing] a shelter . . . within a neighbourhood with provision for piped water, sanitation, drainage, transport, healthcare, education and child development. Also a home, workplace and living environment protected from environmental hazards . . .*

■ Political needs – *includ[ing] freedom to participate in national and local politics and in decisions regarding management and development of one's home and neighbourhood, within a broader framework which ensures respect for civil and political rights and the implementation of environmental legislation.*

. . . without compromising the ability of future generations to meet their own needs

■ *minimizing use or waste of non-renewable resources – fossil fuels . . . scarce mineral resources . . . cultural, historical and natural assets within cities that are irreplaceable and thus non-renewable – for instance, historic districts and parks and natural landscapes*

■ *sustainable use of finite renewable resources – [e.g.] . . . freshwater resources . . . Keeping to a sustainable ecological footprint in terms of land area on which city-based producers and consumers draw for agricultural and forest products and biomass fuels*

■ *biodegradable wastes not overtaking capacities of renewable sinks (e.g. . . . a river . . .)*

■ *non-biodegradable wastes/emissions not overtaxing (finite) capacity of local and global sinks to absorb or dilute them without adverse effects (e.g. persistent pesticides; greenhouse gases and stratospheric ozone depleting chemicals).*

The activities located in cities and the utilities on which they depend are inherently consumers of natural resources. Inevitably, therefore, urban development means that natural capital will be depleted. There is, nevertheless, scope for improving environmental protection and quality and for less wasteful resource use by, for example: increasing densities where appropriate to reduce the energy consumed in transport; and converting open-ended waste disposal systems to closed loops by reuse and recycling. Of particular importance when considering environmental sustainability in the context of cities is what Haughton (1999) terms 'transfrontier responsibility', which requires that local policies should take account of the environmental impacts of activities carried out in one jurisdictional domain, in areas beyond its boundaries. Thus most of the resources used in cities are drawn from areas beyond their boundaries, and the wastes generated by the activities carried on in them may be discharged into local or global sinks. The former includes groundwater and rivers; the latter the oceans, as well as contributions to air pollution and greenhouse gases.

Although Satterthwaite (1997a) argues for restricting the use of the term 'sustainability' to 'environmental or ecological sustainability', in practice, in the absence of any other word with precisely the same meaning, the term is also commonly applied to other aspects of the development process. Some of these uses are quite problematic. For example, 'sustainability' may be applied to development, defined as continued economic growth. The potential incompatibility between the resource-using and waste-generating effects of economic growth and environmental sustainability are often recognized, and arguments for more appropriate patterns of economic development advanced, but the pressures of global competition, the conditionalities of international financial institutions and the lack of effective regulation of private sector companies mean that as the economies of poorer countries grow, the adverse environmental impacts are also likely to increase. Thus rather than being an end, sustainability may be seen as a desirable constraint on other goals such as economic growth (Marcuse, 1998).

In linking development with sustainability, both inter- and intra-generational equity are implied. However, economic growth (achieving and maintaining a baseline level of economic welfare) does not guarantee increased equity and reduced poverty. To reinforce the importance of the latter, the terms 'sustainable' or 'secure' are increasingly attached to the concept of livelihoods. The latter emphasizes reduced vulnerability (the ability to recover from shocks or stresses and maintain or enhance assets), while the former gives greater priority to not damaging the natural resource base on which rural livelihoods depend (Carney, 1998; Rakodi with Lloyd-Jones, 2002).

To reflect the importance of human rights, basic needs satisfaction and the aggregate of human capabilities, and to ensure that patterns of economic development are compatible with people's cultural and social values and lifestyles, the concept of 'social sustainability' is sometimes used. However, this may easily come to mean 'acceptable within the status quo' when social change (redistribution of wealth and power) is what is needed to achieve lasting poverty reduction. Sustainability and social justice may or may not be compatible, so that sustainability can best be used '. . . to emphasize the criterion of long-term political and social viability in the assessment of otherwise desirable programmes and not as a goal replacing social justice' (Marcuse, 1998, p. 111). In practice, sources often seem to confuse means with ends. For example, Basiago (1999) suggests that social sustainability encompasses 'notions of equity, empowerment, accessibility, participation, sharing, cultural identity, and institutional stability' (p. 149).

Finally, the term sustainability is also used with reference to the processes and structures responsible for organizing aspects of the process of development. Most broadly, institutional sustainability refers to the rules by which society is organized and human interaction guided (Valentin and Spangenberg, 2000). Administrative sustainability means ensuring that an organization, the tasks for which it is responsible, or the services it provides continue to function over the long term, and may subsume financial sustainability. It is likely to be positively correlated with economic growth, but also to depend on whether decision-making processes secure the support of the key sections of society, effectiveness and efficiency are rewarded, and the division of responsibilities and resources between levels of government and public sector agencies and other development actors is appropriate. It implies procedural equity, that is:

> . . . that regulatory and participatory systems should be devised and applied to ensure that all people are treated openly and fairly . . . [This does not just include] legalistic and bureaucratic procedures for establishing and enforcing obligations and rights [but] . . . needs to embrace wider processes of public engagement, where multiple democratic and participative forms and channels are brought into play to foster participation and engagement with processes of change.

> *(Haughton, 1999, p. 234).*

SUSTAINABLE URBAN SETTLEMENTS?

We have already noted that the collections of activities that take place in cities and towns are of necessity resource-consuming and waste-generating. In what sense, then, is it valid to refer to 'sustainable urban settlements', as the title of this book does? It can be argued that:

> It is not cities or urbanization that sustainable development seeks to sustain but [instead it aims] to meet human needs in settlements of all sizes without depleting environmental capital. This means seeking an institutional and regulatory framework in which democratic and accountable city and municipal authorities ensure that the needs of the people within their boundaries are addressed while minimising the transferring of environmental costs to other people or ecosystems or into the future.

> *(Satterthwaite, 1997a).*

Municipal governments are potentially in a good position to advance the goals of sustainable development because of their roles as direct or indirect providers of services, regulators, planners, builders, consumers and revenue generators. However, there are limits on their capacity to act, because of their limited autonomy and responsibilities, and even more limited resources. Consumption patterns are largely determined by market forces, and what scope there is for influencing and regulating these lies at the international and national rather than city level. Nevertheless, the populations concentrated in cities, especially their richer members, do make a major contribution to consumption. Although measures to reduce that consumption by more economical development processes and increased recycling are desirable, economic forces in the current global economy are, Gleeson and Low suggest:

> . . . *working precisely in the opposite direction. A world of individual cities . . . competing for 'growth' [defined purely as business activity] within a global market framework is not one which, in the long term, appears capable of ecological sustainability.*

> (Gleeson and Low, 2000, p. 23).

Moreover, the global and national institutional contexts are currently incapable of regulating the transfer of environmental risk and implementing policies for ecological sustainability.

In addition, in many countries there is only half-hearted commitment to decentralization, and devolved responsibilities are rarely matched by revenue-generation capacity or resource transfers. Vested interests resist constraints on their production and consumption activities. In addition, there are 'difficulties in converting buildings, settlement patterns, urban systems and energy, transport and waste disposal systems that developed during the last 40 years of low oil prices which are not easily modified for much reduced fossil fuel use' (Satterthwaite, 1997a). Nevertheless, this book is largely concerned with the scope and prospects for achieving physical patterns of urban development that contribute to the overall goal of sustainable development. However, sustainable development has economic, social and political as well as environmental dimensions, so attention will also be given to the organizational arrangements, actors and their capabilities, and processes of achieving change.

BUILDING URBAN SETTLEMENTS

In the context of sustainable development, the aims of 'city-builders' should be to produce and maintain physical patterns of urban development that provide a conducive environment for the economic, social and cultural activities that take place in cities; resulting in healthy, safe and pleasant living and working environments for all urban residents; and contributing to more environmentally sustainable consumption and waste management. This is not easy.

First, the built environment has a long life, and there is considerable inertia in inherited patterns, buildings and infrastructure installations. Second, there are conflicting interests within cities, between different types of economic activity and income groups, and with respect to any tract of land. Third, many of the concepts, ideas and tools that are currently informing the debate on sustainable urban development are, as in the past, emerging from Northern experience (for example, compact cities; see Jenks and Burgess, 2000), and are not necessarily appropriate or helpful in dealing with the environmental priorities of Southern cities. Fourth, much of the resource use and waste disposal affects areas beyond the city boundaries, and it is tempting for local politicians to ignore this wider ecological footprint of the city in their attempts to attract investment and deliver improved services and environmental quality to their constituents. Fifth, the capacity of public sector agencies, especially municipal government, to plan and manage development, devise and enforce regulations, and provide infrastructure and services, is limited, especially in the face of international pressures that reduce their room for manoeuvre, and in low-income cities.

It is possible to identify more appropriate approaches to planning and management than currently adopted; priority actions that can both improve the quality of the living environment, and help satisfy wider environmental aims; and guiding principles for future development that can learn from the experience of countries which are currently struggling to clean up the legacy of industrialization and to reduce the environmental impact of a reliance on fossil fuel-intensive patterns of energy and transport use. It is with these organizational arrangements and processes, environmental policies and living conditions that the papers in this collection are concerned. They deal with continuity and change; with renewal, adaptation and new development; and with a range of sectors, especially industry, housing and land.

THEMES AND CONTRIBUTIONS

The chapters that follow contribute to debates around one or more of a number of themes: processes and organizational arrangements for agenda-setting, policy formulation, planning and management; issues and responsibilities at the city and local levels; how to achieve more environmentally sound and equitable housing and living environments; and questions of social justice, social change and cultural suitability.

Part I contains a set of papers that explore processes of urban environmental management with respect to housing and economic activities. All examine some of the environmental implications of major urban land-users – housing, industry and other economic activities. More particularly, they focus on some of the policies, legislative instruments, planning processes and regulatory procedures that attempt to secure compatibility between land and building uses and improved urban environments.

Rizwan Hameed and Jeremy Raemaekers identify the main locations of industry in Lahore, Pakistan, and analyse the impact of their activities on adjacent residential communities and the physical environment. They then describe and assess the pollution control and land-use planning regimes regulating development, seeking explanations for their generally poor performance and assessing prospects for the future. David Shaw and his colleagues explore some of the institutional arrangements being used in Shanghai to try to deliver both rapid economic growth and a good-quality environment. They review the administrative arrangements for environmental planning and management in the municipal area, as well as a range of policies and actions, before presenting a detailed case study of the Waigaoqiao Free Trade Zone in the Pudong New Area. Orapim Pimcharoen and David Shaw examine the use of environmental impact assessment in Thailand, with respect to both its quality and its effectiveness in relation to wider planning and decision-making processes. Finally, findings are presented from an international comparative study of the effects of home-based enterprises on the residential environment: Graham Tipple, Justine Coulson and Peter Kellett describe the characteristics, benefits for their operators and effects on domestic living space and local environmental conditions of home-based enterprises in selected low-income residential areas in Cochabamba, New Delhi, Surabaya and Pretoria, and explore the implications of their findings for policy and practice.

The chapters included in Part II are also concerned with the production of livable environments, but focus on issues of institutional, social and cultural sustainability. Peter Brand is concerned with urban environmental management as a social practice, examining the extent to which the municipal government of Medellin in Colombia has employed the environment as a solution to the city's social problems and tensions. He does this by analysing the role of discourse in creating meanings of the environment and the ways in which those meanings have been employed in conflict management and the legitimation of urban government.

Many governments and development agencies have, in recent years, been increasingly concerned with poverty reduction. In this context, Carole Rakodi focuses less on the content of policies to reduce urban poverty than on a potential approach to building sustainability capacity for poverty reduction. She analyses the implications of our current understanding of the characteristics and causes of urban poverty for policy; defines the notion of 'sustainable capacity'; and suggests a process by which this might be built at municipal and community levels. Paul Jenkins is also concerned with the political and institutional mechanisms to achieve social, economic and environmentally sustainable urban development. He examines how the interests of different actors (the state and individual households) can be balanced, in particular through the mediating role of civil society. His arguments are illustrated by a comparison of housing policy in Mozambique and South Africa, both southern African countries undergoing transition from authoritarian regimes.

On the whole, the first seven chapters in this volume are concerned with national or city-level policies, legislation and management systems, although some include specific case studies of areas within cities, and others refer to the impact on residential communities of environmental problems and policies and their potential role in decision-making, alongside other forms of civil society organizations. The institutional and social sustainability of local development processes that rely on CBOs and NGOs is the primary focus of the next two chapters. Denise Martins Lopes and Carole Rakodi analyse the extent to which the community-support activities of an NGO in Florianópolis, Brazil succeeded in building lasting community capacity for organization and action. Harry Smith examines a 'community self-management' (*autogestión comunitaria*) initiative in a large, low-income settlement in San José de Costa Rica, assessing whether this government-led approach opened up a real space for negotiation, or was simply a new form of co-optation designed to deal with social unrest.

Continuing this section's concern with social sustainability, the final chapter examines the way in which cultural values and social organization are reflected in residential environments, some of the difficulties that arise if they are not, and how people can adapt even unpropitious house designs to better suit their social needs. Mashary Al-Naim analyses the *fereej*, a mechanism used by people in Hofuf, Saudi Arabia to create a living environment based on shared values and habits, describes some of the recent developments that have affected traditional housing areas, identifies some ways in which people have tried to adapt new house designs and residential layouts, and briefly explores the implications of his findings for the design and production of the residential built environment.

The common thread running through the third part of the book is change: managing the continuous evolution of the urban built environment; securing and maintaining appropriate changes to policy and practice; and developing new working relationships between the actors in the urban development process. First, Sam Romaya stresses the importance of achieving a balance between planning for urban growth and managing the changing demands on the existing built environment of urban settlements. He outlines a planning approach, and identifies a specific tool which could help to ensure that environmental sustainability objectives are integrated into decision-making, illustrating his arguments with reference to Cairo. Focusing specifically on the densely settled core of cities, Tony Lloyd-Jones and Sarah Carmona draw on a comparative study of inner-city neighbourhoods in Delhi, Jakarta and Recife to suggest an approach to redevelopment that does not displace existing poor occupants. By adopting a participatory approach and building a partnership between landowners, developers, residents and local government, they argue that it is possible to use the high land values in central areas to help generate economically viable redevelopment which includes housing and space for economic activities for poor residents.

The obstacles to progressive and lasting changes in policy and practice are illustrated by M.R. Dallalpour Mohammadi's analysis of urban housing policy in Iran from the 1960s to the present day. He identifies the strengths and weaknesses of successive housing policies, and assesses whether the necessary parallel changes in the institutional framework, financial arrangements and land policy were initiated and sustained. Schilderman and Lowe are also concerned with the development of new approaches to housing, specifically with the reform of legislative frameworks in order to improve poor people's access to legal shelter and livelihoods. They draw on experiences of housing standard revision processes, especially in Kenya and Zimbabwe, to identify the characteristics of innovative and successful approaches to revision and efforts to stimulate the uptake of new procedures and standards.

The need to develop partnerships and alliances to secure appropriate change in regulatory systems for housing is emphasized by Schilderman and Lowe, and is also the theme of the final chapter. Geoffrey Payne reviews different types of public–private partnerships in urban land development, exploring the reasons why public agencies might involve private operators in order to increase the supply of urban land for development, and the effectiveness and outcomes of a variety of partnership arrangements. Finally, he identifies some of the criteria and conditions for developing the new working relationships necessary for successful partnerships.

In the concluding chapter, some of the common themes and findings with respect to sustainability in its various dimensions are drawn out. In addition, some important issues relevant to sustainable urban settlements which are not tackled in this volume, as well as outstanding research questions, are identified. Finally, while recognizing that different circumstances require different solutions, some of the key requirements for building urban settlements that provide satisfactory environments for both economic activity and everyday life, as well as managing the impacts of urban development on the natural environment, are presented.

PART I

URBAN ENVIRONMENTAL MANAGEMENT, EMPLOYMENT AND HOUSING

CHAPTER ONE

Housing and industry in Lahore, Pakistan: good or bad neighbours?

Rizwan Hameed and Jeremy Raemaekers[1]

INTRODUCTION

In many expanding cities of industrializing countries, poorer resident communities are exposed to pollution from nearby industry. In a new report, the World Bank (2000a) argues that, using new and flexible approaches to pollution abatement, developing nations can achieve the magic trick of leap-frogging to clean industrial development, by-passing the dirty middle phase through which all nations have hitherto passed. In this chapter we consider whether the Bank's optimism is likely to be justified in Pakistan, a nation in the early stages of industrialization. We look at the city of Lahore as an example.

As town planners, we consider the problem not simply as one of pollution abatement within the remit of the pollution control regime, but also as one of the spatial mixing of industry with housing within the remit of the land-use planning regime. In terms of sustainable development, the goal can be defined as securing industrial growth that generates wealth and employment, while lowering industrial pollution intensity and achieving a more equal distribution of the residual pollution burden among residential communities that differ in wealth.

First, we provide some contextual background and outline our methodological approach. The pollution control and land-use planning regimes regulating development are described, their operation assessed, and explanations sought for their generally poor performance. Finally, prospects for the future are discussed.

The nation and the city

Pakistan is a nation in the early stages of industrialization: industry accounts for a quarter of its output, about the same as farming and half as much as services. Its per capita GNP is US$470 (World Bank, 2000b). This places it below the level of wealth at which we can expect to see pollution intensity fall as national income rises (Mani and Wheeler, 1998; Wheeler, 2000: Figure 9; World Bank, 2000a: Figure 1.5).

Although only 2 per cent of Pakistan is urban, it boasts several mighty cities. Lahore is the country's second city, and the ancient capital of the Punjab. It is home to some 5 million people and is growing at around 3 per cent a year. Forty per cent of its people live in *katchi abadis*, settlements built without planning or building approval. Lahore lies on the Indian border, on the River Ravi. A quarter of its output is from manufacturing, particularly textiles, metal parts and food processing. In 1997 the city region held about 850 large-scale factories (large-scale is a euphemism, being a census class which covers all units employing 20 or more people; most lie at the bottom end of the scale). Between them, these factories employed 120 000 workers (Government of the Punjab, 1998).

Methods

Field information was collected during 1997 and 1998. Surveys of the distribution of industry in the city region identified 15 clusters (Figure 1.1). These were defined as geographical concentrations of primarily large-scale industrial units. They were identified from a combination of the development plans prepared for Lahore, an industrial location map prepared by the Environmental Protection Department Punjab in the late 1980s, interviews with officials of this agency and the various planning agencies, and field reconnaissance. The clusters were defined by judging best fit, rather than by any statistical cluster analysis. With the exception of two industrial estates (clusters 9 and 11 in Figure 1.1), clusters include other land uses, especially housing, along with industry.

The clusters were used to select firms and residential communities for guided interviews. Representatives (usually owners or managers) of 23 large firms from across the 15 clusters were interviewed. The firms were chosen to cover different ages, types of ownership and waste streams, but all were situated close to housing. One residential community from each cluster was also interviewed, in groups of five to seven people. The communities interviewed were those surrounding the factories of the firms interviewed. We were thus able to cross-check information from adjacent firms and communities.

Officials of regulatory regimes at federal, provincial and local levels were interviewed to gain access to data, identify cases, clarify institutional and legislative issues, and seek explanations of operational weaknesses. Updates on the progress of legislation, etc. have been obtained from Internet sources, especially the website of the Environmental Technology Programme for Industry (www.etpi.org.pk).

REGIMES REGULATING DEVELOPMENT

Pollution control authorities

Pakistan is a federation of provinces. Provinces are split into divisions, which are divided into districts. As in many nations, district administrations have general powers to act against public nuisances, but there is also a dedicated pollution control agency operating in Lahore under the provincial environ-

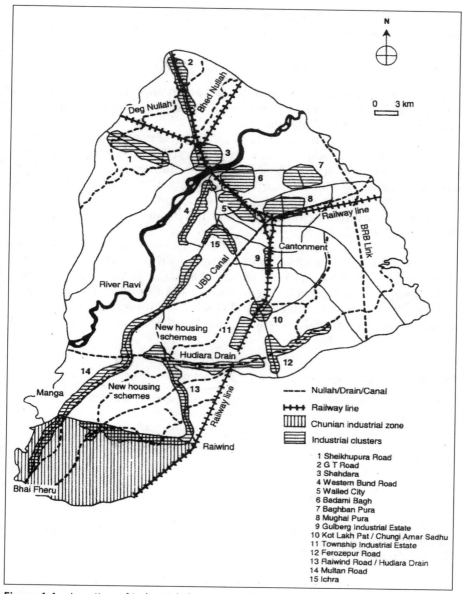

Figure 1.1 Location of industrial clusters in Lahore Metropolitan Region
Source: authors

ment ministry. This agency, the Environment Protection Department Punjab (EPDP), functions under the Pakistan Environmental Protection Act 1997. Its remit includes pollution monitoring, public education and awareness, advising local government on environmental issues and problems, coordinating with various nation-building departments on environmental matters, administering environmental impact assessment[2] for new industries, and enforcing national environmental quality standards.

Land-use planning authorities

Whereas there is only one pollution control agency operating in Lahore, the land-use planning regime is much more complex (Table 1.1; Figure 1.2). This requires a little explanation.

In Pakistan, the urbanized parts of districts are governed by municipal committees or corporations, while those parts that are still rural remain under the district councils. Thus the 343 km² built-up part of Lahore District is governed by Metropolitan Corporation Lahore, and the remaining rural parts by District Council Lahore. The Corporation has held planning and building control functions since 1960, but the district councils received them only in 1997.

Overlying this structure is the 2269 km² Lahore Metropolitan Region (referred to here as the city region). It was delineated under the Lahore Development Authority Act 1975, which created the Authority as successor to a city improvement trust set up under British rule in 1935. The city region includes the built-up part of Lahore District (the Corporation area) and the remaining rural parts of the district (under District Council Lahore), as well

Table 1.1   The planning authorities in Lahore Metropolitan Region

Name	Jurisdiction	Acquired planning powers in	Reports to
Lahore Development Authority	Entire metropolitan region except the cantonment	1975	Punjab Department of Housing, Urban Development and Public Development and Public Health Engineering
Metropolitan Corporation Lahore	Within the city limits except the military cantonment	1960	Punjab Department of Local Government and Rural Development
Cantonment Board	Military cantonment within the city limits	?	Military authorities
District councils	Metropolitan region not covered by Metropolitan Corporation Lahore or Cantonment Board	1997	Punjab Department of Local Government and Rural Development

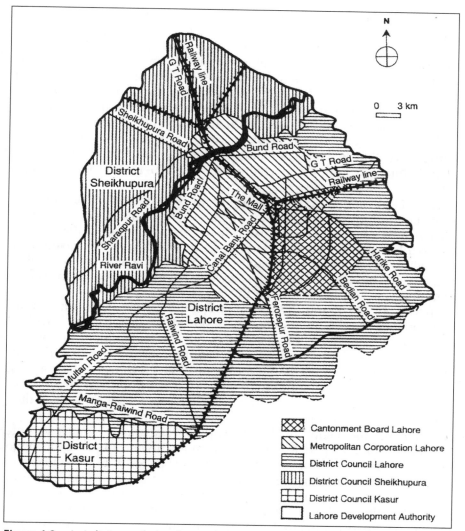

Figure 1.2   Jurisdictions of planning authorities in Lahore Metropolitan Region
Source: authors

as part of the neighbouring rural Sheikhupura District to the north across the River Ravi, and an area to the south in Kasur District.

Lahore Development Authority is charged with a range of functions, including: preparation, updating and implementation of the Metropolitan Development Plan; exercising land-use and building control; preparation, implementation and enforcement of schemes for environmental improvement, housing, transport, health and education facilities; preservation of objects or places of historical importance; and creation of agencies such as the Water and Sanitation Agency.

The Development Authority thus holds planning powers in parallel with the Metropolitan Corporation itself throughout the Corporation's area, and with Lahore, Sheikhupura and Kasur District Councils outside the Corporation's area; moreover, it reports to a different superior. The Corporation and the District Councils report to the provincial Department of Local Government and Rural Development, and the Corporation is headed by an elected Mayor. The Authority, however, falls under the provincial Housing, Urban Development and Public Health Engineering Department. These two departments are headed by different ministers. Irrespective of formal lines of reporting, the Authority incidentally derives great influence from being chaired by the Chief Minister of Punjab Province.

There is still another complication – in the east of the Corporation's territory lies the Cantonment, an island of 93 km^2, controlled by its own Board. This area was set up under British rule, under the control of the military. Its Board deals with all matters relating to planning and development, and with delivery and maintenance of infrastructure services and public amenities. The Cantonment has always been excluded from spatial planning exercises carried out for the city as whole.

Apart from EPDP and the planning authorities, the Punjab Industries and Minerals Development Department (PI&MDD) has also been involved in guiding the location of industry, through the requirement to obtain a 'no-objection certificate' (permit) for location clearance. The PI&MDD was charged with preventing haphazard industrial growth, on the basis of which it has been trying to guide industry away from residential areas. However, its remit is strategic rather than local, and it has no explicit duty to secure pollution abatement.

To sum up: the institutional framework for regulation of industry in the city region contains parallel land-use planning organizations reporting to different provincial departments – clearly a recipe for trouble – and a pollution control regime that answers to a different minister from either of these (although that is not unusual). There is also potential for the industrial promotion authority to act in concert with the land-use planning regime to influence industrial location – although it was never intended to operate at a fine-grained level, lacks explicit links to the other regulators, and reports to yet another minister.

HOW WELL DO THE REGIMES WORK?

Industrial pollution

As is often the case in developing countries, there is little accessible systematic evidence about local industrial pollution in the city region, but the information presented below provides strong circumstantial evidence (Government of Pakistan/IUCN, 1992; EPA Punjab, 1993; Allauddin, 1994;

MELGRD, 1997, 2001; Younas et al. 1997; Ahmad, 2000; Khan, undated, 2001a,b).

A briefing by the Federal EPA in July 2000 reported levels of suspended particulate matter in three Pakistani cities, including Lahore, as 6.4 times above World Health Organization air quality guidelines. For the most part, carbon monoxide, sulphur dioxide, nitrogen oxide and ozone were found to be at acceptable levels. Industrial air emissions have made up a rising proportion of total air pollution in the Lahore city region, despite the rapid rise of motor traffic yielding high emissions: the tonnage of suspended particulate matter attributable to industry increased from 57 per cent of the total in 1985 to 73 per cent in 1993. Steel re-rolling mills and furnaces are important sources. A similar story is told of air pollution in the tannery communities of Sialkot, not far to the north-east of Lahore, where it is held responsible for much of the heavy load of respiratory disease. The country's generally dusty conditions and low wind speeds aggravate particulate air pollution.

Turning to liquid discharges, industries discharge effluent untreated into the municipal sewers or the nearest available natural water body. The River Ravi receives over 200 million gallons of raw sewage daily, generating a biological oxygen demand of 350 tonnes per day, or 300 mg per litre compared with a limit of 9 mg per litre. At least 1100 industries in the region add untreated waste water containing acids, alkali, ammonia and chlorine, as well as an estimated 15 tonnes per day of heavy metals. The flow in the river varies by a factor of 100, which means that at low flow it amounts to a sewage drain. At low flow the river has been found to be completely devoid of dissolved oxygen downstream of the city.

Samples of waste water collected from various industries show contamination levels in all cases exceeding the national environmental quality standards. For example, in waste water taken from textile plants, electroplating industries and metal parts fabricating units, chemical oxygen demand was found to range from three to five times the national standard. Similarly, samples from pulp and paper board mills yielded an average sulphide level six times the standard. Recent technical reports on particular industrial sectors show effluent outputs from factories typically way above the national standards, sometimes by two orders of magnitude.

This situation poses a health threat because the river is used in the city region, and downstream of it, for irrigation, recreation, livestock watering and domestic purposes. More than 23 per cent of the land around the city is irrigated by municipal sewage water and sludge, laced with metals such as cadmium, chromium and lead. The river is also used directly for drinking water, although fortunately not to a large extent, because the abundant aquifer in its catchment means that most of the city's water is drawn from tube wells. However, as the aquifer is itself to some extent recharged from the river, the river's load of untreated industrial effluent may partly account for the documented contamination of the city's water supply drawn from the aquifer, including concentrations of heavy metals.

Apart from being discharged untreated into sewers and water bodies, industrial effluent is also often discharged directly on to land, for example along G T Road and Sheikhupura Road in the north-west of the city, and along Multan Road in the south, exposing surrounding residents to the risk of heavy metal and chemical poisoning. Solid industrial wastes also contribute to land pollution. Such wastes are either dumped with municipal solid wastes (often in low-lying areas without using modern sanitary landfill techniques), or fly-tipped (sometimes immediately outside the premises and sometimes on to open land), or burned at any convenient location.

Mixing of industry with housing

Inappropriate mixing of polluting industries and housing has arisen in the city region, both with housing surrounding existing factories, and with factories opening near existing housing (Qadeer, 1983, p. 206). In 11 of the 15 communities we interviewed, most houses were built without approval (Table 1.2). It should be noted that building permission and planning permission are fused into one process. Development control was strongest in those communities falling under the Lahore Development Authority, which is the land-use planning agency with the best staffing and other resources. It was weakest on the outskirts of the region, under District Council Lahore and District Council Sheikhupura, which until 1997 lacked the powers to exercise building control, and still lack the staff capacity to make their own development plans.

WHY DON'T THE REGULATORY REGIMES WORK BETTER?

Pollution control regime

Why has EPDP not effectively controlled industrial nuisance? First, the national environmental quality standards have never been activated. The federal Environment Protection Act of 1997 created the powers needed by the provincial EPDP, but activation depended on the federal pollution control agency (which does not implement action on the ground) delegating powers to EPDP, and this was delayed until late 1999. National environmental quality standards were created in 1993, and revised in 1997 in cooperation with industry to be more realistic in the Pakistani context. However, EPDP could not apply them pending their approval by a top-level federal council, which also caused a delay, probably because of the business interests of the then political leadership. This council finally approved the standards in August 1999, but as of June 2001 the standards still could not be applied because the regulations for implementing the 1997 Act had yet to be finalized.

Lacking the necessary powers itself, EPDP has sought the cooperation of those who do have powers. Thus it has asked district administrations and

Table 1.2 Permission status of housing and factories in industrial clusters of Lahore Metropolitan Region, and comparison with development plan policies

Industrial cluster (related community)	Permission status		Land-use policies applicable to the area	
	Housing	Industrial firm	1972 Master plan	1980 Structure plan*
Sheikhupura Road (Kot Abdul Malik Area)	No approval at all from DCS	Obtained manufacturing licence from DCS**	Green belt	Policies 1, 2 and 3 apply
G.T. Road (Kala Shah Kaku)	No approval at all from DCS	No permission required at that time	Green belt	Policies 1, 2 and 3 apply
Shahdara (Islam Pura)	No approval at all from MCL	Unable to confirm	Green belt plus some industrial area (rounded off as many factories were already operating)	Policies 1, 2 and 3 apply
Western Bund Road (Zarfishan Street, Ravi Road)	Some with and some without approval from MCL	With approval from PI&MDD	Residential	Policies 1, 2 and 3 apply
Walled City (Sara-e-Sultan)	Mostly without approval from MCL	Unable to confirm	Commercial	Policies 1, 2 and 3 apply
Badami Bagh (Data Nagar)	Mostly without approval from MCL	With approval from MCL	Residential plus industrial area (rounded off since many factories were already operating)	Policies 1, 2 and 3 apply
Baghban Pura (Shalimar Town)	Mostly with approval from MCL	With approval from PI&MDD	Residential plus recreational	Policies 1, 2 and 3 apply

Table 1.2   Permission status of housing and factories in industrial clusters of Lahore Metropolitan Region, and comparison with development plan policies *contd.*

Industrial cluster (related community)	Permission status		Land-use policies applicable to the area	
	Housing	Industrial firm	1972 Master plan	1980 Structure plan*
Mughal Pura (Crown Baghban Pura, Shalimar Link Road)	Mostly with approval from MCL	Unable to confirm	Residential	Nothing specific about the area, but policies 2 and 3 may apply
Gulberg Industrial Estate (Gulberg II and the adjacent area)	Almost all with approval from LDA	With approval from LIT	Residential plus industrial estate	Residential plus industrial estate
Kot Lakh Pat/Chungi Amar Sadhu (Bostan Colony)	Mostly without approval from MCL	With approval from MCL and PI&MDD	Industrial area (rounded off since many factories were already operating)	Policies 1, 2 and 3 apply
Township Industrial Estate (Lahore Township Scheme)	Almost all with approval from LDA	With approval from LDA	Residential plus industrial estate	Residential plus industrial estate
Ferozepur Road (Dullu Kalan)	No approval at all from DCL	With approval from PI&MDD	Green belt	Expansion area for accommodating future growth
Raiwind Road/Hudiara Drain (Bhatta Pind)	No approval at all from DCL	Obtained manufacturing licence from DCL**	Green belt	Expansion area for accommodating future growth

	No approval at all from DCL	Obtained manufacturing licence from DCL**	Green belt	Policies 1, 2 and 3 apply
Multan Road (Chung)				
Ichra (Zaildar Park)	Some with and some without approval from MCL	With approval from MCL	Residential	Nothing specific about the area, but policies 2 and 3 may apply

MCL = Metropolitan Corporation Lahore
LDA = Lahore Development Authority
LIT = Lahore Industries Trust
DCL = District Council Lahore
DCS = District Council Sheikhupura
PI&MDD = Punjab Industries and Minerals Development Department

* Policy 1, existing concentration of industry may continue, but with improvements in traffic, transport and physical infrastructure through preparation of local plans; Policy 2, pollution or other hazards should be removed, as far as possible at the polluter's expense; policy 3, relocation of particular industry types may be considered when essential for environmental, health, safety and other such considerations.

** Note that this does not constitute a location clearance permit. It is an instrument to levy tax.

Sources: interviews with communities and industrial firms; Government of Punjab (1973); Lahore Development Authority et al. (1980).

Metropolitan Corporation Lahore to prosecute offenders under their public nuisance powers. Despite some instances of cooperation, this has produced little effect overall, partly because of corruption within those organizations, and partly because of the endemic protraction of litigation. EPDP has also sought the help of the industrial promotion body PI&MDD. EPDP asked PI&MDD to request firms seeking its location clearance also to seek an environmental impact statement clearance from EPDP, but again some PI&MDD area offices have not complied. Latterly the locational role of PI&MDD has been reduced as part of the federal government's policy of deregulating industry.

These external obstacles are compounded by internal constraints, the greatest of which is the lack of competent staff. EPDP has a staff of some 270, but only seven are inspectors, responsible for 50 000 industrial units in Punjab Province. Efforts to train staff have been undermined by a vicious circle of low motivation, underfunding and poor results, symbolized by the constant replacement of the agency's director general, resulting in trained staff leaving to find work elsewhere. Resources are, as ever, also short: personal computers have been purchased, but they are not being used productively, and records are still kept in brown paper files, obviating rapid and targeted analysis.

Land-use planning regime

Conflicting planning policies apply to a given locality, arising from the concurrent operation of two development plans followed by overlapping agencies (Table 1.2, right column). Metropolitan Corporation Lahore follows the Master Plan for Lahore, drafted in 1966 and sanctioned in 1972 as the Corporation's statutory guiding document (Government of the Punjab, 1973). Lahore Development Authority soon perceived that the Master Plan was not useful to it because the Plan had no force beyond the municipal limits where most growth was taking place, in the green belt proposed by the Plan. Therefore, in 1979 the Authority drafted a Structure Plan for the entire city region, which ignored the Master Plan's green belt (Lahore Development Authority et al., 1980). The 1972 Master Plan could not be updated because there was no legal provision for this. The 1980 Structure Plan was more realistic, but was broad-brush, assuming that it would be interpreted locally through local plans. Local plans have, however, never been made. Again, this is partly because the sanctioning statute does not specify that they must be.

This unworkable situation is at last being addressed by revising the Structure Plan, under the title of Integrated Master Plan for Lahore (Lahore Development Authority/National Engineering Services Pakistan, 1998). The intention is that, following consultation with the Corporation, this will be adopted as the sole plan for the city region. The new draft Plan for the first time includes a separate chapter on the environment, which makes a handful of specific proposals for industrial location in the style of a master plan, but lacks generally applicable policies in the style of a structure plan. As of April 2001, the draft was being revised to accommodate objections by the Development Authority.

Yet more important is the Devolution Plan of the military government, operative from August 2001. This will sweep away the current institutions, installing a single strategic planning and building control authority managing the whole of Lahore District. If this happens, there will then be a single authority operating a single strategic plan.

Unfortunately, this will not by itself remove all sources of contradiction in the control of development. This is because there is also contention about whether the planning authority or other licensing agencies have the final say on granting location clearance to industry. For example, PI&MDD licensed factories to set up in Zarfishan Street and Shalimar Town, in contravention of the 1972 Master Plan followed by the Corporation as planning authority (Table 1.2).

This confusion not only creates problems, but also interferes with the planning authority's ability to put them right if complaints are lodged. All the planning authorities have the power to close down or require relocation of an unauthorized factory, and the Development Authority also has the power to relocate undesirable development. In practice, these powers are virtually never used, for several reasons. One reason is that, in the event that one agency approves and another refuses clearance, the applicant can play them off against each other through the courts – effectively kicking the case into the long grass.

Finally, some of the mixing of industry with housing simply arose before regulatory powers were created. For example, the factory at Kala Shah Kaku was set up in 1962 in the territory of District Council Sheikhupura, which did not obtain planning powers until more than three decades later; and in 1962 PI&MDD also lacked powers to grant location clearance.

These problems of controlling building of factories are complemented in the case of housing by doubts about whether permission to build is required at all. Questioning of residents indicated that some built without permission because, outside the municipal limits, none was required – district councils acquired control powers only in 1997. Inside the municipal limits, where permission has been required at least since the 1960s, the Metropolitan Corporation and the Development Authority have proved unable to hold back the formation of *katchi abadis*, which have later been regularized by government. This post hoc regularization has led people to believe that permissions were not required in the first place (Table 1.3).

The representatives of some communities, where some or most residents had gone through the process of obtaining a building permit, expressed their dissatisfaction with the regulations and the approval process. They pointed out that people do not seek house planning approval because of difficulty in understanding the regulations and procedures, and due to corruption and delays in the process. Some commented that those on a low

Table 1.3   Reasons for not obtaining permission to build a house in Lahore

Reasons given by spokespersons of 13 communities in Lahore*	Number of communities
Many houses date back to pre-Partition (1947) days	2
No need as it is a rural area	5
Building regulations are too strict and not affordable	2
Procedure to obtain approval is time-consuming and complicated	4
It is difficult to get approval without paying a bribe	5
It is in a *katchi abadi*	3
Most people neither know about regulations nor feel the need for approval	5
Plan preparation is costly and difficult	3

*More than one response may be given by each community.

income do not seek permission because the standards do not allow low-cost houses – a common complaint in developing countries. Others argued that finding an architect who could design the house for a low fee is also difficult, and that people on a low income have neither the funds nor the desire to spend money on preparing a house plan to obtain building clearance.

When asked how people deal with building inspectors, respondents invariably replied that inspectors rarely visit. If they do, people appease them with bribes. If the inspector refuses a bribe and reports an unapproved house, a fine is usually levied, on payment of which the house plan subsequently submitted is approved.

Industry

Even without effective external regulation, industry might better regulate itself. Why does it not do so? It is easy to take a cynical view that industry takes advantage, both of apparent immunity from prosecution arising from the ability to intimidate and buy off complainants and officials, and also of poor people's willingness to tolerate nuisance because they need to live close to sources of work. But such a view is too simplistic. In fact, interviews with factory owners and managers revealed that they agreed with the desirability of controlling pollution, but were often ignorant of the problems it causes, of options for abating it, and of the costs of those options (Hameed and Raemaekers, 2002).

A similar defence can be offered of industry's attitude to planning regulation. In the first place, we have evidence that PI&MDD has granted post facto location approval to factories on payment of a nominal regularization fee; and that the federal government has allowed unauthorized factories to obtain import licences for raw material, machinery and spare parts after obtaining post facto location approval. This sends the message to industry that location approval does not matter.

Second, housing moves in close to factories as much as the other way about: according to residents themselves, housing had been located close to existing factories in nine of our 15 clusters. Residents cited proximity to employment, as well as to other conveniences, as important determinants of choice. This must raise doubts in factory owners' minds about the seriousness with which residents view industrial nuisance.

When asked about the proximity of housing and industry, factory owners and managers defended themselves by arguing variously that: at the time they set up the area was empty (seven cases); there were already factories in the area (two); there were only a few scattered houses nearby (one); the nearest housing was at a reasonable distance (one) and still is (one); the factory was in a planned industrial estate (two); or the area was declared in 1947, when the nation was founded, as an industrial zone (one). All also stated that no government agency had taken any action to prevent or remedy the growth of housing around their factories in later years.

It is no surprise that, under these circumstances, industry feels little moral responsibility to clean up its act. It can readily argue that it is meeting the prime social need at this point in the nation's development by providing wealth, jobs and even a focus for services.

PROSPECTS

Piece by piece, the regulatory jigsaw is being put in place in Pakistan.
In pollution control:

- the Environmental Protection Act 1997, which among other things enables the introduction of pollution taxes
- the recent devolution of powers from the federal environmental protection agency to the provincial EPDP
- the possibility that the national environmental quality standards, already approved, will finally be activated.

In planning control:

- the award of planning powers to district councils in 1997
- the proposed rationalization of the Lahore planning authorities and their plans, described above.

In the legal arena:

- the designation of environmental magistrates under the 1997 Act
- the institution in 1999 of environmental tribunals to hear complaints and award penalties or compensation
- the creation under the military regime of anti-corruption cells in public services, to which clients can complain.

Alas, the environmental tribunals, which seemed to offer real hope for environmental justice, have already failed to live up to their promise. Only two were set up, of which only one ever operated, in Lahore itself. It soon ceased to function for want of office space, equipment and staff.

Market signals are more hopeful. Willy-nilly, parts of Pakistani industry are being subjected to market forces favouring a more environmentally responsible image (Khan, undated). Pakistan is now a major exporter to the West of textiles, leather and sports goods, etc., all of which are susceptible to such pressure (witness television documentaries on football manufacture), and the Lahore Chamber of Commerce and Industry told us that there is an urgent need to make industrialists aware of green consumerism in their international trading. The World Trade Organization is requiring that by 2004 nothing will be imported from exporters who do not follow the ISO 14000 environmental management standards adopted in the importing nations.

Joint foreign enterprises are another route by which environmental management standards might be introduced into Pakistani industry. Our sample of 23 firms contained three indigenous exporting firms and three joint foreign enterprises. Thus a quarter of the sample, which was random with respect to these variables, is in categories potentially subject to market pressures to raise standards, suggesting a positive prospect nationwide in this regard.

Pakistani industry itself has taken up the environmental agenda at the highest level. The Federation of Pakistan Chambers of Commerce and Industries, with Dutch technical assistance, has developed the Environmental Technology Programme for Industry, a five-year programme (1996–2001) including demonstration projects (Hameed and Raemaekers, 2002). Government policy is that industry should itself monitor and report its own emissions. A pilot scheme on 50 factories was completed in March 2001, and it is now intended to apply the approach universally (MELGRD, 2001, p. 17).

Apart from regulation, market signals and a voluntary approach, the last arrow in the abatement quiver is pressure from civil society. The role of civil society has been well researched in developed countries (Groeneweger et al., 1996), and the World Bank (2000a) enthuses about the potential of people power in developing countries, citing extensive evidence. These optimistic results, however, hail from countries that are more industrialized, richer, more literate, and with more foreign direct investment than Pakistan (Table 1.4). They are not echoed by our survey of Lahore. We found that 10 out of 15 communities had complained, but that only four had produced some effect. Also, collective as against individual protest was more likely among better-off communities, while any sort of protest was least likely among the poorer ones (Hameed and Raemaekers, 2001).

Table 1.4   Comparison of indicators between Pakistan and case study countries from World Bank (2000a)

	Wealth: GNP/capita, US$,1999	Industrial-ization: industry as %GDP, 1999	Foreign direct investment: million US$, 1998	Education: public spending on education, %GNP, 1997	Literacy: % adults illiterate, male/female 1998
Argentina	7,600	32	6,150	3.5	3/3
Brazil	4,420	29	31,913	5.1	16/16
China	780	50	43,751	**2.3**	9/25
Colombia	2,250	**24**	3,038	4.1	9/9
Indonesia	580	45	−356*	**1.4**	9/20
Korea	8,490	44	5,415	3.7	1/4
Malaysia	3,400	44	5,000	4.9	9/18
Mexico	4,400	27	10,238	4.9	7/11
Philippines	1,020	31	1,713	3.4	5/5
Thailand	1,960	40	6,941	4.8	3/7
Pakistan	470	25	500	2.7	42/71

Figures in bold = cases where a country performs 'worse' than Pakistan.
*The 1998 figure is atypical for Indonesia and reflects the East Asian financial crisis of the time.
Source: World Bank (2000b).

CONCLUSIONS

So does our case study encourage optimism about tackling local industrial nuisance in Lahore, and by extrapolation, in other fast-growing cities of developing countries in the early stages of industrialization? Our views of the good and bad news for Lahore are summarized in Box 1.1.

What worries us is the following scenario. Suppose that, for the variety of causes alluded to in this chapter, the overall environmental performance of Pakistani industry is radically improved by action among the larger enterprises in key sectors. Big factories clean up and are concentrated in planned industrial estates with effective pollution treatment plant. People at the top of industry, government and environmental organizations go away happy that, in the round, national industry is delivering income and jobs at an internationally and nationally acceptable cost to the environment. At this point, the inexorable logic of economic cost–benefit calculations calls a halt: it is just not worth pursuing further, smaller-scale, diffuse and therefore expensive clean-up into the labyrinth of the urban jungle. Yet clean-up has not trickled down to the numerous smaller enterprises scattered through residential areas, which cause much misery to ordinary people, and which face such simple constraints as lack of space for an effluent treatment plant (a genuine constraint even in a major concentration of a leading industrial sector, the tanneries of Sialkot; Ahmad, 2000).

Box 1.1   Prognosis for reduction of local industrial nuisance in Lahore

Reasons to be cheerful	**But . . .**
Current military regime is not so beholden to industrial interests, and is campaigning against corruption.	Already the only environmental tribunal that ever operated has ceased to do so. Also, the shorter-term benefits of a drive against corruption must be weighed against the longer-term damage of undermining democratic processes.
The pollution command-and-control regime is gradually being pieced together.	Every time one hurdle to implementation is jumped, another appears – the latest being approval at the highest level of regulations for implementing the Environmental Protection Act.
Industry-led programmes to raise capacity for environmental management.	Will they seek to, and can they, reach small and medium enterprises that cause local nuisances? Or will they be content to improve sectoral performances by targeting the big fish?
Some protest action by civil society.	But little success, and the poor still suffer more. Very low literacy rate is not propitious.
Market forces signal to industry the need to clean up.	But only some of industry is subject to them.
Some movement towards introducing market-based instruments to supplement command-and-control.	But if regulators cannot operate command-and-control effectively, what chance is there that they can manage market-based instruments?
Updating and rationalization of land-use development plan is well under way.	But not there yet. Effect depends on rationalizing planning authorities as as well.
Planning authorities to be rationalized under national Devolution Plan.	If it happens. To be effective also needs regularizing relationships with other permitting agencies.

In this bleak scenario there remain two hopes. The first lies in vastly improved development control to keep housing and industry apart. But in the big picture the prognosis for this has to be poor, even if we assume institutions will be rationalized. Already some 40 per cent of housing in Lahore was built without permissions. The housing shortfall in Pakistan was estimated in 1998 at 4.3 million units, and the gap between supply and demand is growing (MELGRD, 2001, p. 31). There is little sign that this structural reality will change soon.

The second hope lies in community mobilization to exert pressure on factories directly, or indirectly by pressurizing the environmental protection agencies. But this is bound to be an uphill struggle when literacy is so low,[3] and when many of those adversely affected by factories depend on them in some way for their livelihood.

CHAPTER TWO

Urban growth and development in Shanghai: towards responsive institutional arrangements for environmental planning and management

Dave Shaw, Peter J.B. Brown, David W. Massey and Xiangrong Wang[1]

INTRODUCTION

Most of the world's rapidly growing cities face acute dilemmas in reconciling the different dimensions of a sustainable approach to their immediate policy issues and long-term development. This is certainly true within China, where a policy unashamedly based on rapid economic growth is being pursued with great vigour. Shanghai is China's largest metropolis, and since 1990 its Mayor and Municipal Government have set ambitious economic, social and physical development targets designed to recreate the city as an international economic, financial and trade centre, ranking among the world's leading cities by 2010. The city's master plan was updated and revised in 1998 to help provide the physical structure for the successful implementation of this strategy (Zheng, 2000). Dramatic changes have also been designed to improve environmental conditions in terms of air and water quality, noise levels, waste management and green space.

The successful delivery of the new development strategy depends, among other matters, on Shanghai's institutional structures and processes, and their responsiveness to the need to create a socially and environmentally as well as economically sustainable world-class city. Shanghai's position as a municipality responsible only to Beijing has given it a head start in opportunities for implementing new organizational arrangements. At the same time, the city inherited a standard set of comprehensive and rather traditional, albeit sophisticated, administrative and political decision-making structures appropriate to a centrally planned economy, which needed revising to meet the new conditions of the 'open-door' policies of the 1980s and 1990s. These factors, together with the effects of the loosening of established economic organizational arrangements, have provided the city with a number of institutional challenges. These include the need to catch up on international experience and expertise; the difficulties of balancing economic, social and environmental priorities; and the requirement to create institutional mechanisms that can coordinate the different strands of development administration effectively as well as efficiently. While there is much that is unique and particular about Shanghai, these issues are relevant to many cities elsewhere in the developing world.

This chapter explores some of the institutional arrangements being used in Shanghai to try to deliver both rapid economic growth and a good quality environment. It begins by establishing a conceptual framework in which various approaches to sustainable development can be appraised, before moving to consider the particular tensions of an environmental management approach to sustainable development in China. The discussion then focuses on the case of Shanghai, commencing with a general review of the arrangements for environmental planning and management in the municipal area. It continues with a review of empirical work on the early experience of the Waigaoqiao Free Trade Zone (FTZ) in the city's Pudong New Area. We conclude that there is a need to operate a more coherent environmental policy and to ensure that it is firmly implemented, if Shanghai is to achieve its goal of sustainable development and the status of an international economic metropolis.

SUSTAINABLE DEVELOPMENT: A CONCEPTUAL FRAMEWORK

Without doubt, one of the most fundamental changes to affect policy-makers in the last decade of the millennium was the almost universal adoption of the concept of 'sustainable development'. Indeed it is evident that nearly all programmes and policy initiatives are now justified in terms of sustainable development. In many ways the term has become an oxymoron (Rogers, 1993), used to justify almost any form of human activity, whether promoting development or, at the other end of the spectrum, preventing development and protecting the environment. Nevertheless, this diversity of uses does not diminish the gravity of the issues and the need for policies and action.

In the discussions leading to the 1997 UNCED meeting in New York to review the achievements of the Earth Summit in Rio five years earlier, the UK government proposed a fivefold agenda designed to promote the objectives of global sustainability. This forms the basis of a conceptual framework (Box 2.1) against which to judge policy, action and progress in diverse approaches to sustainable development as a guiding principle for change. It comprises recognition of the need for urgency, shared responsibility, accountability, pressure points, and lifestyles and dissemination. While it is hard to disagree with such general considerations, a key question is still the extent to which the most rapidly developing economies and urbanizing societies are able and, indeed, willing to adopt the practice of sustainable development. The limited success of the Kyoto discussions perhaps serves as a rather bleak reminder of this fundamental difficulty.

Box 2.1   An agenda to promote the objectives of global sustainability

- Urgency – immediate and substantive action.
- Shared responsibility – although with the developed world accepting its prime responsibility.
- Accountability – the critical value of monitoring measuring and reviewing environmental impacts.
- Pressure points – the need for international systems to address global priority areas.
- Lifestyles and dissemination – the need for sustainable development to be part of everyday reality for individuals.

Source: DoE, 1996a.

ENVIRONMENTAL MANAGEMENT OR ECONOMIC GROWTH: THE CHINESE DILEMMA

The precise meaning of sustainable development has been, and continues to be, a subject of intense debate. If the rhetoric is stripped away, sustainable development is about achieving a balance between, or reconciling, diverse environmental, economic and social interests. The weight and importance attached to each of these elements is, in part, a function of individual and collective values, attitudes and ethics, leading to the adoption of different positions in relation to the environment. Such views lie on a continuum from a technocentric to an ecocentric perspective. Such variations in value systems and perspectives lead to various interpretations of the concept of sustainable development. One of the positive outcomes of the debate is that many individuals and agencies now appear to be considering the environmental implications of their actions. O'Riordan (1995) describes this as an 'environmental management perspective'.

Although a range of differing perspectives relating to sustainable development can be conceptualized, sustainable development implies a balance between economic, social and environmental dimensions. However, in the UK, for example, an emerging tension is apparent between central government's interpretation of sustainable development, as expressed in various national policy statements, and what is emerging from Local Agenda 21 programmes, primarily although not exclusively in urban areas. The UK government interprets sustainable development very much in terms of protection of the natural environment, with further economic development providing the necessary resources to achieve this. At the local level there is greater concern with a social agenda, and thus a very different interpretation of sustainable development is evident (see Shaw and Kidd, 1996 for a fuller discussion).

In China and other rapidly developing economies, such tensions are equally readily apparent and extremely difficult to resolve. China was a signatory to the Declaration arising out of the 1992 Earth Summit in Rio, which committed it to the development of policies and programmes that are compatible and consistent with the aims of sustainable development. Indeed, in July 1994 it formally launched its own Agenda 21 strategy, *Population, Environment and Development in the Twenty-first Century*, which was intended to be a national blueprint of strategies and counter-measures for sustainable development (Tremayne, 1996). In a critical review of this document, Bradbury and Kirkby (1996) have identified a number of issues (Box 2.2) that help explain why, despite this rhetoric, China has adopted an unashamedly economic development perspective. Nevertheless, sustainable development remains a fundamental strategy objective as part of China's modernization programme, in both the *Ninth Five-year Plan* and the *Outline for the Long-Term Target for 2010* (IOSCOPRC, 1996). In these circumstances, tensions between development and the environment are bound to be particularly acute. As China becomes increasingly modernized, market-orientated and integrated into the global economy, consumption patterns, lifestyles and material aspirations are going to be increasingly driven by western standards, fuelling the demand for yet more development. As will be seen, it is possible to argue that the economic imperatives are, if anything, even more apparent at the local level.

Box 2.2 Factors influencing China's development policies

- Population growth from 1.2 billion in the early 1990s to 1.3 billion in 2000, and expected to reach 1.5–1.6 billion by 2050.
- A political economy in transition which, despite spectacular growth (the size of the national economy having increased threefold since 1980), exhibits enormous regional differences, with most development focused in the densely settled coastal areas.
- Massive urbanization.
- High unemployment in both urban and rural areas. Some 100 million rural workers are estimated to be unemployed, to whom must be added tens of millions who formerly worked in urban state sector industries that are increasingly having to operate without subsidies.
- Concerns related to the ability of social welfare to keep pace with national economic growth.
- Growing provincial-, county- and local-level administrative autonomy, which has not been paralleled by effective implementation of government policy and control, especially in relation to environmental protection.
- An absence of environmental pressure groups and low general awareness of environmental issues.

ENVIRONMENTAL PLANNING AND MANAGEMENT IN SHANGHAI

National government provides a framework within which the lower tiers of administration operate. The Constitution of the People's Republic of China provides that 'the state protects and improves the living environmental and ecological environment, and prevents and remedies pollution and other public hazards . . .The state ensures the rational use of resources . . . The damage of natural resources by any organization or individual of whatever means is prohibited' (IOSCOPRC, 1996). In fulfilling these objectives, the state defines the rights and duties of all levels of government with respect to their environmental performance, which will be judged against nationally prescribed standards.

The Shanghai Municipal Government (SMG) is designated as one of three municipalities which do not relate to central government through a provincial authority, but which instead enjoy direct relations with Beijing. While this makes its actions subject to closer scrutiny in the capital than other large Chinese cities, since the 1980s and, more particularly, since 1990, this status has also given it greater freedom for institutional innovation. Within the SMG, the Shanghai Municipal Environmental Protection Bureau (SMEPB) has been designated as the competent body to deal with all environmental protection issues across the whole of the municipality. The SMEPB is not an independent regulatory body, but its work is overseen as one of the constituent parts of the Urban and Rural Planning Construction Commission, whose other bureaux include real estate and land administration, and urban planning. The SMEPB has wide-ranging powers and responsibilities at the level of the municipality, although significant tasks are devolved to rural county and urban district counterparts, which by no means makes hierarchical coordination and regulation easy.

The SMEPB is responsible for producing environmental plans (including *The Shanghai Environmental Management Plan*, 1994) and drafting regulations and policies for the Municipal Government (including local standards). It also has administrative duties (such as collecting discharge fees from enterprises, which provide a source of internal revenue, and issuing discharge licences). Its functions also include emergency and risk management, processing and approving projects requiring an environmental impact assessment (EIA; Tang et al., 1997), and monitoring environmental quality across the Shanghai municipal area.

The SMEPB functions internally through a series of departments with specific responsibility for General Administration, Human Resources, Planning (environmental issues and finance), Science and Technology, Law and Policy, Pollution Control 1 (air quality and solid waste), Pollution Control 2 (water quality), Management Support and Monitoring (including new projects), and International Cooperation. Associated with, but separate from, the SMEPB are a number of related administrative institutions and other agencies that have important specialist roles in environmental management, ranging from research to education/publicity and fee collection. These other bodies include the Shanghai Academy of Environmental Science, the Shanghai Environmental Education and Publishing Committee, and the Shanghai Fee Collection Office.

Shanghai suffers from very serious environmental problems, and is taking active steps to implement remedial policies to address some of the most serious issues (Wu, 1996). It faces a dilemma: how can it deal with environmental degradation (a legacy from its past) and, at the same time, address new environmental challenges? Despite the drive for economic growth, environmental policy is a real concern for the SMG. This is reflected in the increasing proportion of Shanghai's GDP directed towards environmental issues. By 1998 this was set to rise to 3.0 per cent (US$1 billion), from 1.7 per cent in 1995 (US$602 million). Shanghai's Mayor Xu Kuangdi stated his determination that Shanghai would join the world's top environmentally sound cities by 2010 (Anon., 1997a).

In dealing with its industrial legacy of atmospheric pollution (including smoke and dust; Zheng, 1998, pp. 62–64) and water pollution, Shanghai is actively pursuing a policy of combining economic adjustment with training and operational measures to reduce end-of-pipe discharges from existing industries. There is an ongoing switch from heavy to lighter manufacturing processes, which can involve either the closure of polluting factories or their relocation from the older areas of the central city to outer locations (where stricter pollution controls are operated). This restructuring is, in part, being promoted by the drive towards greater economic self-reliance of plants, with many inefficient, highly polluting, formerly state-owned enterprises being forced to close on grounds of their non-viability.

Another atmospheric pollution problem for Shanghai has been its reliance on high sulphur-content coal for its electricity-generating stations and millions of coal-burning domestic stoves. One part of the response has been to move to lower emission targets for new power stations, for instance at Waigaoqiao, with advance planning for natural gas from the East China Sea as a replacement fuel source. This policy has been complemented by the SMG's clearance of older housing, and new house-building programmes that have resulted in the loss of many domestic stoves from traditional dwellings. Through these and related policies, it is estimated that since the early 1990s, Shanghai has managed to halt environmental deterioration, with pollution discharges below the 1990 level, while GDP has doubled (Anon., 1997a).

Significant action has also been taken by the £300 million Shanghai Environment Project (supported by the World Bank), which seeks to protect Shanghai's fresh water supply by a complex integrated package of measures. The package includes a new water intake for potable water upstream on the Huangpu at Daqiao, together with a water analysis laboratory. Its other elements comprise a sewage treatment works in Songjiang County to avoid pollution going into the new water intake, and a major West Trunk

intercepting sewer designed to take discharges from 33 of the main industrial polluters in the older parts of the central city. The interceptor is predicated on the polluting industries meeting at least national discharge
standards through internal pretreatment before materials are received. The
West Trunk sewer runs under the Huangpu to the north of the Pudong New
Area and thence to an offshore outlet to take advantage of the dilution
potential of the Yangtze River (Figure 2.1). Elsewhere, efforts are being
made to improve surface waters heavily polluted through industrial and
sewage discharges, for instance through the Suzhou Creek Rehabilitation
Project (Downey, 2001, p. 5), which comprises sewage treatment works to
reduce inputs to the Creek together with an oxygenation programme. The
Project also includes research into municipal domestic waste and night soil
management, coordinated by the Sanitary Administration Bureau.

However, while Shanghai's environment has been seen to be improving
in relation to its traditional smoke- and water-based pollutants, economic
development and increased vehicle movement are creating new environmental problems. Emerging concentrations of ozone and nitrous oxide in
the densely built-up central city have caused particular concern. The
response has been both technical, in terms of improved monitoring capabilities, and policy orientated. Following a research study led by staff of
the Shanghai Municipal Research Institute of Environmental Protection
Services, the SMEPB proposed that all vehicles in Shanghai should switch
to unleaded petrol (Anon., 1997b). A local regulation was passed for Shanghai and four other major cities, resulting in leaded petrol being phased out
within a three-month period. Thus, from 1 January 1998 all cars were
expected to run on unleaded fuel. This will help to alleviate the problem
rather than resolve it, but indicates the speed and effect that particular
measures can have if there is the political will to implement them.

The SMEPB is also responsible for processing major projects requiring
an EIA. In this case 'major' is seen in terms of the level of investment, and
relates to any project estimated to cost more than US$30 million. How-
ever, how stringent such reviews are in practice must be questionable
when a staff of fewer than 10 is available to handle several hundred projects requiring an EIA each year (Tang et al., 1997). Other projects are
determined by more localized authorities within a prescribed framework.
Thus the SMEPB has set targets for the total amount of pollution that will
be permitted, and the relevant authorities are expected to make decisions
within this framework.

At the level of the SMEPB, there is clearly a great deal of work and effort
going into addressing the very serious environmental management problems facing Shanghai. However, at the same time there are at least three
factors that reduce the effectiveness of the more centralized actions. The
first relates to contradictory aspects of the approaches adopted; the second
to the procedures for enforcement and penalties for exceeding licence
agreements; and the third to the degree of autonomy vested in lower-level
authorities.

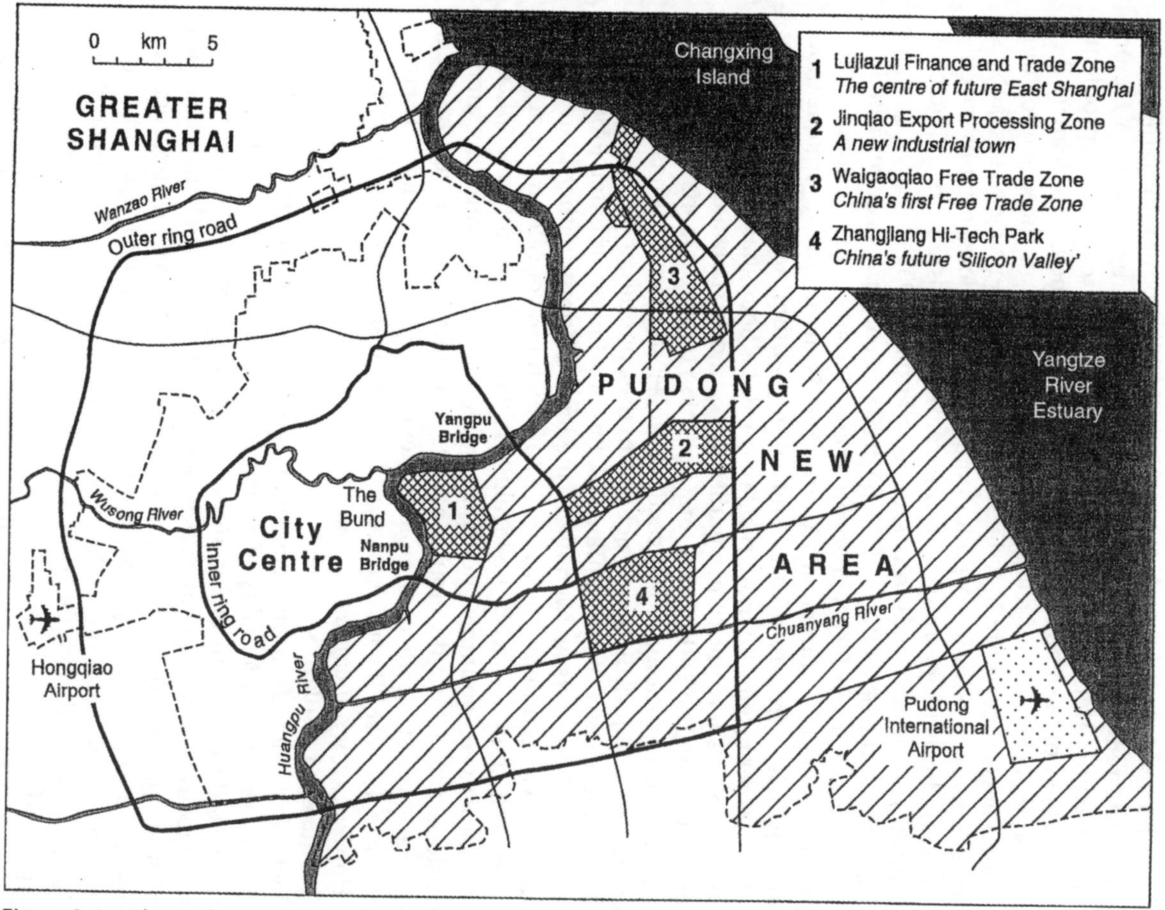
0 km 5
GREATER SHANGHAI
Changxing Island
1 Lujiazui Finance and Trade Zone
The centre of future East Shanghai
2 Jinqiao Export Processing Zone
A new industrial town
3 Waigaoqiao Free Trade Zone
China's first Free Trade Zone
4 Zhangjiang Hi-Tech Park
China's future 'Silicon Valley'
Wanzao River
Outer ring road
Yangtze River Estuary
PUDONG NEW AREA
Yangpu Bridge
The Bund
City Centre
Nanpu Bridge
Wusong River
Inner ring road
Chuanyang River
Hongqiao Airport
Huangpu River
Pudong International Airport

Figure 2.1 The Pudong New Area in Shanghai and the four key development zones
Source: authors

Lo and Yip (1999) suggest that while Shanghai's style of EIA regulation is legalistic, the process is, in practice, dominated by informal politics, notwithstanding the lack of popular participation.

In theory, manufacturing firms are expected to ensure that they do not discharge above a certain level. No permit or fee is required as long as the company or site remains within the specified discharge regulations. A fee or licence is required for exceeding these threshold levels. However, the problem arises because of the fee structure, which is neither sufficient to clean up the pollution caused, nor sufficiently punitive to act as an incentive for the adoption of cleaner technology. In other words, the licensing system acts as a disincentive to the control of pollution. There is also a long-established culture and tradition of ignoring environmental regulations, and the capacity of the SMEPB to enforce conditions is weak (Lo and Yip, 1999).

In addition, the best efforts of the SMEPB can sometimes be thwarted by the activities of lower levels of governance. In terms of institutional structure, the Shanghai Municipal Government is an umbrella organization within which there are district and county authorities. The six county authorities represent the more rural parts of the Shanghai Municipal area, and elsewhere there are 13 urban districts and one special administrative area in Pudong. The SMEPB sets total pollution targets or loads which these lower authorities should not exceed. However, in practice it has very limited powers and jurisdiction to act within the counties and districts. While each of these lower-level authorities has an Environmental Protection Bureau, its director is answerable to the local authority rather than to the Municipal Government. Decisions as to which new development actually occurs ultimately rest with the locality. As there is inevitably a lot of competition between counties and districts to attract new inward investment, decisions about new developments are not infrequently made on local political grounds, with economic imperatives being dominant. There is very little the SMEPB can do to overrule such local decision-making.

However, when it comes to major strategic decisions the SMEPB can try to mediate, particularly if projects may generate significant trans-boundary effects. One such example occurred when Jiangsu Province, immediately adjacent to the Municipality of Shanghai, wanted to promote substantial industrial development along the shores of Dienshan Lake. The proposal was perceived as vital to Jiangsu's prosperity. However, Dienshan Lake is a major supplier of fresh water to Shanghai, and the SMG was particularly concerned to prevent any development that might pollute this important resource. In this case the matter was referred to the national government, which considered that the proposed development strategy was wholly inappropriate.

Shanghai has also developed institutional mechanisms to draw in international experience and expertise to work on its environmental protection master plans, programmes and projects. These often involve the international development ministries/agencies of national governments (e.g. Australia, Japan); private consulting firms (e.g. PKK Kinhill, Mott

MacDonald; McLemore, 1995); and international financial agencies (e.g. the World Bank). The range and depth of Shanghai's requirements vary considerably, as do the relationships established. Some are one-off events; others demonstrate a build-up of experience and practice. What seems important in the latter is that the commissioned work involves local capacity-building through a combination of seconding Shanghainese staff to local project offices, joint working, demonstration projects, in situ training, and specialist study programmes and visits overseas. These 'soft' arrangements are an important but relatively unstudied aspect of institutional innovation in environmental planning and management in Shanghai.

Within Shanghai's counties and districts, there are also a number of development zone agencies, which are themselves regulatory authorities able to determine which companies are permitted to develop within their boundaries. Once again, broad environmental standards are set against which proposals should be judged. The relevant higher authority must also approve the detailed plan for an area. However, the agency then has autonomy to decide what should be permitted, with few effective sanctions on either the regulating authority or the development itself. The Waigaoqiao FTZ in Shanghai's Pudong New Area provides an illuminating case study, in which the interrelationships between economic imperatives and environmental quality in Shanghai can be examined.

PUDONG AND CHINA'S OPEN DOOR POLICY

Shanghai has a long history as one of the most cosmopolitan and powerful cities in China, and is seen by many commentators as being a key barometer of China's economic development (Yeung and Sung, 1996; Barnes et al., 1997; Murphey, 1998). However, it was nearly a decade after China's new open door policy was initiated in 1978 that Shanghai began to be promoted politically as a potential motor for change, and increased national support was secured for the city (Brown et al., 1995). Thus it was only in the early 1990s that central government policy changed, and it was decided to give national support to the local promotion of the city's development so that it could take on a new role as a world metropolis (Wu, 1998).

Today, Shanghai has a population of about 14.9 million, of whom 13.9 million are registered, and has experienced double-figure growth of its GDP over much of the past decade. A significant part of this economic growth is focused on a series of development zones, several of which are located in the Pudong New Area (Hodder, 1996). The Pudong New Area is a 522 km^2 triangular zone located on the eastern banks of the Huangpu River, between the main city of Shanghai (Puxi) and the Yangtze River (Figure 2.1). Apart from a relatively narrow strip of existing development along the Huangpu River, the Pudong New Area provides plenty of greenfield sites ripe for development, especially as new river crossings have improved the accessibility of the area (MacPherson, 1994).

The official line is that 'Pudong development will promote the regeneration and development of west Shanghai, restore Shanghai's function as a national economic centre, and lay the foundation for Shanghai to become one of the economic financial and trade centres in the Far East' (Zhao, 1993, p. 5). To this end, the essential underlying strategy is that the government should spare no expense in supporting the area's development, in both political and financial terms. It is implicit in the strategy that the industrial sectors in the Pudong should be free from the 'three wastes' of atmospheric, water and solid waste pollution (the Pudong New Area should benefit from high environmental quality). McLemore (1995, p. 30) has described how environmental considerations were a continuing theme in strategic planning process for the Pudong New Area in the early to mid-1990s. The resulting strategy provides for the new, modern development in the Pudong (east bank) to contrast with much of the rest of Shanghai (the Puxi, west bank), where environmental problems have traditionally been particularly acute. As noted above, these include the legacy of an outdated industrial base, inadequate waste collection and treatment systems, over-reliance on coal as an energy resource, and an environmental planning and management system not yet capable of addressing these problems (Lam and Tao, 1996).

As part of the overall development strategy for the Pudong, four key development sub-areas have been identified (Figure 2.1):

- the Lujiazui Finance and Trade Zone is to provide the centre for finance, trade and commerce, intended to help to restore the pre-eminence that Shanghai enjoyed as an economic centre in the far East in the 1930s and 1940s (Sun, 1994)
- the Jinqiao Export Processing Zone is being developed as an export processing base
- the Waigaoqiao FTZ is intended to serve as a large-scale, multi-functional free trade zone for the west coast of the Pacific
- the Zhangjiang Hi Tech Park is intended to harness the intellectual and research resources concentrated in the Shanghai area.

Two types of agency play an important role in the development and regulatory processes in these development zones. First, a public administration for the zone is responsible for creating the detailed planning framework and ensuring that development proposals conform to it, that the activity is compatible with the zone, and that municipal and national building regulations and environmental pollution control requirements are satisfied. Second, one or more development corporations are responsible for attracting inward investment and for managing the development process. They are usually assisted in this process by a wide range of financial incentives and other inducements, although the package of measures available varies from zone to zone. Clearly, these two institutional components have to work together closely and in some zones (such as Zhangjiang) the functions have been combined into one agency.

Evidence of new, large-scale development is to be found throughout Shanghai. By 1996 more than 500 key construction sites had been established across the city, and more than 100 major projects had required an environmental impact assessment (SMEPB, 1997). By focusing primarily on the Waigaoqiao FTZ, some of the environmental consequences of this rapid urban growth can be examined.

The Waigaoqiao FTZ

Initial ideas for the development of a new port facility on the Yangtze River at Waigaoqiao date from the mid–1980s. These were superseded in the late 1980s by the decision to make the Pudong New Area a state-led development area. The port and its associated landward area was designated a free trade zone in 1990, enjoying the greatest degree of preferential policies in China, and forming 'the largest regional international trade centre beyond Chinese customs but within China's territory' (Li, 1995, p. 14).

The Shanghai Municipal Government itself has been the overall guiding institution for the Waigaoqiao FTZ. In the 1990s, the SMG organized most of its special development responsibilities through the Pudong New Area Administration, which was absorbed into a new local government for the New Area in 2000. As Tsao (1996, pp. 100–102) has noted, the Area Administration was organized on a simplified basis, with one Bureau covering Comprehensive Planning and Land, and a separate but related Bureau taking responsibility for Urban Construction, including environmental protection along with public facilities and traffic issues. The Pudong New Area Government, following the principle of 'small government providing complete services', has structured its work into three composite bureaux, including an Environmental Protection and Urban Management Bureau (PNA, 2000).

The Pudong New Area Administration established a separate FTZ Administration Committee for Waigaoqiao. The Committee's basic responsibilities include drawing up, implementing and revising a development plan for the FTZ, making local by-laws, approving construction projects (including environmental considerations), and taking charge generally of the Zone's development administration, the provision of public utilities and public welfare. The FTZ's environmental protection staff thus have both horizontal working relationships in relation to the construction requirements of the Administrative Committee and the local development corporations, and vertical relationships with other environmental staff in the New Area Administration and the SMG. In addition, a number of FTZ Development Corporations, including the Xin Development Company (SWFTZXDC, 2001) and the Zone 3 Development Company (SWFTZ3UDC, 1995) were set up to construct infrastructure, manage real estate projects, provide support services for firms, assist in the establishment of enterprises, and organize the provision of utilities.

The process of infrastructure and site development in Waigaoqiao FTZ was so rapid that by March 1995, foreign investors had been attracted to the first phase from 39 countries and 22 major localities in China itself. An estimated 1552 investment projects were reported to have been approved, with investment commitments of US$2.5 billion. More than 100 construction sites were active, and over 200 buildings were reported to be under construction, while the volume of buildings under construction and completed amounted to 3 million m², of which more than 1 million m² was occupied (SWFTZ3UDC, 1995, p. 25). This rapid growth continued during the mid-1990s, so that by the end of 1997 some 3000 companies were located in the FTZ, employing about 30 000 people.

Environmental management and the Waigaoqiao FTZ

The rapid urban development in Shanghai and its key development zones has led to questions as to how far environmental management and the ideas of sustainable development are helping to shape the development process. The findings presented here are based on work to establish and evaluate the baseline environmental position of the FTZ for the Waigaoqiao Free Trade Zone Administrative Committee. They also raise wider questions in relation to the environmental planning and management regime in the Pudong New Area and the wider Shanghai municipal region. The detailed results of an evaluation of the baseline environmental impacts of development in the Waigaoqiao FTZ are discussed elsewhere (Brown et al., 1995; Massey et al., 1997; Wang et al., 1998). The key findings in relation to pollution control, creating a quality environment, and transport and sustainability are discussed here.

Although the existing developed riverside along the Pudong's western margins contained polluting heavy industry, the New Area, including Waigaoqiao, was intended from the start to be the environmental opposite of the heavily polluted Puxi. The SMG's Planning Commission, in its *Guidelines of Industries and Investment of Shanghai Pudong New Area*, specified (section 3[2]) that 'industries which produce substantial amounts of *Sanfei* (three types of waste [water, atmospheric and solid wastes]) and fail to meet environmental protection requirements for waste discharge after efforts for pollution control are made' shall be restricted or prohibited (Planning Commission, 1990). While there is room in the wording for discretion, in regulatory terms the general direction of the policy is clear enough. It also carries implications that infrastructure investment and administrative measures would be in place to deal with industrial and domestic waste, and that existing sources of pollution would be tackled in the future. Using the *Guidelines*, The FTZ Administration's construction and environmental protection office has been careful to ensure that new factories seeking to operate within the FTZ will not emit significant discharges into the atmosphere or watercourses, through regulating new development on the principle of best technology not entailing excessive cost. Thus the regulatory framework and administrative processes for new development should help to minimize its environmental impacts. The evaluation showed that, despite these measures, the FTZ was still facing some serious environmental problems.

Pollution control

The Pudong New Area starts from a generally better environmental base-line than the older and most densely built-up parts of the central city on the west bank of the Huangpu (Puxi), due to its location and general lack of development. In its development, moreover, the New Area is required to set new environmental standards for Shanghai. This requires action on two fronts: remedial action connected with current problems related to the older industrial areas along the Huangpu river (such as the oil refinery complex); and action to secure higher standards in the newly developing zones from the start. The then Shanghai Environmental Protection Bureau (SEPB) reported that air quality was better in the south and east of the New Area than the north and west (the location of older, heavy industry), where it noted serious pollution levels, surpassing not only national standards but even levels in Puxi (Sun, 1994, p. 22). However, the figures for the Pudong are generalized across the whole area, and in order to establish whether the FTZ had been achieving the higher environmental quality required for the new project, a team from East China Normal University was asked to evaluate the environmental conditions in the FTZ itself (Wang et al., 1998).

From the perspective of air quality, the results indicated that the FTZ enjoys very good (first/second class) quality against the relevant national standards. The higher levels of totally suspended particulates were considered to be largely a result of the construction going on in the area. From a water quality perspective, the situation was somewhat different. Surface water quality generally in Pudong is thought to be low, and there are some concerns about heavy metals and groundwater contamination in an area with a high permanent water table – typically approximately 1 m below the ground surface in many places. The water quality monitoring observations indicated 'poor' to 'very poor' quality (between 3 and 4 on an environmental standard scale of 1–5), especially at the surface. These levels were particularly noticeable at sampling points along the stretch of the north–south Gauqiaoguang Canal, which forms the eastern edge of the FTZ and receives flows from the highly polluted east–west Chuanyang Canal, and at points adjacent to the port, although scores for biological and chemical oxygen demand were lower here than along the canal.

Creating a quality environment

Monitoring a set of local habitats in Waigaoqiao revealed that little biodiversity existed within what had previously been a long-established area of intensive agriculture. While this might suggest potential for establishing a new, more broadly based biodiversity, in practice the main focus of policy has been on securing an attractive and visibly green business park character for the area. Planning for the FTZ is based on a series of detailed binding plans produced by the FTZ administration and approved by the Pudong New Area Administration. Development plans should conform to precise specifications, one of which is that, within the first phase, 30 per cent of the area should be left as green space and along the roads standardized green space widths should be designated, depending on the position of the road within a hierarchical framework. Beyond such specifications, which are admittedly extremely generous in comparison to Shanghai's previous practice, no specific landscape or ecological strategy was established for the Zone as a whole. Thus, a shrub and grass landscape has been established within individual development plots, and some tree planting has taken place along the infrastructure corridors. The development looks exactly like the master plan model, although in practice at a higher density than originally envisaged. However, a deeper eco-environmental greening opportunity has perhaps been lost.

Transport and sustainability

One of the most worrying aspects of the Waigaoqiao development lies in its implications for medium- and longer-term transport and energy consumption. The FTZ is accompanied by relatively little residential development, and much of the housing that has been built was for farmers displaced when the land was designated for development. Thus, as the FTZ continues to expand towards the expected 100 000 employees, the question arises as to how they are going to get from the central city of Shanghai (Puxi) on the west bank to Waigaoqiao. Currently most are bussed by their employers from the city to the FTZ. There are no formal plans for any integrated public transport system able to accommodate the intended massive flows of people. It must be questionable whether the bus-based approach, which appears to ignore the need to restrain demand for vehicle use, will be sustainable as more of the FTZ becomes operational, employment densities build up, and the Shanghai-based labour force swells the commuting tide.

CONCLUSIONS

Although it shared in a slowing of growth as a result of the Asian economic crisis of the late 1990s, Shanghai is nonetheless one of the most rapidly developing cities in the world. Such growth creates its own environmental problems. However, much of Shanghai's new development is, at least in comparison to much of its existing industry, relatively environmentally friendly. Within the city's key development zones in the Pudong New Area, attempts are being made to attract only specific types of non-polluting activity – with some degree of success. However, some aspects of the environmental quality of one of the principal development zones, the Waigaoqiao FTZ, were found to be poor because of current construction work or older, more polluting activities elsewhere in the metropolitan area. This finding raises questions about the ways relevant bodies cooperate and integrate their activities, both horizontally and vertically, within the city as a whole. On both counts the institutional framework for environmental management appears to be weak, with much decision-making and autonomy resting with the lowest authorities. There are conflicts between counties and districts within the Municipal Government area (and, indeed, between China's provinces), with mechanisms of mediation appearing to be relatively weak. The lower-tier authorities have considerable autonomy to pursue objectives other than those set by the SMEPB. Furthermore, the enforcement mechanisms for pollution control seem to be particularly weak. If Shanghai is to continue its current growth in anything like a sustainable manner, there is an urgent need to ensure that environmental policy is both more coherent and implemented, and enforced consistently by all levels of government. It has been suggested that, in order to try to promote more effective horizontal and vertical integration, a new authority should be established within the SMG, charged with setting municipality-wide objectives for the year 2010. These would inform decisions in all the sectoral departments of the SMG, by providing an agreed and accepted corporate environmental framework. The challenges are great, and the need for a more holistic approach with effective coordination of effort is readily apparent.

CHAPTER THREE

Rational environmental decision-making: some lessons from Thailand's EIA experience

Orapim Pimcharoen and David Shaw

INTRODUCTION

From a global perspective, the concept of sustainable development has been emerging as an acknowledged and accepted goal of most countries in the world. Notwithstanding the fact that the concept of sustainable development is not amenable to a simple or agreed definition, many global declarations recognize the need to employ various tools and techniques to deliver this objective. One such tool is environmental impact assessment (EIA) (WCED, 1987; Hinrichsen, 1987).

Environmental impact assessment is a systematic, technical and rational process that should help decision makers to determine the appropriateness or otherwise of large-scale development projects (Glasson et al., 1994). As a planning process, EIA is a unique blend of scientific and artistic disciplines (Wood, 1995), combining technical and administrative processes. The technical aspects of EIA research have tended to focus on improving the quality of the product. This is often evaluated through reference to the environmental impact statement (EIS). While there is no doubting that many environmental statements have acknowledged weaknesses, technical and rational research perspectives suggest that improvements in the quality of EIS will inevitably lead to better decision-making. In contrast, much less research emphasis has been placed on examining EIA as an administrative process. Each EIA system is unique, reflecting local legal, administrative and political contexts (Culhane, 1993). Important questions need to be asked about how EIA is integrated into various decision-making processes, and what impact EIA procedures have on decision-making. If EIA practice is going to contribute to the global goal of sustainable development, then it must be fully integrated into the decision-making and planning frameworks of particular localities.

Administrative aspects of any EIA system, particularly the institutional structure within which it operates and the strength of environmental law, including enforcement, are critical in evaluating and understanding the effectiveness of EIA as a tool in the project planning decision-making process (Gilpin, 1995). It has been argued that the American EIA system has operated effectively because supportive forces, both inside and outside government, have worked closely together to ensure effective implementation, in part through the encouragement of appropriate changes in organizational behaviour (Taylor, 1984; Clark, 1993). While EIA might be considered a technical or rational tool, it is only when the political will is sufficiently strong to ensure that the operational machinery (in terms of both administration and enforcement) is in place that an EIA process is likely to have any significant influence on the project decision-making process.

While EIA processes and procedures have been widely adopted, the influence of EIA on decision-making is very variable. In countries that appear to have well established and reasonably mature planning systems, EIA practices appear to be relatively easy to adopt and integrate into existing processes and procedures. This is the case for the Netherlands and France (Weston, 1997). Some countries (including Australia, Canada and the Philippines) have introduced new, specific EIA legislation that establishes requirements, institutions and procedures, while others, with well-established land-use planning systems, have responded by adapting existing environmental and planning legislation (e.g. UK) (Sadler, 1995; Barrow, 1997).

Many developing countries have followed the lead set by the USA and have essentially attempted to copy their practices and procedures (UN, 1990). Some of the pressure for introducing EIA practices has come from donor organizations and their requirement that the resources they provide should be used in a sustainable and environmentally-friendly manner. In many instances, donors have created separate, formalized EIA systems that run in parallel to other decision-making processes (related to, for example, project planning or pollution control). However, little is known or understood regarding the effectiveness of such processes in influencing or shaping decision-making.

This chapter seeks to shed some light on the administrative aspects of decision-making by focusing on Thailand. The chapter is divided into three parts. First, we review the formal EIA procedures in Thailand, describing both the legislative and administrative framework. The second part of the chapter briefly reviews the numbers and types of EIA in Thailand, and suggests that, from a technical quality assurance perspective, the independent scrutiny of statements ensures that the quality of environmental impact statements associated with approved projects is reasonably good. However, closer examination of the practice of EIA in Thailand suggests that the EIA process runs in parallel with pollution control mechanisms and, moreover, often has no impact on the decision to construct a particular project. We conclude by suggesting that much more emphasis needs to be placed on understanding what impact an EIA process actually has on decision-making, always recognizing that an EIA system is embedded within the political and cultural context of the country in which the legislation is enacted and implemented.

ENVIRONMENTAL IMPACT ASSESSMENT IN THAILAND

Before outlining the formal EIA procedures in Thailand, a brief description of the national context is given.

An overview of Thailand

Nearly 80 per cent of Thailand's 60 million people live in rural areas (NSO, 1997). Bangkok is the capital, and the centre of Thailand's administrative and financial system, international trade and investment in business, and tourism. It is one of the fastest growing cities in Asia, and experiences all the accompanying problems of rapid growth.

In the recent past, most of Thailand consisted of many small, relatively self-sufficient rural communities, which depended on the natural resources surrounding them. The national economy relied on the export of native crops. The sustainable use of natural resources was a fundamental aspect of rural life, and a close relationship between local farmers, their activities and resource protection developed. Over the past two decades, however, Thailand has undergone a dramatic transformation, with a rapid increase in industrial development and urbanization. Thailand's transition to an export-oriented economy took off in the early 1980s (TDRI, 1996). However, this economic growth and industrial development has been achieved at the expense of the environment and the natural resource base of the country. At the national level, the migration of large numbers of people to the cities and the growth in industrial activity has resulted in major pollution problems in the capital and other major cities. In rural areas the expansion of agricultural production has resulted in the clearance of forests, which are one of the most precious resources of the country. In the early 1990s some 160 000 hectares of forest were being cleared annually, with only 26 000 hectares of replanting (TDRI, 1996). Because of a growing awareness of the environmental degradation that development was causing, EIA was first formally introduced in the mid-1970s, although EIA activity in Thailand predated the formal enactment of legislation. In 1972, following a World Bank suggestion, a partial EIA was undertaken that focused on the ecological impacts of the Srinakarind Hydropower Dam, a project proposed by the Electricity Generating Authority of Thailand (AIT, 1972; World Bank, 1974). It was the associated financial aid from a donor organization that first introduced the idea of EIA into Thailand, but this was soon to be followed by more formal legislation.

Introducing the Thai EIA process

Key elements of an EIA process include its legal basis, the allocation of organizational responsibility, and the procedures to be followed. These are discussed in turn.

Legislative framework

Following the enactment of the National Environmental Quality Act (NEQA) in 1975, an EIA system was formally introduced in Thailand, pre-dating much of the EIA legislation in European countries. The legislation created a new official body, the Office of National Environmental Board (ONEB), responsible for determining which projects would require an EIA. Initially only large-scale projects promoted, designed and implemented by state enterprises were subject to EIA requirements (MOSTE, 1981). How-ever, it was soon realized that there was a fundamental flaw in this forma-tive legislation – the ONEB was only an advisory body and did not have any regulatory powers of its own (UN, 1990; Sriburi, 1995).

The first amendment of the NEQA in 1978 extended the scope of projects requiring an EIA to include dam and reservoir projects, as well as various private sector projects. The ONEB was given responsibility for formally reviewing the quality of submitted statements.

A second amendment to the NEQA was adopted in 1992. The Ministry of Science, Technology and Environment (MOSTE), with the approval of the ONEB, was given power to issue notices prescribing the nature, type, size and location of projects or activities of government agencies, state enter-prises or private organizations that should be subject to EIA procedures. Project proponents are required to submit an EIA report to the Office of Environmental Policy and Planning (OEPP), a department within MOSTE, for consideration and, more importantly, approval before any designated project can proceed.

Paralleling the approach adopted elsewhere, Thailand has identified a positive list of projects that are subject to an EIA procedure. There are basically two types: those that are likely to have significant environmental impacts because of their size, scale or nature; and those that are located in particularly sensitive environments. The list was initially approved in 1981 with 11 specified project types, and this was subsequently amended, in 1992 and 1996, in response to growing environmental concerns, so that now there are 22 project types requiring an EIA (Table 3.1). An interesting feature of the listing is that where thresholds are specified, these are absolutes, with the result that many developers seek to circumvent the regulations. For example, a number of small individual hotel projects of 79 bedrooms or less have been built together in a complex to avoid the 80-bedroom threshold. The cumulative effect of several small projects has, therefore, escaped assessment.

Organizational involvement

The statements are prepared using a fairly standard approach which describes the project, analyses environmental conditions, predicts the environmental impacts associated with project construction and oper-ation, suggests appropriate avoidance or mitigation measures for the more

Table 3.1   Projects requiring EIA in Thailand

Types of projects or activities	Criteria
1 Dam or reservoir	Storage volume of at least 100 million m³ or storage surface area of at least 15 km²
2 Irrigation	Irrigated area of 12 800 hectares or more
3 Commercial airport	All sizes
4 Hotel or resort	Numbering 80 bedrooms or more
5 Mass transit system and expressway projects	All sizes
6 Mining	All sizes
7 Industrial estates	All sizes
8 Commercial port or harbour	Capacity for vessels of 500 ton gross or more
9 Thermal power plant	Capacity of 10 MW or more
10 Industries (eight types)	
– Petrochemical industry	Using raw materials produced from oil refinery and/or natural gas separation unit with a production capacity of 100 tons/day or more
– Oil refinery	All sizes
– Natural gas separation processing	All sizes
– Chlor-alkaline industry requiring sodium chloride as raw material	Production capacity of each or combined of 100 tons/day or more
– Iron and/or steel industry	Production capacity of 100 tons/day or more
– Cement industry	All sizes
– Smelting industry other than iron and steel	Production capacity of 50 tons/day or more
– Paper pulp industry	Production capacity of 50 tons/day or more
11 All projects in watershed area classified as Class 1B by the Cabinet Resolution	All sizes
12 Coastal reclamation	All sizes
13 Large buildings	Buildings with a height of at least 23 m or total floor area more than 10 000 m²
14 Residential condominium	80 or more units
15 Land allocation or housing project	500 or more land plots or a total land area of more than 16 hectares
16 Hospital located:	
– In area adjacent to rivers, coastal areas, lakes, or beaches	30 or more patient beds
– In area other than above	60 or more patient beds
17 Pesticide industry or industry producing active ingredients by chemical process	All sizes

18	Chemical fertilizer industry which uses chemical process in production	All sizes
19	Highway or road passing through the following areas	All projects
	– Wildlife sanctuary and non-hunting areas	
	– National Parks	
	– Watershed area	
	– Mangrove forest designated as National Forest Preserve	
	– Coastal area within 50 m of maximum sea level	
20	Waste disposal plant	All sizes
21	Sugar and related products industries	All sizes
22	Petroleum development	All sizes
	– Surveying/drilling	
	– Petroleum and oil pipeline transportation	

Source: MOSTE (1981, 1992, 1996).

serious and adverse impacts, and identifies suitable monitoring proced-ures. Such reports are submitted to the OEPP, the government department responsible for the administration of the EIA process, for review and approval. Within the OEPP there are 12 separate divisions. The Environ-mental Impact Evaluation Division (EIED) is directly responsible for administering the EIA process. In addition, there are other stakeholders who have an important role in Thai EIA procedures.

- The project proponent is usually a government agency, state enter-prise or private sector organization whose proposed project/activity falls under notification for the types or sizes of projects that require an EIA. The project proponent is responsible for the prepar-ation of the EIA report, although this task is usually subcontracted to consultants.
- Since December 1984, it is a requirement that any EIA report must be prepared by a consultancy company which is registered with the OEPP. Currently, 55 consultancy companies are licensed to conduct EIAs in Thailand, with the licences normally being valid for five years. This licensing procedure and, where necessary, the cancelling of a licence, are important mechanisms designed to control the quality of consultants and thus, indirectly, the quality of EIA studies and reports (OEPP, 1995).
- An independent Technical Expert Review Committee (TERC) is responsible for reviewing the quality of all submitted EISs. While the EIS is subject to a preliminary review by the OEPP to ensure

conformity with the guidelines, it is the TERC that provides more crit-ical technical analysis. Within the TERC there are five panels (water resources, transportation, mining, industrial, residential groups), one for each of the most significant project types. Each group comprises 16 individuals who are appointed by the National Environmental Board. Some are specialists in relevant disciplines, others represent the permitting agency, and at least two are drawn from the NGO sec-tor. The TERC can and does reject EIA reports, and may ask the pro-ject proponent or its consultant to revise a report or provide additional information before a decision can be made. The TERC is, therefore, a semi-independent quality assurance mechanism.

■ The permitting agency is the body charged with the power and duty to consider and grant permission for any project. Such decisions are dependent on EIA approval. However, when the EIS approval process exceeds the timescale laid down by law, the EIS is deemed to have been approved unless an extension to the review period has been agreed. In approving an EIS, the TERC may identify conditions to be applied to the consent, and these must be included in any permission granted by the permitting agency. If the project pro-ponent is a government agency or state enterprise, the final decision-maker is the Cabinet, otherwise the permitting agencies are national agencies such as the Departments of Harbours, Mineral Resources, or Industry, or relevant local authorities (the Bangkok Metropolitan Government and the 75 other provincial local authorities).

The EIA process

Once an EIS has been submitted, two alternative procedures are followed, depending on whether the report is on a private project or one initiated by the government or a state enterprise. If the project is a private initiative, the EIS is always submitted to the EIED (a department within the OEPP; Figure 3.1). The EIED then has 30 days to conduct a preliminary review and pre-pare a report for the project proponent and the TERC. This review checks that the statement conforms to the guidelines, rather than evaluating the quality and validity of the proposal. If the EIED considers that the state-ment is deficient, it can be returned to the project proponent or its con-sultant for revision. Once the statement has satisfied the EIED, the statement, along with any preliminary comments, is forwarded to the appropriate expert group within the TERC. This sub-group then has 45 days to consider the EIS. If the EIS is approved, the relevant permitting agencies are able to grant permission for the project to operate, subject to comply-ing with any mitigation measures and ensuring appropriate monitoring programmes are in place. If the report is not approved, the project propon-ent has to revise the proposal or submit additional information to satisfy the TERC's requirements. Until the TERC approves a statement, any permitting agency has to withhold the relevant licences.

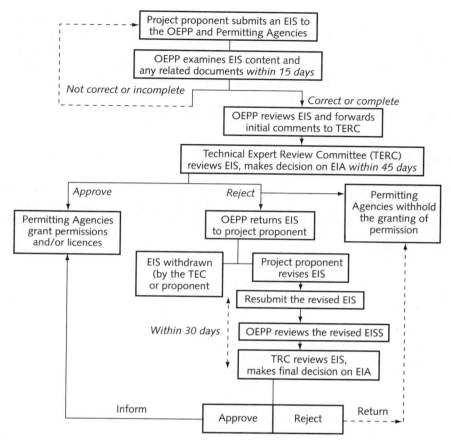

Figure 3.1 The EIA approval process for private projects and projects that do not require Cabinet approval. *Source:* OEPP (1995)

Most of the rules and regulations governing the EIS approval process focus on the length of time the review of a statement should take. This is so that EIA procedures do not delay the development process unnecessarily. The OEPP is responsible for overseeing the EIA approval process. Before 1992, the OEPP was required to complete the review of an EIS within 90 days, and then had a further 30 days from the date of any resubmission. In 1992, aware of some of the problems and criticisms of the EIA approval process, the NEQA introduced fundamental reforms. Responsibility for the technical review of EISs was transferred from the OEPP to the TERC. The period for reviewing a statement was shortened from 90 to 75 days, and for all projects the EIA is to be integrated into the project design as early as possible, ideally forming part of the feasibility study. These reforms recognized the limited role that an EIA prepared late in the process can have on decision-making, and suggested that EIA had become a bureaucratic hurdle instead of an integral part of project design.

In the case of government or state enterprise projects, where the permitting agency is the Cabinet, the process is different. By law the EIA process is required to start much earlier, and the OEPP sets the terms of reference on a case-by-case basis. It is the National Environmental Board which is responsible for assuring that the statement conforms with the guidelines and is of sufficient quality. Furthermore, there are no set time limits on how long the review of the statement may take (Figure 3.2).

EIA IN PRACTICE

The above review of the legislative process and procedures demonstrates that EIA is seen as an important environmental management tool in Thailand. But how does EIA work in practice? There appear to be good quality control mechanisms with respect to the statements themselves, but does the EIA process actually aid decision-making?

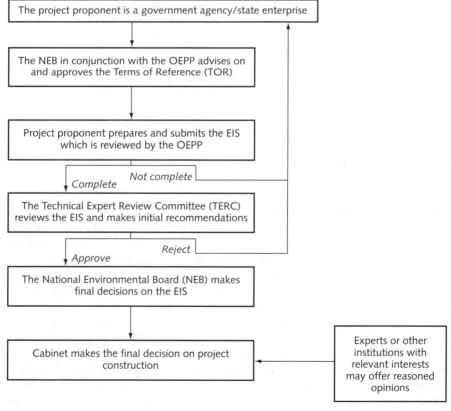

Figure 3.2   EIA approval process for projects requiring Cabinet approval
Source: OEPP (1995)

Because of the OEPP's formal involvement in the processing of EISs in Thailand, it has a comprehensive record of statements and relevant decisions. By collating records showing the nature, size and scale of all projects that have required an EIA, the date the EISs were submitted, and the timing and outcomes of EIA review processes, a systematic overview of EIA in Thailand was established (Pimcharoen, 2001).

Between 1982 and 1997, official records suggest that 4615 project proposals were subject to EIA procedures. Two factors account for the annual increase in the number of projects subject to EIA procedures. First, the number of project types covered by the EIA legislation has expanded; second, investor confidence is reflected in the strength of the national and regional economy. In the early 1990s, project EIS submissions averaged between 200 and 300 statements per annum. The mid-1990s saw a significant fall in the number of large-scale development projects, coinciding with the collapse of the Thai economy. More recently, following economic recovery, the number of statements has exceeded 350 per annum

In addition to the increasing number of projects subject to an EIA, there has been a switch between different categories of project over time. In the formative years the most common project type requiring an EIS was mining, with well over 1500 proposals submitted. More recently, the Thai government has effectively prohibited such private sector projects because of the environmental damage caused, unless the proposal is critical to the needs of the construction industry. Therefore the number of mining EISs has become insignificant. Instead, different sectors of the economy are becoming increasingly subject to EIA procedures, notably large-scale housing and industrial development projects.

For a private sector project, the EIA is initially scrutinized by the OEPP and then by one of five expert groups of the TERC. These groups are relatively small organizations, so how do they manage this heavy and increasing case load? With very few exceptions, statements are considered within the prescribed time periods, and a significant number of statements are rejected on at least one occasion. A rejection by the TERC means that the permitting agency must withhold the relevant licences. On a year-by-year basis, about one-third of all EIS submissions are initially rejected by the TERC. Many are subsequently resubmitted, until the authorities are satisfied. Often this may involve two or three resubmissions. Very few projects appear not to have proceeded in the end because of an initial adverse or poor EIS. Only about 2 per cent of all projects for which an EIS has been submitted (about 100 schemes) have been rejected and the project proposal formally withdrawn or a statement never resubmitted.

What this initial survey confirmed was that EIA is an accepted and important part of project development in Thailand. The system appears to be based on independent verification, which resulted in a significant number of statements being rejected, at least initially. Thus there is clear evidence that the system placed a great deal of emphasis on the quality of a statement, with some suggestion that the requirements of the regulatory agencies, as they became more familiar with the process and more conscious of the impacts of certain types of projects, were becoming stricter. The number of EIS statements that were deemed unsatisfactory increased from 28 per cent in 1992 to 43 per cent in 1996 (OEPP, 1997). Thus, from a technical point of view it appears that the system is demanding high-quality EISs from project proponents and their consultants. But what impact do such statements actually have on decision-making? The statements submitted may be extremely comprehensive and technically competent, but if they have little impact on decision-making, their role must be questioned.

In order to explore this question, a number of case studies were chosen for more detailed analysis: three industrial projects and three large housing projects. Full details of these case studies can be found elsewhere (Pimcharoen, 2001). This paper reports briefly on some of the key findings. The case study analysis involved a number of stages. The project files were explored to establish the chronology of events; the EISs were reviewed to assess the quality of the product; and structured interviews were held with key stakeholders involved in the process to obtain their views and perspectives on the EIA procedures. In evaluating the process, it is useful to divide it into two parts. The technical process refers to the way the statements are prepared, while the administrative process refers to how the public authorities use and consider the EIA in decision-making. These processes are complementary. The evaluation suggests that there are shortcomings in the EIA process in Thailand, particularly from an administrative perspective.

There are robust quality assurance mechanisms in evaluating the statements themselves. This is evidenced by the number of statements that are initially rejected as being incomplete or inaccurate. However, the detailed case study work revealed a number of limitations with respect to technical aspects of the process, giving rise to a view, at least on the part of the project proponents, that EIA is an unnecessary bureaucratic hurdle that involves additional cost and delay without adding any value to the project. There are a number of components to this perspective. Many project proponents initiate an EIA at the end of the project design process, often after a construction permit has been granted. When delays are encountered because submitted statements are rejected on one or more occasions, the project proponents describe the process as unnecessarily bureaucratic. Often the consultants specialize in particular types of projects, and tend to apply a formulaic approach, replicating previous statements that have been approved elsewhere without due consideration of local conditions. As a result, because of a lack of adequate scoping, significant impacts may be omitted.

On many occasions, project construction has started before the EIA review has been completed (or, in some cases, even started), and therefore there is no opportunity realistically to consider alternatives. For example, a cement factory in Lampong Province promoted by Thai Cement PLC was subject to EIA procedures. The EIA process started six months after construction of the plant began, in January 1994, and the EIS was eventually approved in October 1994. The EIS approval was critical in enabling the Operating Licence to be granted, in November 1994. Such a delay inevitably means that the only way to deal with significant environmental impacts is through mitigation measures and/or attaching strict monitoring conditions to licences.

However, in practice the monitoring is often not undertaken, and on those rare occasions when it is, it is not carried out in a systematic and regular manner by suitably qualified staff. This is a function of both an institutional framework unwilling and unable to enforce the conditions, and a lack of suitably qualified and trained individuals to carry out the monitoring. From a project proponent's perspective, once an operating licence has been approved, monitoring of impacts is perceived as an unnecessary burden for little or no perceived benefit, especially when the chance of the regulatory authorities rescinding the operating licence is extremely remote. This is largely a function of the limited resources allocated to enforcement agencies. Thus, while the law suggests strict environmental protection, national policy promotes rapid economic growth, and enforcement regimes are lax. Thus project proponents often ignore conditions that they perceive to be unnecessarily burdensome or that will incur unnecessary costs.

Even if some of these technical problems could be overcome, there are still significant problems in incorporating EIA within the Thai planning process. Perhaps the biggest problem is the way the EIA system fails to relate to the land-use planning system. There are numerous examples where projects are granted planning permission, and indeed actually constructed, before EIA procedures have been satisfactorily concluded. Where the EIA process can have an impact is in delaying the operation or occupation of a building until the EIA procedures have been satisfactorily completed. For example, construction permission for a housing project in Ratburana District, to the west of Bangkok, was granted in September 1993. However, it was not until December 1993 that the project proponent commissioned consultants to carry out an EIA. It then took nine months to prepare the statement, which was initially rejected by the OEPP because it failed to satisfy the basic guidelines. It was resubmitted in December 1994 and eventually approved in February 1995. The whole EIA process lasted 15 months and was not finalized until after the houses had been built. Before houses can be occupied, an Occupation Permit is needed, and in this case it was withheld until the TERC finally approved the EIS.

For industrial properties, not only Occupation Permits but also Operating Licences are required. The latter ensure that the necessary pollution control licences have been obtained before production begins. Once gained, these Operating Licences must be withheld until the EIS has been approved. They may also include conditions that anticipate various mitigation measures. Pollution control licences usually operate over a five-year timescale, and in theory can be revoked at any time if any of the operational conditions are breached. However, in practice revocation has never happened.

So first, there are at least three decision-making processes that can relate to EIA procedures; and second, the link between an EIA process and land-use planning is extremely tenuous. Local authorities are responsible for planning and construction permits, and they usually alert project propon-ents to the need for an EIA, although often after planning permission has been granted. The EIA process is administered by an agency of central gov-ernment (OEPP), and a semi-independent technical review panel (TERC) evaluates the quality of a statement. Both bodies can and do reject submit-ted statements, and may require further information and/or additional mitigation measures before they approve an EIS. For those projects falling within the jurisdiction of an EIA procedure, the approval of an EIS by the TERC is a necessary prerequisite for an Operating Licence to be issued by one of six different central government ministries, depending on the type of project in question. Thus the EIA process appears to be extremely bureaucratic and technical in nature. The EIA is intended to be an antici-patory tool, but in the Thai situation it is difficult to see how the process is effectively integrated into decision-making processes at a sufficiently early stage in project design and development to be effective in preventing or mitigating adverse environmental impacts.

CONCLUSIONS

The EIA procedures have been designed to minimize the environmental impacts resulting from the implementation and operation of large-scale projects. In general, in Thailand environmental concerns have been a sec-ondary priority, overshadowed by the overriding priority of economic development. This has led to a lack of awareness among project propon-ents and permitting agencies of the potential benefits of the EIA process. Such perspectives are often compounded by a lack of political will, so that projects are often approved before an EIA process has started, yet alone been completed.

As a result, EIA has tended to be used to mitigate the expected negative environmental impacts of large-scale projects, rather than as a project planning tool or decision makers' assistant to achieve sustainable develop-ment. Project proponents perceive EIA as a bureaucratic hurdle, which is accepted as a necessary evil in order to obtain project permission, rather than a tool that could be used in the design process to minimize the adverse environmental effects generated by their projects.

Despite the generally good technical quality of EISs, EIA is likely to have little if any impact on protecting the environment. Although there is still scope for improving the quality of EISs, this is unlikely to change the situation. What is clear is that EIA needs to be incorporated into decision-making more effectively and consistently, in order to influence decisions about whether a project ought to proceed, where it should be located, and how it should be designed. To achieve this there will have to be a fundamental change in the attitudes not only of project proponents, but also of administrators in a variety of agencies, and of politicians.

CHAPTER FOUR

The effects of home-based enterprises on the residential environment in developing countries

Graham Tipple, Justine Coulson and Peter Kellett

INTRODUCTION

For many households in developing world cities, home-based enterprises (HBEs) are essential for a sustainable livelihood. The effect of Structural Adjustment Programmes and other economic events during the last 20 years of the twentieth century have reduced the scale of the formal sector, and have driven many people to earn their living in the already active informal sector. Because setting up shops or workshops can be both complex bureaucratically (de Soto, 1989) and prohibitively costly, new and long-standing micro-enterprises benefit from being in the only space households can use without further cost: their domestic space. Thus HBEs are important, and are likely to be increasingly so, in developing countries. Their success can contribute significantly to sustainable economic development.

However, HBEs tend to be unpopular with regulatory authorities dealing with employment conditions, land-use planning or building control. They are perceived to be generators of poor working conditions, and there is some literature documenting problems faced by out-workers who carry out part of a larger industrial process within their homes (e.g. Bhatt, 1989). It is assumed that the HBE will impinge on already scarce domestic space to an extent that is harmful to the resident household. In fact, where there is legislation allowing some enterprises in residential buildings, there is often a stipulation as to the maximum amount of space to be used. For example, the regulations developed for Pretoria before the end of apartheid to govern HBEs in the white suburbs allow for a maximum of 30 per cent of the gross floor area of a dwelling to be used for a home business. There are no exact space stipulations in the Act of 1984 for Black Communities. Part 8.2 simply states that:

> the occupant of a residential building may practise the social and religious activities and their occupations, professions or trades including retail trade on the property on which such residential building is erected provided that: the dominant use of the property shall remain residential. . .

The negative externalities and threats to the environment arising from industrial uses are well documented in the literature, recently by Robins and Kumar (1999) and Hameed and Raemaekers (1999). From this arises a perception of the dangers of mixing industrial and domestic uses. However, hints that it is not necessarily, or even regularly, the case that HBEs create poor environments can be found in the rather sparse literature on the interface between HBEs and the housing environment. Strassmann (1987) found that HBE operators in low-income settlements had better dwellings than those without HBEs. The dwellings were one-third more valuable, they occupied larger sites, they had more floor space, and they were more likely to have sewer connections. He characterized the HBE operators as the elite of the low-income settlements.

This chapter uses data from a four-country comparative study of HBEs to highlight some of the environmental issues raised by their presence.[1] The study areas were in Bolivia (*La zona sur* in Cochabamba), India (Bhumeheen Camp, New Delhi), Indonesia (Kampung Banya Urip, Surabaya) and South Africa (East Mamelodi, Pretoria). In each study, about 150 households with HBEs and about 75 without HBEs, living in the same study areas, were interviewed. Renting was not included in our study as, although it is a valid HBE, it involves no change of use from residential and so does not present the challenge to planning orthodoxy posed by, say, steel fabricating or pig-keeping.

In this chapter we summarize some of the quantitative data from the case studies. We show that many of the fears that inform policy banning productive enterprise in the home are based on misunderstandings of the nature of most HBEs. We find that people living in poverty seem to be content to put up with not only the problems they may cause through running HBEs, but also those caused by the HBEs of their neighbours. The benefits they derive from being able to make a living and using services offered in HBEs generally appear to outweigh any environmental concerns they may have. Thus we believe that regulations prohibiting the use of domestic space for business enterprises are inappropriate, as they are incongruent with the needs, priorities, practices and attitudes of the people occupying large proportions of our growing cities.

CHARACTERISTICS OF HOME-BASED ENTERPRISES

First, the characteristics of the HBEs in the study are described, and their employment and income benefits identified. Second, the homes in which HBEs operate are described and their effects on domestic living space and environmental conditions identified. Finally, some elements of a strategy to facilitate income generation in the home are suggested.

Types of enterprise

By far the most common HBE is the small shop selling daily household necessities for people who do not have a refrigerator or much storage space: fresh food, bottled drinks, snacks, soap, candles, rice, canned food, cigarettes (both in packets and single 'sticks'), etc. (Figure 4.1). In the South African shop shown, crime is such a problem that all the goods must be visible from the steel-grilled serving window on the right. There is also a range of more specialized shops: second-hand clothes, paraffin/kerosene, fish, meat, vegetables, sweets, soft drinks, as well as ice cream shops, small cafés and teashops, and beer bars. Many entrepreneurs make food for sale outside, either in the street or at places of work or schools. Services are represented by repair shops for clothes, shoes, cars, cookers, and footballs; personal services such as day-care crèches, sewing clothes and furnishings to order, hairdressers or barbers, doctors or traditional healers, photographers, dentists and dressmakers; rental of videos and party equipment; and office services such as band bookings, telephones, photocopying and assistance with legal documents. Production HBEs are often concerned with clothing manufacture: in the examples shown in Figure 4.2, an Indonesian woman sews in a room occupied by herself, her husband and three children, but the Bolivian clothing workshop is more sophisticated, manufacturing export-quality T-shirts. In addition to clothing, there were also manufacturers, assemblers or finishers of knitwear, embroidery, electronic components, shoes, masks, golf gloves, bags, jewellery, paper packages, shuttlecocks, and stone monuments; brick-making, upholstery, welding and woodwork; and a flour mill.

Figure 4.1 A small shop in South Africa selling daily requirements
Source: Centre for Architectural Research and Development Overseas, University of Newcastle-upon-Tyne

Figure 4.2   Home-based manufacturing: above, sewing in the living room in Indonesia; below, a clothing workshop in Bolivia
Source: CARDO, University of Newcastle-upon-Tyne

In *La zona sur*, Cochabamba, the production HBEs are overwhelmingly concerned with clothing manufacture, mainly of denim jeans and jackets, children's wear, dresses and T-shirts. There are also manufacturers of knitwear, shoes, bags, jewellery, and stone monuments. In Bhumeeheen Camp, Delhi, the most common production activities are outworking based on piecework in embroidery. There are also clusters of TV tuner-assemblers and thread-cutters. Outworking is not as important in the Indian case as might be expected from the literature (Bhatt, 1989), or from areas studied by others (Lall, 1994). In Banya Urip, Surabaya, there are several production HBEs manufacturing traditional Javanese furniture, decorated bird cages for export, masks of various kinds, and shoe uppers. There are many HBEs making rattan and wooden handicrafts or clothing to order, as well as a few niche market HBEs: a feather artist and farmers of crickets.

In the South Africa sample, the activities in our Mamelodi study areas are very strongly concentrated on providing daily needs and household services to local residents. Several HBEs make and sell traditional beer, usually providing a rudimentary place to sit and drink the litre measures. Services include traditional healers (*sangoma*). There is little manufacturing of items for sale to a wider market, only occasional HBEs in brickmaking, upholstery, welding and woodwork. One or two HBEs recycle metal into local charcoal stoves.

Employment and income benefits

It is evident in all our case studies that HBEs greatly increase employment opportunities for low-income households, especially for women. In all our case studies, at least 50 per cent more women work in HBE-operating households than in those without an HBE. There are also improvements in work participation for men, except in South Africa where slightly fewer men work in HBE households than non-HBE households.

Three out of four of our case studies show respectable increases in income for HBE households in comparison with their non-HBE-operating neighbours, especially at the means. In all three samples, HBE households are between a quarter and a third better off than their non-HBE counterparts at the means. In our fourth sample, in Bolivia, there is such a difference between HBEs and non-HBEs (the former are 150 per cent higher) that we suspect a sampling error has exaggerated the real difference.

Where they occur, HBEs are obviously very important contributors towards household incomes. In all the case studies, HBEs generate between half and three-quarters of their households' incomes. In the India and Indonesia samples, they provide about half the households' incomes. In Bolivia and South Africa, however, they are the chief income sources for the households that have them. In South Africa, more than half of HBE households have no other income. In the other three samples, between 33 per cent (in Indonesia) and 41 per cent (in Bolivia) have no other income. Thus HBEs are important for the households' incomes and quality of life. Without them, many would be severely hampered, and it would be beneficial if policy could take account of this when considering any harmful effects they may have.

ENVIRONMENTAL EFFECTS OF HOME-BASED ENTERPRISES

In this section, we examine the homes in which enterprises operate and the implications of this use for the space available to households, their access to services and their environmental impacts.

Homes used for enterprises

First, the condition and size of dwellings used for HBEs is described and compared with those without, leading into an assessment of the use of space for economic activities.

Condition and size of dwellings

Unlike Strassmann's (1987) sample, in our samples HBEs do not necessarily operate in better-quality dwellings than those occupied by non-HBEs (Table 4.1). The building technologies used in the case study countries can be grouped to gain some comparability. Bolivian adobe, a mud technology, can be classified as permanent and equivalent to blocks or bricks because, in practice, it is comparable. In a similar vein, wood and tin (metal of all kinds but mainly galvanized iron) in Indonesia and South Africa are defined as temporary. In our Bolivia case study, all occupy permanent dwellings; in India and Bolivia, slightly more non-HBE households occupy more permanent structures; but in South Africa, HBEs seem to occupy better-quality dwellings. Whatever the balance, there is no support for any assertion that HBEs are concentrated in the worst dwellings.

Table 4.1   Type of dwellings (percentage)

Dwelling type	Country			
	Bolivia	India	Indonesia	South Africa
Dwellings with HBEs				
Brick, block, adobe, permanent, 'pucca'	100.0	63.3	91.4	21.9
Semi-permanent, 'semi-pucca'		30.0	8.6	
Wood, tin, temporary, 'kutcha'		6.7		78.1
Non-HBE operators				
Brick, block, adobe, permanent, 'pucca'	100.0	69.3	98.7	15.6
Semi-permanent, 'semi-pucca'		28.0	1.3	
Wood, tin, temporary, 'kutcha'		2.7		84.4

The amount of space used by HBEs, and its proportion to the whole dwelling, are important issues in assessing the impact of HBEs on the living environment. Our India sample has very small dwellings, with means of 10.8 m² and 2.1 rooms for HBE households (Tables 4.2 and 4.3). These dwellings cover the whole of the plots, abutting other dwellings at the rear and sides. They accommodate a mean of 5.3 people and the HBE. The paucity of open space and the narrowness of the streets exacerbate the crowding, but also demonstrate that – at least in India – lack of space is not an obstacle to operating an HBE. The non-HBE sample has even smaller dwellings (by about 20 per cent or 2.2 m² less at the mean).

In the Bolivia sample, the HBE operators have about twice as much indoor space as non-HBE households, with a mean of four rooms rather than only 2.5. In Indonesia, the HBE operators have about 7 m² more space but no more rooms than non-HBE operators. In the South Africa sample, HBE operators have about a quarter more space than non-HBE operators (6 m² more at the mean) and one room more. As HBE operators have more indoor space than their non-HBE neighbours, this is strong evidence that HBEs generate better living conditions. However, we shall see below how far the presence of the HBE removes this advantage.

Table 4.2 Area of rooms (m²)

Dwelling type	Country			
	Bolivia	India	Indonesia	South Africa
Dwellings with HBEs				
Mean	72.8	10.8	59.1	28.1
Median	62.0	9.0	53.5	24.5
Non-HBE operators				
Mean	36.9	8.4	51.8	22.2
Median	25.0	7.7	47.3	20.5

Table 4.3 Number of rooms occupied

Dwelling type	Country			
	Bolivia	India	Indonesia	South Africa
HBE operators				
Mean	4.0	2.1	5.9	5.0
Median	4.0	2.0	6.0	5.0
Non-HBE operators				
Mean	2.5	1.8	6.0	4.2
Median	2.0	2.0	5.0	4.0

Use of space for HBEs

There is a great deal of difference among the samples with respect to the number of rooms and area used only for HBEs and the proportion of the dwelling that this represents. The larger dwellings in Bolivia and Indonesia contain more dedicated space than the smaller dwellings in India and South Africa. Both the former have a whole room dedicated to the enterprise at the median (and means of two-thirds or four-fifths of a room, respectively) while the latter two have no specialized rooms at the median, and means of only a small fraction of a room (one-third and one-fifth, respectively). In terms of space, the pattern is the same, although the Bolivia sample has a substantial lead over the Indonesian (a mean three times higher). The India and South Africa samples devote very small spaces indeed (means of less than 2 m²) exclusively to their HBEs.

The number of rooms and areas used for both domestic and enterprise uses – the fungible space (Lipton, 1980) – is greater, however, and follows a different pattern among the samples. Of the two that had the most rooms and areas used exclusively for HBEs, the Bolivia sample has relatively little jointly used space: 20 per cent of a room and 4 m² at the means. Indonesia, however, has two-thirds of a room and 8 m² at the means – about the same as the space used exclusively for HBEs. The smaller users of exclusive HBE spaces have more jointly used space. In the India sample, means of two-thirds of a room and 3 m² are jointly used, while in the South Africa sample there is joint use of almost a whole room and 5 m².

In order to assess the impact of HBEs on the space available, we have calculated net rooms and spaces used by including sole-use HBE rooms or space at parity, and mixed rooms or space used as half. We feel that this reflects at least some of the reality of room use, assuming that the HBE may 'get in the way' of domestic life in those rooms that are shared, but that economic activity does not prevent at least partial domestic use. The balance is likely to vary between great inconvenience where there is a fixed machine and little inconvenience where the paraphernalia of business can be shelved, both of which occurred in our pilot study in India (Kellett and Tipple, 2000).

There is little doubt that the ideal for most HBE households would be spatial separation between domestic and production activities, and many interviewees expressed their wish to develop a room for business use. However, in reality this is difficult to achieve for many, given the limited space and financial resources. The one strategy that is open to them is to be flexible about domestic arrangements.

It is informative to compare HBE operators' net domestic space with that of non-HBEs, to see whether HBEs cause crowding or not. Recall that HBEs have larger dwellings than non-HBEs in all the case studies. There are two patterns in our net domestic space data (Table 4.4). In India and Indonesia, the HBEs reduce the space available to about 80 per cent, roughly equivalent to that available to non-HBE households. In Bolivia and South Africa,

Table 4.4   Net domestic space* used for HBEs (percentage frequencies)

Dwelling type	Country			
	Bolivia	India	Indonesia	South Africa
Dwellings with HBEs (m²)				
Mean	47.6	6.7	46.8	23.4
Median	40.0	4.5	42.5	19.5
Percentage of dwelling area				
Mean	65.8	61.2	81.4	80.7
Median	66.7	54.2	85.7	83.2
Non-HBEs (m²)				
Mean	36.9	8.4	51.8	22.9
Median	25.0	7.7	47.3	20.5

*HBE space and half mixed space

HBE operators still have more space than non-HBE operators. Where plots are very small (in India), HBE operators reserve only 61 per cent of their space for net domestic uses at the mean, and little more than half at the median.

In order to demonstrate how crowded the accommodation is when there is an HBE, we can assess the net domestic space per person (Table 4.5). The larger household sizes for HBE operators in India and South Africa influence the outcomes. In India, HBE households are almost 10 per cent (0.4 persons) larger at the mean, while those in South Africa are a whole person larger at the mean than non-HBE households. In the India sample, a mean of only 1.3 m² of net space per person is available for HBE operators, representing very crowded accommodation. However, the South Africa sample shows in excess of 5 m² per person, and the other two case studies have more than 10 m² per person. Only one of the case studies (Bolivia) continues to show HBE operators with more space per person than non-HBE operators. This is largely owing to the very much larger premises occupied by the HBE sample. In the other case study areas, the differences are small at the medians but greater at the means (more than 2 m² per person in both the Indonesia and South Africa samples).

Table 4.5   Area (m²) of net domestic space per person

Dwelling type	Country			
	Bolivia	India	Indonesia	South Africa
Dwellings with HBEs				
Mean	11.9	1.3	10.5	5.54
Median	9.0	1.0	9.6	4.0
Non-HBEs				
Mean	8.7	2.0	11.6	7.0
Median	6.0	1.0	10.0	5.4

These data show that, whereas HBE households do have more space than non-HBEs, the effect of the HBE occupying domestic space is to take away that advantage. Thus, the suggestion that HBEs might generate better accommodation than where they are absent is ambiguous. Larger dwellings occur where there are HBEs, so the HBEs are probably helping to improve the housing stock. However, their households usually enjoy less domestic space, so there is no conclusive evidence that HBEs are instrumental in improving residential conditions within the dwellings. The negative effect of HBEs on net domestic space per person appears to be most serious where the original housing conditions give rise to crowded conditions (in our India sample). Thus we may aver that, where poor conditions exist initially, HBEs are likely to have greater effects on crowding than where the original conditions are more spacious.

Access to services

An important aspect of the housing environment is the access that occupants have to essential services. When HBEs are present, there are issues of whether they improve service levels by enabling the provision of better services, or whether they overload services provided only for residential users.

There is a varied relationship between the standard of services enjoyed by HBE and non-HBE households among the samples (Table 4.6). In Bolivia, HBE households enjoy marginally better services than non-HBE households, but they have twice as many telephone connections. In India, both have poor services, but non-HBE households have much poorer water and bathroom availability. Telephones and electricity are marginally more available to non-HBE operators – both of which are counterintuitive. In Indonesia, the non-HBE sample is marginally better serviced than that with HBEs, but both are well serviced. In South Africa,

Table 4.6 Services in houses or on plots of residents with and without HBEs (percentage frequencies)

Services	Country							
	Bolivia		India		Indonesia		South Africa	
	HBE	Non-HBE	HBE	Non-HBE	HBE	Non-HBE	HBE	Non-HBE
Water tap	52.1	48.0	3.3	10.7	82.9	86.7	60.5	61.8
Bath/shower room	32.7	17.3	4.0	10.6	98.7	100.0	9.5	4.4
Flush toilet	87.9	78.7	–	–	97.4	97.3	45.6	48.5
Pit latrine	15.1	20.0	–	–	0.0	0.0	34.7	39.7
Telephone line	53.9	25.3	4.7	5.3	100.0	100.0	4.8	8.8
Electricity	100.0	93.3	95.3	100.0	97.4	100.0	54.4	51.5
Sewerage	72.1	56.0	–	–	100.0	100.0	54.4	51.5
Refuse collection	0.0	0.0	–	–	98.0	98.7	54.4	51.5
Place to receive post	0.0	0.0	91.3	85.3	100.0	100.0	–	–

there is a slightly better servicing record for the non-HBE households, but that is probably a sampling quirk arising from a slightly larger proportion being drawn from an area where full servicing is available. Thus our data show no general improvement in services by virtue of operating an HBE.

This leaves the question of whether HBEs impose unsustainable burdens on residential service provision. This is dealt with below, mainly with regard to waste generation, the presence of machinery (drawing large amounts of power), and traffic generation. However, the nature of the HBE can be used to indicate water-use levels: HBEs that obviously require more water than domestic uses include preparing and serving food; brewing (mainly in South Africa); retailing vegetables, meat and fish; and services such as hairdressing, photography, medical and dental practices. None of these practised at HBE scale is likely to draw more water than can be supplied at domestic pressures through standard pipes. Even brewing uses only one or two oil drums full of water at a time in each HBE.

Waste generation and disposal

Waste generation and disposal are potential problems for HBEs. The waste materials generated by the enterprises investigated include textile offcuts and thread, leather offcuts, sawdust and timber, rubber, bottles, beads, metal (wire and nails), wrappings, plastic bags, sacks, boxes, waste food, dust and ashes, cut hair, diluted hair-perming liquid, and used components. Single HBEs produce a few potentially noxious or hazardous wastes: cadmium, diluted acid, needles and soiled dressings, razor blades, electronic components, chemical powders, coal dust, dye, fish waste, and oil.

Waste products are generally disposed of in the same way as domestic wastes. Where collection systems are unorganized or ineffective (in India and half the South Africa sample), HBEs may exacerbate the problems. However, some operators also recycle wastes, reducing the overall problem. They may simply collect bottles, paper, plastic, metal, etc., and sell them on. In Bolivia, for example, agents call round to buy waste material. Some use it as their raw material in making baby clothes or papier-mâché masks, stuffing pillows, manufacturing local stoves, making footwear out of rubber offcuts, etc. Some wastes, especially wood and rattan offcuts, are used as fuel. Waste food may be fed to animals kept around the house. Packaging such as sacks and bags is reused for storage; cloth, rattan and wood may be burnt for cooking or warmth in cold seasons. Polythene bags are also reused. The burning of wood, cloth, etc. for heating in winter or for cooking adds pollution to the atmosphere, but probably no more than would be produced by other fuel sources. Cadmium, produced in one Indian enterprise, is recycled by its producer. A user of styrofoam in Indonesia mixes waste pieces with fuel and makes glue for his own use. Very little is thrown away.

Use of machinery

Noise nuisance generated by HBEs is one of the arguments used against them, in that, in the minds of advocates of zoning, they may disturb the calmness that characterizes residential areas. Machinery use is an indicator of the likely noise nuisance generated by HBEs. As we shall see from the types of machinery used, noise levels are fairly low.

Our samples fall into two sets with respect to machine use. Over 40 per cent of the HBEs sampled in Bolivia and India have some form of machinery, however small. Machinery is much less common in the Indonesia sample and, especially, in the South Africa study area. Most own whatever machinery they use. By far the most common are sewing machines, with some hemming and overlock machines. There are a few printing presses, and some compressors. Metal working, welding and cutting machines are used in metal fabricating workshops, and carpenters may have some mechanized tools. An occasional HBE has a plastics moulding press or similar specialized machine. There are a few sound systems, and several items of hairdressing equipment. Photocopiers, gaming machines, video machines, computers, and other hi-tech equipment are used in some HBEs. Refrigerators and freezers are present in some shops. Some of these machines are likely to draw more power than is available under domestic supplies, but few generate significant amounts of noise.

Traffic generation

As with machinery noise and power demand, traffic generation is thought to be a harmful effect of HBEs. However, it is usually only the extra, supposedly heavy, traffic to the HBE that is considered. The reduction in traffic from localizing work and services in neighbourhoods can be considered as a positive effect of HBEs.

Perhaps the most crucial rows in Table 4.7 are the last two, the motorized vehicle journeys generated by HBEs. As we can see, these are very few in

Table 4.7 Most important mode of transport of supplies to HBEs (percentage frequencies)

Mode of transport	Country			
	Bolivia	India	Indonesia	South Africa
No supplies delivered	6.0	1.2	2.8	4.5
On foot	1.0	57.4	28.5	9.1
By animal	0.5	17.9	0.0	0.0
By non-motorized vehicle	5.5	18.5	11.7	2.6
By public transport	48.5	4.9	20.7	61.7
By light motorized vehicle	29.0	1.2	35.8	21.4
By heavy vehicle	9.5	0.0	0.6	0.6

India, and comprise between one-fifth and two-fifths of deliveries else-where. Public transport is an important mode in Bolivia and South Africa. Walking and other non-motorized forms predominate in India, and are important (40 per cent or so) in Indonesia; in both cases, streets inside the settlements are very narrow. Thus it is evident that there is some increase in traffic as a result of HBEs, but the fears about extra traffic and heavy vehicles penetrating residential areas are not well founded.

Some elements of a strategy to facilitate income generation in the home

The two most important elements of strategic assistance to HBEs are the acceptance of HBEs as valuable to the national, city, neighbourhood and household economies; and a change in the mind-set that sees them as anti-thetical to residential peace and quiet.

Often, HBEs are simply not valued or accounted for in the national economy. Their enormous contribution to people's lives is counted as worthless. This is partly because they are statistically invisible, which arises from their illegality and the fear of their operators that they will be closed down or harassed for *ex gratia* payments. With a hospitable atti-tude towards HBEs would come more trust on the part of operators and, after a grace period when trust is being established, an ability to include them in national statistics.

The Utopian dream of suburban residential areas, full of happily dozing households and quietly playing children, is so far from the reality of low-income neighbourhoods as to be useless in policy formulation. Such areas are vigorous, changing, challenging and productive places within which households draw layered screens around themselves to create islands of relative peace and privacy.

A mind-set that expects HBEs in residential areas would allow for:

- service levels suitable for the loads required by small enterprises
- plots large enough to work on
- dwellings a whole room larger than planned-for occupancy rates would indicate
- dwelling costs that take account of the potential income from an HBE.

The last two points deal with expectation, rather than provision or compul-sion. Householders with HBEs might be expected to have larger and more costly dwellings than where HBEs are absent, but should not be compelled to have them through prescriptive policies on housing standards.

Mains services should be provided with HBEs in mind. Their presence is not necessary for HBEs to operate, but it is likely that any problems caused by the presence of HBEs will be minimized if appropriate levels of services are installed. For example, our study suggests that inefficiencies in the municipal waste disposal systems will be exacerbated by the presence of HBEs. Thus it is important to expect higher levels of waste generation than mere domestic uses would generate, but not necessarily different types of waste. It may be desirable to install industrial levels of electrical voltage where HBEs are likely to be in manufacturing, for example, in towns specializing in particular industries (Lall, 1994).

Small plot sizes impose no bar on the establishment of HBEs. However, it is evident that an HBE has a more marked effect on domestic space when plots are very small. Thus, as indicated in Tipple's work on post-occupancy housing extensions (Tipple, 2000), plots should not all be small in the expectation that they will accommodate a single household. Instead, just as some plots might be large enough to permit cultivation or the construction of rooms for rent, space for an HBE should be included in the design.

There are, undoubtedly, HBEs that are unacceptable in residential areas, but there are very few examples in the study. Neither leather tanning (Mahmud, 2001) nor pig-keeping occurred, but there were a few kerosene sellers using inappropriately dangerous technology (open drums). If there are good reasons to prevent particular uses on health and safety grounds, these should be proscribed. However, for the rest, we contend that our data show them to be no great damagers of the residential environment. They tend to reduce space within the home to slightly poorer levels than their non-HBE neighbours enjoy. They have some marginal effects on the environment, and may impose unplanned-for burdens on services. But they are nowhere near the villains that planning rules imply.

We believe that HBEs expose the unhelpful nature of planning and building regulations for the livelihoods of people living in poverty. In line with Schilderman and Lowe (Chapter 14, this volume), our data demonstrate that current standards and procedures are unaffordable for informal sector entrepreneurs trying to maintain an economic advantage by working from home. In addition, the prohibition of most HBEs is clearly contrary to the opinions and priorities of their neighbours. Those that may be problematic are those that generate danger (including, in the South African case, those that attract crime) or excessive noise, smoke, dust, odour, etc. These, however, are in a minority. There are, moreover, problems with prescriptive regulations, including those that list acceptable uses, as they are likely to hamper newly emerging fields of endeavour, for example, cricket farming in Indonesia. There is little doubt that non-conformity to regulations leaves HBE operators open to extortionary practices by officials and agents who offer protection from prosecution, and renders enterprises ineligible for formal loans and other assistance.

The evidence suggests, then, not merely a general acceptance that HBEs are valid in low-income residential areas, but also that they should be encouraged. Local land-use and development control should be passed down to the local level, although the appropriate agent of control will vary from one country or city to another, and may be anything from chiefs-in-council to community-based organizations, depending on what is validated at the neighbourhood level and congruent with local norms. How decisions are made should be locally valid, but one approach could be based on whether a majority of immediate neighbours are content that a use should go ahead.

In the past it has been adequate to take account only of planning issues when determining planning decisions. However, sustainable development requires that the relationships between different parts of the policy- and decision-making process are recognized, for example when planning decisions take into account the need for economic development and poverty reduction. The issues exposed by HBEs vividly demonstrate the need to remove sectoral blinkers in decision-making about urban activities. This study has demonstrated that the decision-making process affecting low-income neighbourhoods should take account of the need for households to make a living and that, for many, their dwellings are the only places available for their economic activities.

PART II

ACHIEVING INSTITUTIONAL, SOCIAL AND CULTURAL SUSTAINABILITY

CHAPTER FIVE

Environments of harmony and social conflict: the role of the environment in defusing urban violence in Medellin, Colombia

Peter Brand

INTRODUCTION

As population and manufacturing production surge towards the cities of the developing world in the twenty-first century, so their profile in the sustainability debate has magnified. In the new millennium, the urban poor in less-developed nations will increase their share of the population. The environmental demands caused by this massive shift in population and industry has become a source of global ecological stress with which already hard-pressed local governments are finding it difficult to cope. As a consequence, improved urban management practices in the cities of developing countries will be vital to the search for sustainable development on a global scale. This is the essence of the argument behind the international approaches to sustainable urban development which emerged from the Rio de Janeiro World Summit.

This instrumentalist approach, while undoubtedly inspiring some interesting advances in urban management practice, has so far failed to produce significant net improvements in the urban environment, or to reverse deteriorating global environmental trends. Urban environmental management, as adopted wholesale in Agenda 21 (UNCED, 1993) appears to be set against the negative spatial effects of the neoliberal economics driving globalization (Burgess et al., 1997; Low et al., 2000). The environmental contradictions arising from economic globalization are examined by Zetter (2002). His conclusions concerning the managerial potential of current urban sustainable development policy are pessimistic, and tend to be borne out by recent evidence and projections (see, for example, International Red Cross, 1999; OECD, 1999; UNEP, 1999; World Bank, 1999a).

In the light of this disappointing performance, it is legitimate, indeed necessary, to enquire into urban environmental management as a social practice – not merely its social effects but, above all, as a mechanism for regulating socio-spatial relations in contemporary urban society. Such a theoretical perspective already has considerable practical support. The emphasis given in urban environmental management to local problems, involving decentralized systems of administration, bottom-up participation, local knowledge, social inclusion, culturally sensitive organizations, gender, and so forth, has opened the way to what might be described as a new paradigm for urban management, as evidenced at the 'City Summit' held in Istanbul (UNCHS, 1996b). It should not escape notice that this paradigm is aimed above all at the urban poor and disadvantaged – those excluded from the benefits of globalization and, in many cases, threatening to destabilize the often precarious social order of cities in the developing world.

Whereas from a global viewpoint the urban environment is conceived as a critical problem for planetary ecological survival, this chapter addresses the extent to which city governments are employing the environment as a solution to their internal social malaise. The theoretical argument for such a perspective is outlined, and then applied to an analysis of urban environmental planning and management in Medellin, Colombia. Two key themes examined are the role of discourse in creating meanings of the environment; and the way those meanings can be employed in conflict management and the legitimation of urban government. The case of Medellin, one of the most violent cities in the world, with an innovative and enterprising recent history of environmental management, is an appropriate and fecund example for exploring this approach in practice.

THE SOCIAL CONDITIONS OF URBAN ENVIRONMENTALISM

The socio-spatial effects of globalization

A major theme in current urban debate concerns how the globalizing tendencies of the 'new world order' are reducing the effective sovereignty of national governments and forcing cities to act as protagonists in the international arena. City entrepreneurialism has become the order of the day, but it is a tall order for the majority of cities in the developing world. What most cities are faced with is the much less glamorous need to survive.

Whilst international competition offers glittering prizes, it tends to mask the uneven consequences and often disastrous results of globalization at the urban level. The effects are well known, but it is worthwhile rehearsing some of the most alarming facts: a recent Human Development Report (UNDP, 1999) joined other voices condemning the growing gulf between rich and poor (both within and between nations); some 70 countries are now poorer than they were a decade ago; and the number of people living in absolute poverty could rise from 1.2 billion in 1987 to 1.9 billion in the year 2015, over half of whom will live in large cities in the developing world (World Bank, 1999a). Meanwhile, public expenditure budgets have been reduced under the weight of structural adjustment policies and economic and fiscal crises, unemployment and the informalization of work has increased, and outbreaks of protest and street violence have multiplied from Jakarta to Quito. Crime and violence, as symptoms of social decomposition, are recognized as a serious impediment to development in Latin America (Ayers, 1998). As World Bank Chief Economist Joseph Stiglitz has acknowledged, globalization is a dangerous force, '. . .a great wave that can either capsize nations or carry them forward' (World Bank, 1999b, p. 1) and most urban governments in the developing world are at the very eye of the storm.

One of the results of all this is an acute crisis of urban governance. In the already fraught context of increasing military conflict within many developing countries, social inequality and the dismantling of both traditional and modern welfare institutions are accentuating a breakdown of the social order and undermining civil authority within cities. This is an essential context for developing an adequate understanding of the environmental turn in urban planning and management. As Harvey (1996) clearly argues, any proposal concerning nature/environment is necessarily a social project. While sustainable development has been adopted by global institutions as a strategy for perpetuating capital expansion, city governments appear to be tapping into the discursive, institutional and financial resources of sustainable development policy to help contain the social conflicts and contradictions emerging from that very process.

Rethinking urban environmental politics

Much early theorizing of the politics of the environment centred on the environmental movement itself – its various philosophical origins, political strategies and social implications. However, as governments and businesses turned 'green' as well, a veritable cacophony of voices transformed an already confusing debate into an almost indecipherable one. Recent work has therefore directed its attention to this discursive dispute over the environment (Escobar, 1996; Harvey, 1996), and how environmental issues come to be defined, prioritized, managed and controlled (Hajer, 1995; Dickens, 1996; Eder, 1996; Macnaghten and Urry, 1998; Fischer and Hajer, 1999). This new 'cultural politics' of the environment has raised some interesting new questions, such as the trustworthiness of scientific knowledge, the relations between scientific and governmental institutions, the existence of multiple natures, the relativeness of values in nature, and so forth; in short, the way in which the environment as a problematic entity is constructed and fought over.

The application of this type of analysis to urban affairs has been largely limited to specific issues or disputes, coalescing around the idea of environmental justice (Harvey, 1996; Martinez-Allier, 1997; Marcuse, 1998). Environmental justice, concerned with the equity of the distribution of environmental 'bads', certainly provides a sharp political edge to the abstract goals of the official agenda on quality of life, social inclusion and poverty reduction. The analytical challenge with regard to urban affairs, particularly in developing and transition countries, consists in moving from issue-specific events and the interests involved in them, to a more structural approach incorporating not just disputes over particular development projects, but also the more general question of control over urban space and the management of urban conflict.

A key theme for developing such an approach is privatization. In its widest sense, privatization has brought with it major problems for the public sphere, which in modern society has been represented by the state. Recent transformations in the organization and functions of the neoliberal state have seriously weakened this representative capacity, with profound consequences for urban management. A general tendency towards decentralization has been offset by a massive privatization of goods and services, while at the same time local authorities have had to operate within severe fiscal constraints administered by central government. In fact, local authorities increasingly act as financial mediators, regulating the monetary relations between citizens and the private sector. As direct-supply public agencies disappear, the local state simply administers the (diminishing) flows of public expenditure on housing, health, education, roads, public transport, utilities and so forth, through the regulation of prices, tariffs, subsidies, access according to need, minimum levels of service provision, and so forth.

The point to be emphasized here is that this undermining of universal systems of service provision and the introduction of selective and/or competitive systems erodes the notion of the public interest vested in the state, and forces citizens into a position of self-interest. As a result, the state becomes increasingly remote and merely instrumental with regard to social welfare in privatized, fragmented and inequitable urban society.

The specific issue of the increase in urban crime and violence and the privatization of security can be seen as yet another manifestation of this overall trend. The state is unable to impose effective authority over large areas and sectors of urban social life, and security is privatized as individual citizens, residential communities, private companies, youth gangs, militias, mafias, vigilante groups, and so forth, arm themselves with conventional weapons and technological systems to protect their particular interests. The chronic inadequacies of the neoliberal state are exposed on the streets and in the daily struggle for survival.

The environment as the reconstitution of the public sphere

An inevitable consequence of privatization is that, as the reproduction of social life is determined ever more by the market, local governments are faced with a legitimacy crisis: they can no longer be seen to be effectively protecting the income and welfare of citizens. As command over the reproduction of the material conditions of social life slips from their grasp, city governments are left with a territorial jurisdiction reduced to its purely physical manifestations. Space, now understood as 'environment', is the only area that can be convincingly managed in the name of the public interest (Brand, 1999). While the idea of the common good vested in the environment has gained widespread currency at a global ecological level, it has been relatively underexplored in terms of urban management. This is somewhat surprising, as local environments are the lived space through which abstract notions can be made to appear real and evident, and so gain political import.

The key to the legitimation of local governments through the environment is to separate the spatial from the economic, and achieve a public consensus that the quality of urban life is spatial and autonomous. It is not simply a matter of arguing that space/environment is important in people's lives – it very obviously is – but to convince people that it is *the* most important area and is relatively independent of economic development issues. The nub of this idea is well expressed in the following quotation from World Bank Group President James D. Wolfensohn:

> Growth does not trickle down, so therefore, development efforts must address human needs directly . . . what matters most is moving beyond traditional concepts of economic growth, to putting people – their health, welfare, education, opportunity and inclusion – at the heart of the development agenda for the 21st century.

> (World Bank, 1999b, p. 2).

Given this explicit admission of the structural inequality of contemporary economic development, it is not surprising that health, welfare, opportunity and inclusion are increasingly located, discursively, in the quality of local environments. In effect, the divorcing of people's lives from 'traditional concepts' of economic growth (wealth generation and distribution) assigns those lives to their immediate spatial or environmental dimension: a local and introspective conception of social welfare in a globalized economy, for those unable to benefit from it.

The discursive resources of environmentalism and sustainable development for achieving such a reconceptualization are considerable (Harré et al., 1999). Rather than entering into a theoretical analysis of those resources, the rest of this chapter explores the ways in which they have been adapted and applied in a specific locality with its particular socio-spatial problems.

THE MOBILIZATION OF ENVIRONMENTAL MEANINGS IN MEDELLIN

Medellin is the centre of a metropolitan area of 3 million inhabitants, the second city of Colombia, and the country's traditional industrial centre. During the 1980s the city witnessed a crisis of multiple dimensions. The traditional industrial base was threatened, unemployment soared, political violence erupted, corruption scandals undermined local authority credibility, the flagship Metro project ground to a standstill, the religious authority of the Catholic church waned, family structures were destabilized, and law and order effectively broke down. The detonating factor of all this was the emergence of locally based drugs cartels, which dramatized the challenge to the existing moral, legal and political order. A proud and dynamic city fell to an unprecedented low in self-confidence.

One result was that Medellin acquired international notoriety as one of the most violent cities in the world. The number of violent deaths in Medellin alone reached a peak of 6644 in 1991 (equivalent to one in 400 people), and throughout the 1990s the annual murder rate, at over 400 per 100 000 inhabitants, was the principal cause of death among 15–40-year-old males. The control of violence and the re-establishment of 'peaceful co-existence' became the city's principal challenge. It inspired many innovative responses in terms of political negotiation (going way beyond the normal remit of participation) and new collaborative strategies of urban management.

As innovative as any of these was the way the environment became a medium and a means of reconstituting a sense of social harmony and legitimation of the local state. Although many important physical improvements were implemented over the period, this chapter focuses on the discursive construction of the environment and the values and meanings 'discovered' within it, as both a prior requirement and integral part of those improvements.

Defusing violence in the 1980s

This section briefly describes how the environment was conceived in relation to the city's social crises, using development plans as the main source. Development plans provide a synthesis of the strategic thinking behind specific policies and programmes, and in doing so provide much more than a rationale for concrete actions. Understood as discourse, they contribute to the social significance attributed to urban management practices, establishing meanings that create public issues and legitimate particular forms of local state intervention. In other words, discourse constructs environmental problems, partially on the basis of scientific and technical knowledge, but also in relation to the overall urban problems. This relational aspect is highlighted here.

In the first plan produced during this period, in 1985, the environment played only a marginal role. The plan described the metropolitan area as 'uneven and unbalanced' due to the socio-spatial effects of economic recession and the insufficiencies of state intervention. The environment was conceived in terms of ecology, substantially disconnected from development issues, but emerging on the horizon of long-term interests with regard to the future quality of urban life (Departamento Administrativo de Planeación Metropolitana, 1985).

During the three-year preparation of that metropolitan strategic plan, crime and violence escalated into a major urban problem. A subsequent municipal plan produced in 1986 not only gave statistical form to the environment through the technical description of its material components, but also discursively inserted the environment into the overall picture of the deteriorating social and spatial conditions of life in the city. Insecurity and the precariousness of life were the dominant themes underlying develop- ment strategy. Social and environmental dangers were given an associative relation, articulated to collective well-being through the call for individual responsibility and the need for a change in attitudes and behaviour:

> *A vital concern is that of citizen security, without which the panorama will remain overshadowed by anxiety and fear. This security must be founded on state initiatives on the prevention of crime at its source and the repression of crime in all its forms and manifestations . . . Also of fundamental importance will be those measures designed to prevent tragedies caused by landslides and floods in the high- risk zones already identified in the city, improved disaster management procedures should such events occur, a reduction in road accidents, and better fire prevention and control. To the extent that the community manages to recover a sense of tranquility and become co-author of its own security, it will in turn be able to devote greater energy to building progress in the city and consolidate confidence in the future.*
>
> *(Departamento Administrativo de Planeación Metropolitana, 1986, p. 39).*

At the same time, an enduring division of responsibilities and distribution of power was established. In effect, responsibility for care of the environ- ment, and the remedying of environmental ills, was transferred to all citi- zens, while authority over the environment was located firmly in government hands. In the first instance, authority was determined by sci- entific understanding and technical knowledge of natural resource sys- tems, which tended to wrest understanding of the environment from lay experience. Later, legal and regulatory measures operated by specialist institutions would be established within the local authority in order to impose control over environmental action.

In 1987 a landslide buried 300 homes and killed over 500 people in the Villa Tina sector of the city. A vague public environmental consciousness and latent environmental fear was given dramatic and tragic expression by this environmental 'terrorism', comparable in its magnitude and effects to the social terrorism being experienced by the city. In its aftermath, the en- vironmental question gained considerable momentum, and in the post- Brundtland climate of those times the leader of the city council was to assert that:

> *Together with violence, hunger and social decomposition, the citizen of the twentieth century is witnessing the painful spectacle of the extinction of his natural environment and his own life, in a future scenario which to many seems irremediable . . . This forum will suggest priorities for action. State initiatives must be backed up through education and awareness. Solutions are urgent and there is no time to lose.*
>
> *(Concejo de Medellin, 1989, p. 7).*

The problem of urban violence continued to grow in the following years and intensified into militarized street warfare, bombings and large-scale terrorism in the preparatory period leading up to the approval of the new constitution, which would tackle the issue of extradition (of drugs barons), in 1991. In a desperate social situation, the environment became a metaphor for the moral value of life and the liveability of the city. The latter was not merely a quality-of-life issue, but literally a matter of life and death, of survival. The provincial governor at that time was later to comment that, on taking up office, he found the city 'frightened to death – most of the local elite had fled to other cities or countries' (Anon., 1997d). Security in the city had become a national judicial and military affair; for the re-establishment of law and order on an everyday scale, the local authority turned to the environment. The 1990 plan, for example, argued that the city was suffering:

> . . . serious environmental problems . . . upon which action must be taken in an opportune and appropriate way, in order to avoid Medellin becoming an unliveable city in the very short term . . . The environmental picture – one of pronounced deterioration – makes it imperative that the municipal authority . . . undertake an environmental management programme in accordance with the requirements of urban development and the quality of life of the city's inhabitants.

> *(Departamento Administrativo de Planeación Metropolitana, 1990).*

Establishing a sense of harmony in the 1990s

By the time of the 1993 plan, extradition had been approved and severe blows dealt to the local drugs cartels, and terrorism abated. Despite continuing high levels of murder and violence, a sense of relief invaded the city and, along with it, the need to reconstruct social harmony. Once again urban discourse turned to the environment. During the 1980s urban environmental discourse had appealed to the biological fact of human existence and the cruel forces of nature; now it turned to the exploitation of the more benign values to be found in nature. The Rio de Janeiro summit provided the ideal background for the discursive mobilization of environmental values:

> Planning in Medellin will be undertaken from a human perspective and with a sense of responsibility for future generations, through the adoption of the criterion of sustainable development. In meeting present needs, deficiencies arising from the past will also be addressed, along with the setting of conditions which guarantee peace and prosperity for the people of Medellin in the future.

> The governance of the city will be ruled by the principles of respect for human life and all other forms of life, the integral development of the city's inhabitants, and therefore of the city itself, and will be realized in perfect harmony amongst human beings and between human beings and the ecosystem which surrounds us.

> *(Concejo de Medellin, 1994, p. 97).*

However, these values had to materialize and be expressed in urban space. Discourse needed to be connected to daily life in the city, and environmental values symbolized and integrated into everyday spatial experience. In 1992 the city created the Instituto Mi Río (My River Institute) as an executive arm of environmental management. Its specific remit was river basin management, addressing one of the major sets of environmental problems relating to floods and landslides caused by destabilized water regimes. Its improvement works, including the landscaping of the main river in the central part of the city, and extensive engineering and landscaping works to the many streams that surge menacingly through the barrios, clinging to the steep valley sides, have had an enormous physical and aesthetic impact.

In the context of this chapter, the Institute also became a major vehicle for mobilizing environmental meaning through discourse, and its non-scientific and highly participatory approach facilitated the penetration of these meanings into the popular sectors of the city. The discursive resources for reconstituting a sense of collective interest in a conflictive and fragmented city can be summarized as follows.

The species voice: as urban society fragmented under the weight of violently antagonistic relations, together with the general weakening of the public sphere through privatization, the species denomination – mankind – became the only credible collective noun. Biological identity allowed the problematic idea of a common social identity to be stated as a plausible common species identity. In the evolutionary time horizon of sustainability, the species voice provided a discursive device for expressing human unity which antecedes social structures, side-steps causality, and diverts attention from the widening inequalities in the social conditions of existence. In the following quotation, for example, the species voice allows needs to be expressed in an elemental form:

> *There is now an ever greater awareness amongst* human beings *that water constitutes an essential aspect of both environmental protection and economic growth, as well as being decisive in improving the quality of life.*
>
> (Instituto Mi Río, 1995, p. 21).

Common responsibility: species identity allowed the field of collective responsibility to be redefined in an environmental framework, but not necessarily in an equal and similar way. The species voice was discursively employed to consolidate a sense of universal responsibility and, within it, the determination of the duties and obligations of particular individuals or groups. In particular, environmental education and participation played a pivotal role in translating relations of power and dominance on to the environmental sphere. In the following extract, for example, it is claimed that, just as the physical state of the environment needs monitoring, so does the state of knowledge and appropriate behaviour patterns of the participant population:

It is clear that, given the purpose of assuring the viability of the policies and regulations aimed at preserving and restoring the environment, basic information is needed from the very beginning on the form and intensity of the community perception of environmentally-related phenomena, on the level of community knowledge of relevant regulations and the importance of ecological balance in the aspirations of individual and collective life, and on the level of appropriation of matters concerned with natural resources and the environment in general.

(Universidad de Antioquia, 1994, p. 14).

Natural origins: despite the burgeoning evidence linking environmental problems to questions of poverty and the social discrimination of environmental disasters, discourse in Medellin insisted on the 'naturalness' of such phenomena to human existence, embedded in the deep forces of geology, the surface energy of geomorphological processes or the unpredictability of technological systems. Once the natural origin of the problem had been established, technical management could then be presented as the only and indispensable answer, as illustrated in the following quotation:

Citizens should be aware of the risks to which we are exposed and, consequently, we have to adopt the necessary preventive measures, turn to the governmental organizations created for this purpose, and apply the appropriate technical solutions in each instance.

(Municipio de Medellin, 1996).

Legality/status: local institutions specializing in environmental matters perform the vital function of lending authority to the issue, not just by regulation but also through discursive practice. What is at stake is the status of the environment as a problem, and the legitimacy of the objects and concepts of environmental discourse. To secure and maintain this status within the city, the statements of international organizations provided a rich reserve which could be used selectively to establish the general legitimacy of the environment as a significant urban issue. The following quotation is but one illustration:

A pressing obligation was acquired by the municipality, and particularly the Mi Río Institute, through the declaration of the mayor's conference on the environment held in Marseilles (France) last March: 'The greatest importance needs to be given to information and education at all levels, particularly the young, so as to encourage prevention and awareness'.

(Instituto Mi Río, 1995).

Rationality: with the deterritorialization of the local economy, the chaos undermining urban society, and a weakened local government unable to provide the order traditionally associated with the welfare state, the rational foundations for local intervention in urban affairs became increasingly problematic. Within environmental discourse, to act rationally is to condition social practice to the laws and regularities of natural resource systems. Disorder, self-interest and atavistic aggression appeared to reign everywhere in social life, but the environment provided a plausible repository of rationality: the discursive domain for the re-establishment of the rational action of society upon itself, now mediated through the laws of nature. In this discursive shift the environment became a vital legitimizing factor of public institutions, and a central ground of local politics, as illustrated in the following objective of the 1993 development plan:

> To ensure, through the policy of sustainable development, that an adequate and rational *use is made of human, natural and artificial resources, and all other resources belonging to the city.*

> (Concejo de Medellin, 1994, p. 97; my emphasis).

As a result of this discursive construction of the environment, towards the end of the decade urban environmental management had been firmly established as a way of debating spatial development which could comprehend the urgent social requirements of harmony, solidarity, peaceful co-existence, equity and rationality (Brand, 1998). However, as with any 'discursive formation' (Foucault, 1970), heterogeneity and dispute were its defining characteristics. A broad consensus had been established that the environment was a significant issue which could contribute to resolving the city's social crisis, but opinion differed considerably as to how (creating employment, changing urban 'imaginaries', restoring moral values and respect for life, stimulating social pacts through a functional and symbolic interest in air and water, and so forth), and as to its long-term effectiveness. Furthermore, all urban development projects are now politically contested and legitimized using the discursive resources (both legislative and regulatory) of the environment.

To sum up, the biophysical environment in Medellin suffered many problems over the period examined, especially in relation to air and water pollution, and risk through landslides and floods, and many real improvements were undertaken. However, addressing those problems was not so much an object in itself, in the orthodox natural resource conception of sustainability, as a spatially viable way of facing up to and contributing to the solution of a specifically urban social crisis.

CONCLUSIONS

This brief outline of the construction and mobilization of meaning in the environment in Medellin is an illustration of the general proposal contained in this chapter: that urban environmental management can be, and needs to be, understood as the management of social change. It is argued that the nature of this social project, while supported in the abstract goals and discourse of sustainable development, achieves real, concrete form in the dialectics of socio-spatial change only in particular places. As management practice, urban environmentalism becomes embedded in the power relations of complex urban dynamics. The goal of urban environmental sustainability then becomes a means rather than an end: a means of regulating social practices and containing the contradictions and conflict of contemporary urban life. Medellin is an exaggerated case of deteriorating urban social relations, but its general characteristics will not be unfamiliar to many cities in the developing world, where inequitable societies and emasculated governments combine to produce a crisis of governance.

This chapter has centred on the discursive construction of the environment, and how social relations were redefined environmentally through the affirmation of biological collective identity, a certain submission to nature's forces, the exploitation of nature's 'values', and the positing of the quality of life in nature's moral and functional embrace. Little attention has been given to concrete improvements in real, lived environments. Theses are clearly important. However, their significance depends on the prior construction of meaning which urban development projects materialize and, as it were, bring to life.

The long-term significance of urban environmental management remains open. Urban environmental management has so far proved to be socially and politically effective in terms of legitimizing local government, as well as promoting some highly interesting changes in urban development policy and spatial configuration. A key question is whether, and how long, this can last. The perspective developed here suggests that this will depend not on issues of global ecology or environmental performance indicators, but rather on the continual and credible reconstruction – both discursive and spatial – of urban environmental welfare in the moral void and chasms of social inequality of the neoliberal city.

CHAPTER SIX

Building sustainable capacity for urban poverty reduction

Carole Rakodi

INTRODUCTION

By the late 1980s, it was recognized that structural adjustment policies were, by design, having particularly adverse effects on urban economies and residents (Killick, 1995). In attempts to reduce government budget deficits, reform civil services, liberalize trade and abolish price distortions (especially those that were held to discriminate against rural areas), public services deteriorated, domestic manufacturing was hard hit by competition from imports, widespread retrenchment of wage employment occurred, and real wages declined. As a result, the incidence of urban poverty increased in many adjusting countries and, although the proportion of people categorized as poor generally remained higher in rural areas, urban poverty increased at a faster rate than rural poverty, and the proportion of all poor people living in urban areas increased (Haddad et al., 1999). In some adjusting countries, the adverse effects of adjustment were relatively short term, and renewed economic growth brought with it reduced poverty. In the majority, however, although some research purported to show that many rural people were no worse off (and some were better off) after implementation of adjustment policies (Sahn et al., 1997), the hoped-for benefits of adjustment were slow in manifesting themselves and the incidence of poverty continued to be unacceptably high.

It was, moreover, argued that poverty line analyses underestimate the incidence and severity of urban poverty by failing to allow either for the extra expenditures incurred by urban households, or for the higher costs of those included in household consumption baskets (Satterthwaite, 1997b; see also Ruel et al., 1999). Increasingly, the attention of external funders shifted to the need for structural adjustment policy packages to include both safety nets to protect the poor against the effects of such policies, and longer-term strategies to reduce poverty. Early programmes aimed to mitigate the adverse impacts of structural adjustment, and by 1999 these were institutionalized as Poverty Reduction Strategy Programmes (PRSPs), which all countries seeking IMF and World Bank loans for stabilization and structural adjustment had to have in place. To a varying extent, governments and external financial agencies began to pay attention to urban poverty and the scope for action at the municipal level to be assessed (Vanderschueren et al., 1996; Satterthwaite, 2001).

Attempts to address urban poverty have been initiated in a growing number of countries and cities worldwide (see, for example, Amis, 2001).

Building on earlier conceptual and empirical work and experience of urban projects since the 1970s, a potential approach to building sustainable capacity for urban poverty reduction is outlined in this chapter. This is explicitly normative, although some of the difficulties and dilemmas likely to be encountered in implementing such an approach will be identified. Any attempt to address urban poverty must be based on a sound understanding of its characteristics and causes. First, what our current understanding implies for policy is reviewed. Second, the notion of 'sustainable capacity' is discussed, and a process by which this might be built at municipal and community levels is suggested. This chapter is not primarily concerned with the content of policies to reduce urban poverty, and it is early days for assessing the outcomes of those programmes which have adopted approaches resembling that advocated here. It will be appropriate to refer to the content of policy in what follows, but these elements of the discussion will be indicative rather than comprehensive.

UNDERSTANDING THE CHARACTERISTICS AND CAUSES OF URBAN POVERTY

Urban poverty has, in the past, generally been defined in terms of a poverty line, and this is still the basis for monitoring the incidence of poverty using large-scale sample surveys. Even with methodological refinements (for example to allow for the different cost of the basic basket of foodstuffs and other goods in different regions and cities, to analyse the intensity of poverty, to improve estimates of household income/expenditure, and to use panel studies to detect trends in poverty incidence), sole reliance on poverty line measurements causes a number of problems (Rakodi, 1995a).

- The poverty line is defined by outsiders, and neglects people's own definitions of poverty, which incorporate lack of access to assets and services, ill health, insecurity and political marginalization.
- Poverty line analysis is considered to provide only partial explanations of the causes of persistent poverty and deprivation (and its reduction or deepening). In particular, although poverty line analysis reveals the characteristics of people and households associated with poverty (including low educational levels, lack of skills, poor health, insecure tenure), it does not reveal underlying causes, especially processes of political and social exclusion, and may not examine the relationships between labour market position, health and environmental conditions (Satterthwaite, 1997b; Songsore and McGranahan, 1998). Nor does it usually detect the intergenerational transmission of poverty, which is related to food, health and effective education, or

the immediate triggers of impoverishment, both within households (e.g. illness or bereavement) and external to them (e.g. recession, the impact of policies, eviction). As a corollary, nor is it a satisfactory basis for identifying the determinants of improved well-being for individuals, households and communities.

■ The use of poverty lines may imply that the poor are passively waiting to become beneficiaries of trickle-down effects from economic growth or external interventions, when in practice they are active agents, adopting positive strategies for coping with impoverishment and securing improved well-being (Rakodi, 1995a, 1995b; Moser, 1998), and influencing the political, economic and social actions of government.

Box 6.1   Differentiating the urban poor in Kenya

In preliminary participatory urban appraisals[1] in Kenya in 1996/97, poor residents defined poverty and deprivation as including:

■ low incomes affecting food consumption, and lack of access to income-earning opportunities
■ inadequate access to basic services, particularly water and sanitation
■ inability to afford healthcare and to keep children in school
■ insecurity, including unreliable incomes, crime and violence, and insecure tenure.

They also distinguished between:
The *poor*, who

■ tend to be large families, with many children not attending school
■ eat only one meal a day
■ are often casual workers, lacking even the capital needed to start a micro-enterprise
■ are generally tenants.

The *very poor*, who

■ eat once a day or less
■ rely on begging or occasional work
■ are unable to buy medicine or send children to school
■ are tenants.

The *not so poor*, who

■ are in regular waged employment/earn a regular income
■ eat three meals a day
■ are able to send their children to school
■ may own their own house.

To complement the monitoring of income poverty, therefore, research in the 1990s has relied on people's own perceptions and diagnoses of what it means to be poor, the causes of impoverishment, and the constraints on their ability to achieve improved well-being (Hentschel and Seshagiri, 2000). It is evident from this work that 'poor people' must be differentiated, that poverty is dynamic and not static, and that urban residence is associated with particular experiences of poverty.

In participatory appraisals, poor people themselves differentiate between degrees of deprivation and vulnerability (Box 6.1).

The location in which poor urban households live is influenced by their poverty, but also provides or excludes them from opportunities, thus influencing their chances of becoming trapped in poverty, further impoverished, or better off. Typically resident in informal settlements (although the latter are not necessarily uniformly poor) or, in some parts of the world, living on the streets, in tenements or in public places such as railway stations, poor households are faced with a number of trade-offs: they may choose inner city locations where accommodation is unavailable or extremely cramped at rents they can afford, in order to have relatively easy access to a variety of livelihood opportunities. Alternatively, they may opt for peripheral areas where it is possible to rent more space and even obtain access to land on which to build a house and grow food, but where infrastructure and services are underprovided or absent, and travel costs are high.

Not only do the fortunes of poor people change over time with economic fluctuations, changes in policy and political instability, they also change as a result of the household life cycle, decisions related to personal and household livelihood strategies, and unforeseen stresses and shocks. Often, households are poorest when they contain young children, tying the mother to her home and preventing her from earning, while the children themselves are too young to contribute to the household income. Elderly households lacking support from their relatives may also be among the poorest. When a household cannot afford to send its children to school or to keep them there, or when disease (especially HIV/AIDS) is passed on from parents to children or leaves the latter orphans, poverty is transmitted from generation to generation. Some households are particularly susceptible to shocks and stresses: those with only one working adult or only one source of income, and those living in the most insecure tenure conditions, for example, are vulnerable to further impoverishment. Others are more resilient: those with several members capable of working, with diversified sources of income, able to supplement their incomes with food produced in urban or rural areas, and able to call on supportive kinship or other social relationships. Some households may be unable to respond to opportunities because they contain only one able-bodied adult, lack skills and contacts, or are affected by ill health (Rakodi, 1999a). Others may be able to respond positively, because they have spare labour, as well as access to social, political or financial capital.

Urban residents are susceptible to a variety of pressures associated more with urban than rural life, especially where landlessness is not yet a serious problem (Ruel et al., 1999). In the central areas of cities, the locations where poor people live and work may be subject to commercial pressure for higher-density or non-residential development, susceptible to gentrification, or vulnerable to harassment if formal businesses protest at the competition from street sellers or the poor image conveyed by rough sleepers and pavement dwellers. In peri-urban areas, while better-off farmers and landowners may be well placed to take advantage of urban growth by intensifying production to supply fresh produce to urban markets or by subdividing their land for residential development, the smallest farmers and landless may lack both the capital to respond to these opportunities and the skills to compete in the urban labour market (Rakodi, 1999b). Urban areas are also characterized by a range of environmental hazards, including biological pathogens (disease-causing agents) and their vectors, chemical pollutants and physical hazards, to which poor residents, particularly infants, children and women, are especially vulnerable (Nunan and Satterthwaite, 1999).

Not all the opportunities, constraints, processes of exclusion and risks are amenable to policy intervention – and certainly not at the local level. The limits of policy must be recognized; nevertheless, there is scope for action. Lasting improvements in well-being require increased opportunities (for example, to obtain work and access income-earning activities, acquire land, or become house owners); reduced constraints on the ability of poor households to take advantage of the opportunities available (for

---

Box 6.2   Differentiated needs and multiple responses in Indian cities

Drawing on the lessons of support by the UK Department for International Development (DFID) to slum improvement projects in a number of Indian cities, Loughhead argues that poor households may be improving their situation, coping or becoming further impoverished, and that their priorities in relation to survival, security and quality of life vary depending on the category or trajectory in which they find themselves. For some, developmental or social action measures will be appropriate, while for others, priority needs to be given to social protection (Loughhead and Rakodi, 2002). For the improving poor, social action measures may prioritize education and skills training, credit for enterprise development, and opportunities to participate in decision-making; while social protection might include basic service provision, insurance, enforcement of core labour standards, and savings and loan services. For the declining poor, the social protection measures needed (including free and accessible healthcare, pensions and benefits to meet immediate consumption needs, food subsidies and shelter for the homeless) will be more extensive than feasible actions to improve their asset base.

example, education and skills training, access to capital, more appropriate regulatory frameworks, and an end to harassment by police and municipal inspectors); access to basic services at an affordable cost (piped water, sanitation, energy, education, health); and reduced risk (by improving their security of tenure, making living environments healthier, and providing access to financial services and basic safety nets such as pensions). Interventions must recognize that the needs of poor people and communities vary enormously, so a single policy package will be inappropriate. Instead, policies need to be tailored to the circumstances of particular poor groups and households (Box 6.2). A responsive mode of policy formulation and implementation is therefore required to produce effective and lasting results.

ORGANIZATIONAL CAPACITY FOR URBAN POVERTY REDUCTION

Capacity implies '. . .capability for development work' (Dale, 2000, p. 177) or '. . .the ability to perform appropriate tasks effectively, efficiently and sustainably' (Hilderbrand and Grindle, 1995, p. 445). It may refer to the capabilities (resources and other abilities) of people to improve their own living situations, the capacity of organizations to define and fulfil their objectives, and the presence of widely recognized institutions (organizations with recognized and legitimate roles and tasks, rules of social interaction, laws and regulations). Capacity is generally regarded as a necessary property of organizations, especially those in the public sector, but if it is accepted that there are limits to what the state can and should be expected to do, the capacity of other actors and social organizations is also important. In the context of urban poverty reduction, there is a need to consider the roles of both central and local government, and also the ability of poor people to articulate their needs, claim their rights, solve some problems by their own efforts, and identify and negotiate with appropriate external organizations for other purposes.

Often, neither government agencies nor poor people have the capacity to undertake the relevant tasks and functions, thus a process of organizational and institutional change is required to develop relevant capabilities. The increased capacity which results needs to be lasting – able to cope with and recover from crises, shocks and unexpected developments, to generate resources to support the individual or organization's activities, to plan ahead, and to allocate and use resources to achieve the intended aims. To develop sustainable capacity, the process of change is as important as the content. It will both produce direct results and alter the context in which change occurs, as those involved jointly determine what is to happen and reflect on their experience. The discussion concentrates on poor people and their organizations, and on municipal government.

Poor people and community groups

Most residents in southern towns and cities, even recent migrants, have social ties in the urban centre based on kinship or area of origin. These help with initial searches for work and somewhere to live, and are added to by new social relations developed through work and social organizations such as churches, mosques, trade unions or other trade associations (Beall, 1999). Many residents are transient, moving between rented dwellings as they seek to establish and consolidate their position in town, or to achieve their goals before returning to rural areas. Their social relationships change and shift, forming webs that stretch across the city and beyond to rural areas, other cities and abroad.

However, for many others, especially women, the neighbourhood in which they live becomes the main locus of their social relationships. They may, for example, develop patterns of reciprocal assistance with childcare or financial management. The neighbourhood is where, in societies that practise seclusion, women can move around in what is regarded as semi-public space; where many economic activities occur; where struggles over the control of public space by different social groups for enterprise or socializing are worked out; and where more or less satisfactory solutions are developed to the absence of utilities and services, for example communal wells or purchase of water from vendors, shared pit latrines, informal schools and informal private healthcare practitioners. This is not to say that social relations are harmonious, mutually supportive, incorporate everyone, or enable residents to develop satisfactory relations with the local political and administrative system. Urban neighbourhoods are generally socially mixed, including newcomers and long-established residents, owners and tenants, people from different areas of origin, speaking different languages and perhaps adhering to different religions or denominations. Many contain groups regarded as socially undesirable or disruptive – unemployed young people high on drink or drugs, criminals and gangsters.

Even illegal settlements have to develop relationships with the administrative system – with the police, to avoid eviction and improve law and order; with service providers, in attempts to secure the means of living, improve environmental conditions and perhaps win the right to occupy the land permanently; and with political parties, in the hope that an elected politician can act as a patron and intermediary on behalf of the community (Benjamin, 2000). Leaders emerge in most settlements, but there are as likely to be many leaders as a single one, with rivalry causing insecurity and inhibiting the ability of residents to make strong claims on the political and administrative system (Ward and Chant, 1987). Often, leaders will be identified or imposed by organizations from outside a community (or co-opted) as a means of ensuring social control: delivering votes for a particular political party and ensuring law and order. Examples are the way in which 'slums' are used as 'vote banks' by rival political parties in the ostensibly democratic but thoroughly clientelistic Indian political system (Benjamin, 2000); or the appointment of Chiefs and Assistant Chiefs by the Provincial Administration in Kenyan urban areas, and the requirement that local leaders be acceptable to them. Often, neither residents nor community leaders are fully aware of their legal position with respect to tenure rights or entitlements to services – they know little about the structure of government, which agencies are responsible for what, the powers and limits to power of functionaries and officials, or how NGOs might help when government agencies refuse to recognize them, or threaten them.

The capacity of poor people in specific residential areas, especially informal settlements, to articulate their needs, make claims on the political and administrative system, ensure that interventions are appropriate, and take action for themselves to complement state provision is, therefore, generally limited. It is for these reasons that external interventions to assist the poor by provision of services, regularization or upgrading often include attempts to establish a unified, community-based organizational structure. In principle, the intention is to enable residents to articulate their priorities and play a role in decision-making. However, experience over several decades demonstrates not only that practice generally falls short of this ideal, but also that the process of community organization inevitably raises a number of difficult issues.

First, empowering residents and their organizations so that they can play a role in decision-making changes the balance of power, and may be perceived by existing power-holders as a threat. In practice, the motivation of those in power may be to increase state control over unofficial or illegal areas rather than to enable their residents to make claims on the state. In some countries, community-based organizations (CBOs) have been inextricably linked to the ruling party, as in Zambia, Tanzania and Mozambique in the 1970s. While potentially pro-poor, they are not necessarily democratic and accountable. Control, indoctrination and mobilization are more likely than empowerment to be their prime purposes. A CBO may also be developed to ensure that interventions are appropriate and smoothly implemented, by engaging residents in a process of consultation. Residents' views may or may not be taken into account in decision-making, although a wise agency will take them seriously. Some would argue that this instrumentalist role for CBOs falls too far short of self-determination, while others argue that the need for expertise, city-wide planning and equitable distribution of resources implies that residents are only one of the legitimate participants in decision-making, alongside political representatives and public agencies (e.g. Abbott, 1996). Evans (1996) argues that state–society synergy, based on complementary functions and embeddedness (ties that connect citizens and public officials across the public–private divide), will produce more positive developmental outcomes. The key ingredient in synergistic strategies is '. . ."scaling up" existing social capital to create organizations that are sufficiently encompassing to effectively pursue developmental goals' (Evans, 1996, p. 1130), while egalitarian social structures, robust bureaucracies and rule-based competitive political systems also facilitate the emergence of synergy.

Second, the organizational structure, electoral mechanisms and provisions for accountability are critical in determining the extent to which CBOs are legitimate, lasting, and develop the capacity to represent and act on behalf of residents. In some cases, systems have been imposed with little regard for existing structures of leadership and organization. They may be resented, unworkable, or last only as long as the availability of funding (Phillips, 2002). In other circumstances, while the form such organizations take is handled sensitively, they may be vulnerable if their legal basis is insecure, or their relationship to the formal political system unclear. In Cebu City, in the Philippines, since the downfall of Marcos, national, municipal and sub-municipal (*barangay*) levels of government have all been re-democratized and allocated a share of resources, providing greater scope than before for local control over decision-making (Etemadi, 2000). In Bolivia, the Law of Popular Participation and establishment of *Organizacións Territorial de Base* provide a legal basis for local decision-making (Blackburn and de Toma, 1997). However, in Colombo, Sri Lanka, Community Development Councils, established in association with the government's Million Houses Programme in the late 1980s and early 1990s, which enabled residents and community leaders to work with government officers to identify problems, set priorities and develop solutions, were not sustained in the face of entrenched government institutions, power structures antagonistic to community participation, inadequate legal underpinning, and changes in political control (Russell and Vidler, 2000).

The organizational structure to be adopted needs to be acceptable to, and developed in conjunction with, residents, politicians and parties in the formal political system and local (and perhaps central) government structures. Reaching agreement on the structures, modalities and sharing of power and responsibilities is likely to be a slow process; even if a formal 'legal' agreement is reached, poor residents will need ongoing support, they will have to continually reassert their rights, and renegotiation of the relationships will be necessary as circumstances change. In some residential areas, divergent interests will give rise to conflict and even preclude the establishment of a single organization able to speak for all residents. Where prior experience and capacity are limited, appropriate structures and processes need to be developed in a limited number of areas before replication is attempted. It is more likely that sustainable capacity to organize in order to make their voices heard, influence the political and policy agenda, and make claims on public services will be achieved by poor people in countries with a history of active struggle for democratic rights.

Where residents have a tradition of organization, supported perhaps by trade unions, churches or liberation movements, they may take the necessary initiatives, and the role of government can be to support the replication of local organization and to integrate such organizations into its own processes of decision-making. Participatory Budgeting in Brazilian cities, for example, has developed from a well-established base of community struggle and organization in the context of a wider movement for democratization, although it also has proved vulnerable to shifts in political control (Souza, 2000). Where there is no such tradition, there is a question about who should take the initiative where residents are unable to do so without outside assistance. Where government has been unwilling, NGOs have often taken on this role.

The third issue is related to the role of NGOs. The outcomes of NGO initiatives have been very varied, not unexpectedly given the enormous variation in the motives, origins, types and resources of the organizations involved. Many NGOs are concerned with welfare – plugging the gaps in state-provided services. For many poor residents, especially those living in settlements not provided with services because of their illegal status, such services are important. However, they tend to be supply-driven, and may not match people's own priorities. Nor do such NGOs hold government to account for its own failures, or challenge inappropriate policies. Organizations with development or empowerment objectives are more likely to adopt demand-driven approaches and to support residents (see e.g. Blackburn and de Toma, 1997 on the role of NGOs in developing participatory approaches for *Organizacións Territorial de Base* in Bolivia; also Chapter 8, this volume). However, they have a tendency to take the credit for initiatives which build on existing institutional capacity and social capital, and some find it hard to relinquish control over the organizations they have supported, for example, NGOs over Community Development Councils in Colombo (Russell and Vidler, 2000). The motives of NGOs are not always transparent, their staff may be well paid compared to public sector staff, the resources available to them are often generous compared with either local government or CBOs and, because they need 'success stories' to secure further funding, they may be less than objective about their contribution. For a variety of reasons, levels of trust between NGOs and other local actors vary. Large, well-resourced northern NGOs may be welcomed, or they may be resented by local NGOs and government institutions. So-called GONGOs (government-oriented NGOs) may be suspected by residents and other NGOs, everyone distrusts 'briefcase' NGOs, and government agencies may be suspicious of all NGOs.

Finally, even the best resourced NGOs have limited capacity. They are unlikely to operate in more than a few settlements, sacrificing universal coverage for concentrated effort. Where their support to a community is concentrated, the staff and financial resources available may be unrealistic for either long-term sustainability, or replicability in similar areas citywide. Ultimately, only government agencies can ensure comprehensive organizational structures and universal provision of services. Where such agencies are unused to participatory modes of working and lack the skills and resources to facilitate community organization, action planning and implementation, suitable NGOs can potentially play an important role in developing sustainable and replicable models for developing community organizational capacity, and in building the capacity of local government and less aware or well-resourced NGOs to work with residents. Such NGO involvement in urban poverty reduction should be agreed with, and accountable to, the local agencies and organizations with long-term responsibility; should involve realistic levels of resources to ensure replicability; and should have an explicit exit strategy, to ensure sustainability. Such a role for NGOs does not preclude either the continued involvement of some in service delivery and social welfare, or the need for some to challenge public policy or play an advocacy role on behalf of residents.

Municipal capacity to reduce urban poverty

The capacity of local government to reduce poverty depends on the presence of a responsive political system and organizational or administrative capacity.

Normally, a democratic political system is likely to be more responsive to the needs of poor people than an authoritarian or oligarchical system, but the extent to which this is the case depends on the broader context (especially political history and culture, the ethnic configuration of the country, and ownership and control of key resources such as land); the nature and role of political parties, civil society groups and the media; and the design of mechanisms and procedures for elections, accountability, etc. (Blair, 2000). Much of this depends on national experiences, trends and decisions. However, the workings of a local political system are also influenced by the urban economic and social context; the composition and motivation of local elites and other political actors; and the range of responsibilities, volume of resources and extent of autonomy of the municipal government.

Organizational capacity implies the ability to formulate policy and strategy; plan and manage implementation, operation and maintenance; review progress and performance; and react to both unexpected events and the findings of monitoring and evaluation. It implies the capacity to perform both direct and indirect provider roles, the latter including, in particular, enabling and regulating. Furthermore, it includes three aspects of efficiency: productive efficiency (the ability to optimize the use of resources); allocative efficiency (the ability to respond to the preferences of citizens); and adaptive efficiency (the ability and willingness to learn) (Batley, 1997). Capacity is related to opportunities and constraints in the organizational environment, especially the legal–administrative framework; political practices; central–local government, public–private sector and public sector–civil society relations; and the resources at the organization's disposal, as well as a range of organization-specific variables (Dale, 2000). Attention needs to be paid to structures and mechanisms for policy formulation, planning and management, service delivery, monitoring and evaluation, regulatory functions, and internal and external accountability; to the generation and allocation of financial and other resources; and to staffing numbers, arrangements and capabilities (Batley,

1997; Dale, 2000). Despite attempts at decentralization, local government typically has limited autonomy because of the reluctance of national politicians and central government ministries to lose control.

Nevertheless, in many countries renewed commitment to decentralization and (re-)democratization in recent years has resulted in increased attention to developing local government capacity and improving revenue generation. There is insufficient space here to explore the principles and components of local government reform and their outcomes. Instead, the focus is on how to ensure that changes are both sustainable and pro-poor, and particularly on the role of agencies external to local government in supporting institutional change.

Typically, the impetus for change is associated with a project:

> . . . *a planned intervention for achieving one or more objectives, encompassing a set of interrelated activities which are undertaken during a delimited period of time, using specified human, physical and financial resources.*

> *(Dale, 2000, p. 208).*

Projects are the way in which policies or strategies are broken down into manageable units of activity, and are also typically the vehicle through which external agencies have channelled their funding. If time-defined funding to achieve specified project objectives is to be used for building sustainable capacity to address urban poverty on an ongoing basis, there are a number of implications for project design. The multi-dimensional nature of poverty and deprivation, the importance of responding to the priorities of poor people, and the need for a range of actors to collaborate have been explored above.

If prior evidence of the characteristics of poor people, their needs and preferred solutions does not exist, a process of appraisal and action planning with poor groups needs to be the first stage of a poverty-reduction project. Project activities must then be capable of responding. Inevitably, a wide range of needs and requirements will be identified, requiring a multisectoral response that implies the involvement of many different central and local government departments and/or NGOs. As community organization evolves and priority problems are tackled, other needs are likely to be identified, alternative solutions required, and responses to unforeseen events needed. Blueprint approaches to project design have proved to be inflexible and inappropriate, especially where the objectives include capacity-building at community and organizational levels. The timescale for community organization, participatory planning, collaborative decision-making, the development of new approaches and working relationships, and attitudinal changes is unpredictable. Adaptive approaches, in which the content and procedures can respond to problems or improved information as implementation proceeds, are therefore advocated (Gow and Morss, 1988; Rondinelli, 1993). These alternatives emphasize experimentation, learning, adaptation, participation, flexibility, building local capacities and organic expansion. Process approaches recognize that the achievement of development goals does not simply require solutions thought out by experts: the problems to be solved are complex, much information is not available at the outset, and local people and organizations are actors, not merely beneficiaries or recipients. Two broad approaches may be distinguished: those that aim at empowering people to articulate their own needs and demands; and those that stress the need for project management to be more flexible and adaptive. However, these are differences of emphasis, rather than being mutually exclusive (Bond and Hulme, 1999).

Historically, funders have often pressed for the establishment of special project units, but such arrangements often failed to develop lasting organizational capacity (Rakodi, 1991). To build local ownership and enduring capacity, it is necessary to strengthen existing organizations, with or without major structural reform. Changes to programme content and working practices must deal with entrenched authority structures and attitudes, the need to continue some tasks while changing or introducing others, ongoing responsibility for routine service delivery, revenue generation and regulation, and lack of staff awareness and skills. To progress and institutionalize change takes time, especially when, as is so often the case in local government, existing organizations are weak, underfunded and inadequately staffed. As successive problems are identified and solutions tried, inevitably there will be mistakes and shortfalls between objectives and implementation. Not only does local government lack capacity for both routine service delivery and developmental tasks, but it is also characterized by structural and cultural constraints that hinder innovation, including hierarchical and sectoral organization, and inflexible procedures. The centrality of bureaucratic structures and routine tasks is associated with rewards for consistency rather than risk-taking on the part of managers and staff. In addition, monitoring and evaluation processes are undeveloped, and channels through which the findings of outcome and impact evaluations can be fed back into decision-making are absent. Often, neither the structures and processes nor the incentives available reward the creative thinking and the willingness not to penalize mistakes that characterize a learning organization (IDS Workshop, 1997; Thompson, 1997). Based on the first 11 years experience of a 20-year Norwegian International Development Agency-funded project in Sri Lanka, Bond and Hulme (1999) argue for:

■ 10- to 20-year time frames in order to achieve sustainable institutional strengthening of district-level organizations for development and poverty reduction (see also IDS Workshop, 1997)
■ projects phased to allow for experimentation and iterative improvement of small interventions, or alternatively, funding for a pre-project preparation period to allow communities and local groups to undertake thorough analyses before committing themselves to a project (IDS Workshop, 1997)

■ budgeting and accounting arrangements that permit the planning and implementation of a variety of interventions at different speeds and over different timescales
■ error seen as a chance for learning, rather than an occasion for punishment.

However, they note the tension between these requirements and the ways in which external, especially donor, agencies operate:

> . . . it is hard to see how a commitment to decentralization [and poverty reduction] can be fostered in donor agencies that insist on short time-frames, resist flexibility because of the problems it causes them with monitoring, insist that interventions are assessed in terms of their ability to achieve outputs rapidly and punish partners for their 'errors' rather than scrutinizing how effectively they are learning.

(Bond and Hulme, 1999, p. 1354).

Building the capacity of a bureaucracy demands changes to its working rules in order to allow staff to experiment, learn from mistakes, and respond creatively to changing conditions and new opportunities. Functions and objectives need to be clarified, emphasis placed on interdisciplinary and interdepartmental working, processes of training/learning developed, and incentives devised to reward those who promote and facilitate the process of institutional change.

CONCLUSIONS

Lasting poverty reduction depends to a large extent on national economic fortunes and policies. The design of macro-policies can, however, take account of their impact on real incomes and the demand for urban labour. Still at the national level, meso-policies can help to compensate for any poverty-increasing effects of macro-policies by their impact on disposable incomes through taxes and transfers, their influence on the prices of goods and services consumed by the poor (by means of indirect taxes and subsidies), and their influence on the availability and price of publicly provided goods, especially health, education and water (Stewart, 1995). Urban policies can tackle only local and some meso-level problems, depending on the allocation of responsibility for services (healthcare, primary education, utilities), financing arrangements, and the degree of autonomy of local government. It is hard to make them more than ameliorative if the causes of poverty remain, redistributive issues are not tackled, and/or the effects of macro- and national meso-policies outweigh the impacts of urban programmes. Nevertheless, in many towns and cities there is considerable (and often increasing) scope for local action to reduce poverty and deprivation.

To realize this potential, it is necessary that the design of basic municipal services, regulatory functions and targeted interventions aimed at tackling specific problems experienced by poor people should be based on a sound understanding of the characteristics and causes of poverty and deprivation at the urban level. To ensure that such an understanding is developed, the responses are appropriate, and lasting improvements in well-being are achieved, poor residents need to be able to articulate their needs and assert their claims on resources through the political and administrative systems. For this to happen, and despite the difficulties, systematic local organization is needed, in 'communities', informal settlements and/or at sub-city levels of government. In addition, municipal government and other state and non-state organizations need to be able to respond, as well as to weigh the claims of various local groups and competing policy objectives in order to ensure financial viability and equity. For lasting reduction of urban poverty and deprivation, these structures, processes and actions need to be sustained. This implies both realism and the replication of appropriate models and approaches city-wide. Both require the development of capacity among residents, government and NGOs alike. Given the existing weaknesses and the political, social and economic complexities, a long-term, incremental and halting process is more likely and realistic than dramatic change. Sustainable capacity necessarily implies building on what is there, without expecting a rapid transformation.

CHAPTER SEVEN

The role of civil society in housing policy development: some lessons from Southern Africa

Paul Jenkins

INTRODUCTION[1]

As indicated in the Introduction to this volume, the sustainability of cities in the face of rapid growth and change is the theme of this book. A principal premise of this chapter is that, while socially, economically and environmentally sustainable urban development visions are absolutely necessary, realistic political and institutional mechanisms to achieve these are of equal importance. The chapter focuses on relevant roles for the major actors in urban development – the state, the market and civil society – and how these have different interests that need to be balanced.[2] It has been stated that housing policies and programmes tend to result from political expediency, rather than a rational and informed analysis of the situation and demands of individual households for housing (Willis and Tipple, 1991). We argue here that it is political, institutional and economic realities that guide policy development, and that these generally present significant constraints affecting implementation. A rational and informed political, economic and institutional analysis of the prevailing situation is essential to create housing policies and programmes that are implementable and sustainable.

In this chapter we investigate relationships between the state and individual households, and the possible mediation of these by various forms of civil society. In different political situations there are different possibilities for civil society to act as a channel for the demands of individual households eventually to inform policy, which is of great importance for sustainability. To illustrate the argument, we refer to housing policy in two contrasting but closely linked countries in southern Africa – Mozambique and South Africa, both undergoing transition from authoritarian regimes. We draw on political analysis of Latin America's transition, outline how housing policy has developed in each country, identify some of the key constraints on policy implementation, and relate the findings to a prognosis of the developing political, economic and institutional situations as a basis for assessing sustainability.

THE STATE AND CIVIL SOCIETY IN AFRICA

There is some lack of agreement among political scientists on whether civil society actually exists, and if it does, how it is conceptualized (Harbeson et al., 1994). One of the most concise definitions is that of Victor Azarya, who defines civil society as

> *'. . . a certain area of society, a public area between household and state, where groups constituted at a level beyond the family interact with each other and with the state to pursue their interests'.*

> *(Azarya, 1994, p. 88).*

Despite this debate, many political theorists accept the usefulness of the concept, seeing it as a theoretical rather than empirical construct, which is best understood relationally. They look on civil society as the public realm between state and family, distinguish it from political society, and see it as the base for the legitimation of state power.[3] Civil society is seen by most as having both vertical (state–society) and horizontal (intra-society) relations, the horizontal functions being as important as the vertical ones. However, it is argued by some that civil society should not be primarily identified with its organizational form – as long as our focus on civil society remains only in associational life, we may leave out large numbers of people who do not see association formation as the preferred means to solve problems (Azarya, 1994, p. 96), especially in Africa where civil society has been long submerged and marginalized.

The partial nature of state–society interaction, and the weakness of both state and civil society in the post-colonial African context, are seen as leading to a series of weak political regimes.

> *Ethnic self-determination movements, large-scale societal disengagement, and ethnically based clientelism in numerous African countries indicate the absence of a social contract, and these fundamentally divided societies are more likely to produce civil societies significantly more segmented than European philosophy would suggest, at least in the short run.*

> *(Rothchild and Lawson, 1994, p. 255).*

This position is theoretically underpinned by Peter Ekeh (1975), who holds that while in the West the public realm developed as one public in relation to society, in Africa it developed as two publics because of the disjunction between state and society under colonialism. Ekeh identifies the civic public, dominated by the state and lacking legitimacy (and socially determined constraints); and the primordial public, comprised of ethnic, religious and similar associations which, due to the general alienation of the state from society, evolved separately, with strong relationships to wider social values. However, it is recognized that in Africa horizontally organized groups – such as labour unions, bar associations and women's organizations – are often more influential than vertically organized primordial ones (Rothchild and Lawson, 1994, p. 256).

Outlining the political evolution of civil society in sub-Saharan Africa, Harbeson (1994) points out the highly interventionist command relationships of the colonial state with society, its quasi-military nature, and a fiscal base rooted in high taxation of the peasantry, characteristics that were passed on to newly independent states. The radical reordering of political space imposed under colonial rule deconstructed potential civil societies – 'invented' Africa – leaving only marginal space for civil society.[4] Towards the end of the colonial period, with a lessening of strict colonial scrutiny and repression, a proliferating web of associational life provided a structure for the nationalist challenge. However, the trend in post-Independence politics has been to destroy this public realm and replace it with an 'integral state', in which the state seeks unrestricted domination over civil society. The integral state, however, has often subsequently given way to the 'patrimonial state', characterized by the personalized nature of rule; frequent violations of human rights; lack of clear designation of the powers and roles of central government, because it is subordinated to the patrimonial ruler; and a tendency for individuals to withdraw from the (civic) public realm, thus using an 'exit' rather than 'voice' option. There is mounting evidence that recent stress on the contraction of the state in structural adjustment programmes has accentuated this pattern.[5]

As a background for understanding the potential roles of civil society in Africa, Donald Rothchild and Letitia Lawson have analysed six ideal regime types, or theoretical constructs, in relation to the extent of state control over state–society interaction, and the nature and extent of societal incorporation into the public realm (Box 7.1). They draw on political analysis of Latin American states – particularly their transition from authoritarianism to modernization (O'Donnell et al., 1986). They point out that in Latin America, civil society was consolidated during a period of rapid social and economic change in which interest groups were strong enough to make serious demands on the state. However, when the channels through which these demands were made became institutionalized, populist and

---

Box 7.1   Regime types in relation to state control and societal incorporation

Majoritarian democracy

This is represented by a high degree of societal incorporation and only partial state control over state–society interaction. It is characterized by polyarchical regimes where ruling elites made up of top political leaders and bureaucrats, traditional rulers and their descendants, the leading members of the liberal professions, the rising business bourgeoisie, and top members of the military and police have succeeded in maintaining the 'independence bargain', structuring politics so as to promote open, two- or multi-party competition, for example, Botswana, Mauritius, Gambia and Namibia. These are all small countries in population terms, and are all dominated by a core ethnic group. In these cases democracy legitimates the rule of the power-holders without endangering their continued supremacy.

State populism

Where a ruling elite allows forms of decentralized decision-making, civil society is broadened, but does not develop autonomously. These regimes are characterized by overt state control of processes and mechanisms of state–society interaction, with societal participation tolerated. Historically there have been few examples in Africa. Those that have emerged (Ghana, 1981–83; Burkino Faso, 1983–87; Uganda) have all later been challenged by elites.

Pacted democracy

This is a minimalist form of democracy, where ruling elites allow power-sharing and a degree of popular participation – they operate through an amalgam of authoritarian control and consociational democracy. The 'consociational' democratic model, as developed by Lijphart (1985), has four main aspects: a grand coalition of political leaders from all major societal segments; protection of minority interests by means of a mutual veto rule; utilization of the proportionality principle in the formation of coalitions, appointment of civil servants and allocation of resources; and the preservation of a high degree of segmental autonomy in the management of affairs. This model seeks to reconcile open public participation with elite cooperation in the management of government in socially and culturally divided societies. This form has also been comparatively rare in Africa, but two historical African examples were Jomo Kenyatta's period of rule in Kenya and Paul Biya's in Cameroon.

State corporatism

This form is similar to state populism, in that the state subordinates organized interests in civil society and/or opens specific institutional areas of the state to representatives of civil society. It requires a relatively strong and autonomous state. There is some debate on the extent of these regimes in Africa, depending on the understanding of differences between 'corporatist tendencies' and fully fledged 'corporatist regimes'. A historical example of the latter is Côte d'Ivoire.

Societal disengagement

This form is characterized by the detachment of societal groups from political and economic involvement in the state. State avoidance can develop in more extreme cases into new societal institution-building outside the state, where local societies begin to take back control of activities generally accepted as the responsibility of the central state, such as security and education. A number of examples of this form exist in Africa, one of the more extreme being Tanzania in the 1980s.

State repression

This is a regime where, in order to maintain control and repress any challenge from civil society, the ruling elite applies mechanisms of coercion throughout the political domain. Again, this form is relatively common in Africa, contemporary examples including Kenya, Sudan, Somalia and Liberia.

Source: Rothchild and Lawson (1994).

corporatist regimes began to limit the autonomy of civil society, as they managed the modernization process.

Rothchild and Lawson's analysis refers primarily to the 1980s, raising questions about how this situation changed in the 1990s, and the extent to which the situation in Africa is similar to that in Latin America. Much has been written about governance and improving state–civil society relations in Africa (Hyden, 1992), and this has been at the forefront of political conditionality for continuing international assistance in many countries. However, most analysts agree that the problems of democratic consolidation in the region are enormous, and many '. . . do not expect the current trend toward liberalization in Africa to result in full-blown democratic systems in the larger and more pluralistic countries in the near future' (Bratton and Rothchild, 1992, p. 282).

This chapter argues that, based on political, economic and institutional analysis using some of the concepts related to state–society interaction outlined above, much can be learned about the realities that guide and constrain policy formulation – in this case of housing policy – in Africa. More specifically, it can also help to predict the likelihood of wider social demands being incorporated in these policies. The next section applies such an analysis to Mozambique and then South Africa – two contrasting yet closely linked states and societies in southern Africa.

STATE–SOCIETY RELATIONS AND HOUSING POLICY IN MOZAMBIQUE

State–society relations in Mozambique

In terms of Rothchild and Lawson's typology, Mozambique was, until fairly recently, a case of societal disengagement – although from Independence to the late 1980s the state had exerted its integrating power through a form of state populism, the nature of the 'social contract' that this entailed involved corporatism and, later, clientelism. Since the imposition of colonial rule, a large majority of the population have not engaged with the state except when forced to. While there was widespread willingness to engage with the new state after Independence, the practices of the ruling elite, economic difficulties caused by international pressure and natural disasters, and latterly the civil war led to a rapid return to disengagement by the majority of the population. This has been strengthened by the strong influence of the international agencies and, subsequently, global capital flows, which have undermined state power and also required the dismantling of the state in many areas. The result is a weakly structured society, devastated by war and other forms of social disruption, and a weak state (Abrahamsson and Nilsson, 1995).

In Mozambique, much of the public discourse on civil society has focused on the notion of traditional authority, with its base in the countryside in rural social relations. By contrast, the international community has tended to see recently created national NGOs as the main protagonists of civil society, and these have received substantial support, without which it is unlikely they would survive.[6] Very few of these, however, have emerged as a result of local organization of community interests, most being aid-driven and top-down. It has been argued that 'the notion of "civil society" in Mozambique is yet another in a line of exotic imports, some of which, like the previously dominant discourse of socialism, have not had a happy history locally' (Grest, 1998). The formal institutions of civil society are thus those that Ekeh would term 'modern' or 'civic' – the 'primordial' and 'traditional' institutions, which are much more closely linked to indigenous and local forms of culture and organization (and which in the long term may be much more important for the development of civil society) remain largely unstructured (and unresearched). However, these bodies exist in parallel with the 'modern' sector of civil society, in ways that may be analogous to the distinctions currently drawn between the formal and informal sectors of the economy (Grest, 1998). Their importance for the day-to-day survival of the majority of Mozambicans, including access to shelter, is increasingly noted but has been little investigated. The phenomenon of globalization is particularly marked in the case of Mozambique, due to the ever more important role the international community[7] has come to play in setting national economic and political agendas. The lack of correspondence between these agendas and the realities of political power and social practice at the local level lead, however, to their ineffectiveness.

The state response to household demand for housing in Mozambique is inadequate, as discussed below. Why does the state not respond more adequately? First, the state is bankrupt and survives (economically at least) only due to international intervention. As noted above, this heavily influences policy, as international agencies can, to a great extent, dictate policy objectives through their stranglehold on investment finance. This is beginning to change as private sector finance – mainly regional and multinational – is beginning to be attracted into Mozambique. However, this is, and is likely to continue to be in limited areas, mainly transport, energy, mineral extraction, agriculture and related processing, tourism, and latterly also consumer and financial services for the elite and new economic areas. This means that increasingly, Mozambique has to adjust its policies not only to the conditionalities imposed by the international community, but also to the whims of global capital, in many cases allocating scarce (financial and institutional) resources to create an attractive environment for inward investment. This often means fewer resources for the urban poor, and less supportive policies (Jenkins and Wilkinson, 2002).

In the above context the state needs to isolate itself from, or contain, popular pressure. In the case of Mozambique, the extreme weakness of civil society means that such pressure is articulated in a 'raw' fashion, in which it is difficult to aggregate preferences. Moreover, there is a strong incompatibility between community demands and limited public resources. As there is no overt repression, due partly to the political reforms supported by the international community, the political elite has begun to insulate itself from social opposition through delegation of authority to a technocratic class. This requires an authoritarian regime, which (as argued more fully by Jenkins, 1999a) is being constructed through a form of pacted democracy.

In general, it is essential that the primordial and civic forms of civil society develop both to interact with the restructuring state, challenging it where necessary, and to strengthen social development where the state and the market will not, or cannot, do so. For too long the assumption underlying development theory, policy and practice has been that the state is the primary actor. The reality that this is not so – and indeed is unlikely to be so – is particularly clear in Mozambique, at the 'periphery of the periphery'. However, increasing reliance on the market to drive development is not likely to reach those at the economic periphery, let alone beyond it. On the contrary, there is evidence of growing socio-economic segmentation within countries, the increasing absorption of economic and political elites within global capitalist society, and thus a growing rift between society and the state worldwide.

Housing policy in Mozambique

Mozambique's national housing policy was approved by the parliament in December 1990. This was the country's first explicit housing policy; previously such policy had been implicit within the overall development strategy (Jenkins, 1990; Jenkins and Smith, 2001). This chapter does not allow space to describe the evolution and nature of Mozambique's National Housing Policy (see Jenkins, 1998). However, while technical inputs from national and international personnel stressed the need for an effective housing policy which recognized the enabling role of the state in stimulating private sector and community/individual activity, the approved policy concentrated on privatization of the state housing stock and construction capacity, as well as opening of the residential construction sector to private enterprise. There was little emphasis on state facilitation of the community sector, despite the latter being by far the most important for the population, given the weakness of the private sector and high levels of urban poverty.

Since 1990 there has been little effective implementation of the housing policy, except for continuing divestiture of state housing stock, and some growth in new housing supply by the private sector for the upper end of the market. The Social Housing Programme approved as part of the National Housing Policy has slowly been developed to a very limited extent. Of the two new institutions created to implement this (Instituto Nacional de Habitação e Urbanismo and Fundo de Fomento de Habitação), the first has demarcated less than 1000 residential plots, with another 4000 planned or in progress; and the second has built some 35 houses in total, as well as offering 470 subsidized housing finance packages. It is significant that, although the Programme was approved in 1991, it took until 1995 to create the institutions needed to implement it, and these are still extremely weak. In any case, the appropriateness of a policy of constructing formal dwellings, in urban areas where less than a fifth of the population live in such housing units at present, can be questioned.

The housing policy has, in practice, primarily benefited the political and economic elite, who have been able to purchase state housing with large discounts. Many of these dwellings are then rented out to members of the international community at high rents even by international standards, due to the restricted supply of good quality dwellings. While it is illegal to purchase more than one state unit, there is evidence that a new landlord class is emerging which is doing so (Jenkins, 1999c). On the other hand, although state rents have been adjusted upwards minimally, they are still extremely low in relation to economic rents. This imbalance continues to undermine the housing market, as it is much cheaper to acquire a state unit than to build a new dwelling. The housing market has, however – after a long time – begun to function at the upper end of the scale, despite high interest rates and restrictions on credit availability.

It is thus argued that in these conditions – a weak state and weak market – it is not feasible to reach the urban poor by conventional state interventions in housing, whether at project level (sites and services and upgrading); programme level (targeted subsidies and urban development programmes) or policy level (state facilitation of the housing market). There is no realistic prognosis for the short-to-medium term within which the state or the market can effectively reach the urban poor in terms of shelter at scale, given the acute institutional and economic constraints. In contrast, when the state and the market are as weak as in Mozambique, both historically and contemporarily, underlying social structures are obviously – and crucially – engaged in economic activity, not merely in social and cultural activity. New approaches are needed that are based on the very social mechanisms and structures – often on the fringes of the state and the market – whereby the majority of the population manage to survive. Without these, the urban areas will deteriorate further and become more unsustainable in social, economic and environmental terms.

This chapter now looks at a very different political, economic and institutional situation in the same region, to see how relevant the above analysis might be in a wider context.

STATE–SOCIETY RELATIONS AND HOUSING POLICY IN SOUTH AFRICA

State–society relations in South Africa

Applying the typology in the first section of this chapter to South Africa, under the apartheid regime this was a clear – and extreme – case of state repression. In post-election South Africa the state continues to be strong, as it was under the apartheid regime, but has moved away from a repressive role. But the extent to which it is able to implement a widespread democracy is questionable.

The private sector and the market are also well established in South Africa. Both the state and the market are undergoing restructuring and, although this is guided by national political decisions, it is highly (and increasingly) influenced by global economic forces, with support from the international community. At the macro-economic level, South Africa is currently embarking on a self-inflicted structural adjustment programme as part of a major attempt to attract new investment as the basis for new economic growth. It has to break into the world manufacturing and service markets to achieve this, as its traditional exports (mineral and agricultural products) face either dwindling demand or tariff barriers. In this it is up against tough global competition from better equipped, more experienced and more highly skilled countries with greater internal efficiencies. It also lacks a strong regional market within which to grow, and with which to interact economically. It has a difficult task ahead.

There has been widespread and heated debate on the role of civil society in South Africa, and the new government has incorporated certain elements of civil society in its development programmes – for instance in welfare. However, in other areas, although government policy initially promoted a role for civil society (for example through the Reconstruction and Development Programme, RDP), in practice, and with the renewed macro-economic focus of government policy (through the Growth, Employment and Rehabilitation strategy), this seems to have become secondary. In effect, by pinning development strategy to state redistribution of wealth from economic growth, as opposed to growth based on redistribution of existing wealth, the government has of necessity become extremely developmentalist, as it attempts to break into the global economy on the best possible terms. As detailed elsewhere (Jenkins, 1999a), while the new South African government aspires to majoritarian democracy, to some extent it started out following a state populist line (for example through the RDP), and at present more properly can be described as hovering between pacted democracy and state corporatism. Practices developed in the transition phase and subsequent state action indicate a strong tendency to subordinate the organized interests of civil society, usually through defining specific institutional mechanisms for their participation, in order to make authoritative decisions both to redress the inherited social and economic imbalances, and compete in the global market place to ensure economic growth.

Civil society in South Africa, although strong in comparative regional terms, has found its position eroding. This is clearest in the civic movement, but is also the case for non-governmental organizations (NGOs). The non-governmental movement was promised by government that it would have a strong role in post-election development. However, in practice this has not developed, and there is a widespread distrust on both sides. Organized labour continues to be in a strong political position as part of the current national governing coalition, although this may not last in the medium term. Political society is also quite strong, with a number of well-developed political parties (as well as a number of relatively weak ones) and a strong opposition. In certain regions the latter is the major political force, favouring a confederal path for future state development.

The role of traditional or primordial civil society in South Africa is also complex. As in most colonial states, traditional rulers were used as part of the governing process in the apartheid period, and they represent a relatively strong political force, especially in rural areas. The new government has, to a great extent, co-opted this group politically through mechanisms whereby they have political representation, but little formal direct power. Primordial civil society is also relatively strong in South Africa, although less organized into ethnic and other particularist associations (compared to West Africa), and expressed more through organizations such as the Nativist churches, which indeed exert cultural influence at a regional level. To date these have not exerted any real political influence, and hence no attempt to incorporate them politically has taken place, although the largest churches (such as the Zionist Church) have been courted by both previous and new governments.

Housing policy in South Africa

How has this affected housing policy formulation and implementation? Space does not permit a detailed description of the new housing policy or its development. Descriptions are now fairly readily available (for example, Mackay, 1995; Goodlad, 1996), and there is a growing critique of its implementation (see, for example, Watson et al., 1996; Bond and Tait, 1997; Jenkins, 1997a, 1999b; Laloo, 1998; Tomlinson, 1998; Wilkinson, 1998; Mackay, 1999). As described in detail elsewhere (Jenkins, 1997b, 1999b) the new policy was thrashed out during the period of negotiations (approximately from 1991) leading up to the first elections in 1994. Following the pattern of the general political negotiation process, the policy was developed by a group of institutional participants in a National Housing Forum representing the newly legalized political parties, civil society groupings, the building construction and materials industries, the financial sector, and NGOs.[8] These were mostly relatively powerful lobby groups at the time of transition, although their status has not necessarily been maintained, as noted above. In addition, there was a fair degree of collaboration between sub-groups, such as the African National Congress and the civic movement and financial and construction capital, which has also not been maintained.

The main point is that the nature of the agreements reached was predicated on the process and participants involved. The process of reaching consensus essentially entailed groups with major differences reaching a lowest common denominator in their agreements, beyond which they would not concede. In addition, there were major differences in how language and terms were perceived by different groups. Thus in some cases agreements were reached in which certain groups explicitly indicated that their interpretations, for example of affordability, differed. Hence the agreements that underpinned the new policy development were limited and open to reinterpretation. The participant organizations also varied enormously in their composition, experience and orientation. Some were highly skilled negotiators, some highly skilled technically, some highly skilled mobilizers, some had great political acumen, and some had enormous financial resources, but others had very few of these skills and resources.

The nature of the process which brought these interests together therefore relied to a considerable extent on the full-time consultants who guided the negotiations. The fact that the participant organizations reached agreement at all is a testimony to the commitment of those involved, whether representatives or consultants. However, the nature of the process and the vastly different positions in reality led to a juxtapositioning of essentially antagonistic aims. One such was the desire to promote community development, despite the lack of interest in this on the part of the private developer sector; another was the desire to (re-)engage the private sector in low-income housing finance, of which the financial sector was extremely wary, given past experience and a significant volume of outstanding loans.

Over and above these factors, the policy developed relied predominantly on previously tested mechanisms, and it has taken a long time to promote alternative mechanisms, despite the intensive background study activity in 1992 and 1993, and the wide range of alternatives discussed in Housing Forum working groups. Whole areas of policy are as yet not developed, for instance, mechanisms to promote higher-density development and social rental housing. While this is not surprising in that the policy and subsidy mechanisms were basically developed for implementation by the existing civil service, which had – and has – limited experience of alternatives, in practice the new government has done little to change the situation. It is argued that this is partly due to limited institutional and technical capacity within the civil service, which itself is in the process of restructuring (Jenkins, 1997a; Jenkins and Smith, 2001), but it can also be attributed to the political and economic goals of the new ruling elite and their consociational partners.

The policy concentrates first on a limited number of capital subsidy mechanisms, and second on a variety of institutional and financial arrangements for government to pave the way for private sector delivery. The former are basically extensions of the capital subsidy scheme initiated by the state-sponsored parastatal the Independent Development Trust in 1992, itself derived from experiments undertaken by the Urban Foundation, and not dissimilar to various sites and service financing schemes previously implemented by Provincial Governments. The latter are attempts to more effectively re-engage the private sector, which had previously been engaged in lower-income housing delivery in the early and mid-1980s.

On the whole, it is probably not surprising that a relatively closed process, with a limited number of participants representing extremely varied, large and generally poorly informed constituencies, to a certain extent dominated by consultants and limited by existing institutional capacities, and in a situation of rapid political and social change, produced a policy that now requires not only fairly significant technical adjustment, but also is being moulded by new – or more apparent – political realities.

In this context, the housing policy can be seen as representing an attempt at neo-corporatism, which is unravelling as the various corporate participants (such as the civic movement, NGOs, and the construction and financial sectors) fail to see any advantage in participating in policy implementation. The government has subsequently made a number of amendments to the initial policy, mostly recognizing the role of lower tiers of government, but also attempting to adjust the nature of its relationship with the private sector (Jenkins, 1997a). These have been stimulated by ad hoc specialized Task Teams which have reported to the Minister. There is currently no institution at national government level with clear responsibility for revising the policy in the light of the obstacles to its implementation.[9] The overwhelming driving factor in this sector for the state for most of the post-election period was the politically determined target of 1 million new houses before the next election (2000) – regardless of the actual demand or nature of the supply.[10]

What seems to have resulted, due to institutional weakness as well as political and economic pressures, is an authoritarian political elite, which is restructuring the existing technocratic class created in the apartheid era to ensure it can implement its policies in the face of actual political, and possible social, opposition. The structures that were created to allow a neo-corporatist negotiated process during the transition have been generally jettisoned. However, new and more appropriate mechanisms for state–society interaction over policy are not being developed (Jenkins, 1997b). This is similar to many other sub-Saharan African countries after independence, when the state took over development and subordinated the participation of civil society, with disastrous results in terms of policy, including housing policy. It has generally taken several political terms, during which opposition has slowly become organized, to begin to rectify this marginalization of civil society.

It is still a matter for conjecture, but it increasingly seems that economic growth levels will not attain the 6 per cent targeted by government in the Growth, Employment and Rehabilitation strategy. Thus it has been argued that the result of the current supply-led approach to housing provision will, subject to budgetary constraints, be to provide public support for a limited section of the population, with a growing majority who will not benefit from new development by either the public or private sector. It is suggested here that, despite the declared intention of the new housing policy, in the face of the macro-economic and institutional realities, the state will find it economically and politically difficult to assist lower-income groups (who proportionally are growing fastest in South Africa, particularly in urban areas) at an adequate scale. For most individuals and households in this group, especially those with the lowest incomes, reliance on their own resources is already the dominant mode of socio-economic activity. Although they access government resources where possible, the benefits they receive are limited and their engagement with the formal private economy is minimal.

What is perhaps most important in this context is that the creative energy of the wider population, as potentially channeled by groups within civil society, is not lost, but works with the state and the private sector where possible, and outside the state and the market where necessary. This will entail strengthening both horizontal and vertical structures of civil society, as the continuing weak institutional nature of both the state and civil society present major difficulties in developing alternative approaches in housing delivery, at least in the medium term. This area, as in Mozambique, has been little researched to date, but is of great importance in promoting society-led development.

CONCLUSIONS

Although the political, economic and institutional contexts of Mozambique and South Africa are very different, the result of an analysis based on these factors – and not purely the technical aspects of policy – illustrates the difficulties in developing policies that can be relevant at the macro-economic level in the current global situation; can respond to organized political demands (often from the political elite and other powerful groups); and yet effectively identify and respond to demand from wider society, especially where a significant proportion of people are poor. Reconciling these usually conflicting demands, at a time when there is strong international and national pressure to widen governance regimes, often interpreted solely as creating majoritarian democracy, seems to be leading to the development of authoritarian regimes supported by technocratic elites. In such regimes, civil society is either subordinated through consociational structures, or incorporated in specific institutional areas, giving rise to pacted democracy and state corporatism, respectively.

This chapter has not only attempted to show the importance of sound political, economic and institutional analysis of policy parameters, but also the potential and growing role for the horizontal, as well as the vertical, structures of civil society, despite the dominant global economic context, which is driving increasing segmentation of society across the world. It has stressed that a strong civil society is necessary both to interact vertically with the state, and also to define and implement society-led development in the vacuum created by the growing isolation of the state and the market from large sections of the population. The chapter has stressed the need for research into 'primordial' civil society and its potential role in such strengthening, arguing that in Africa this is more prevalent than 'modern' civil society.

In the field of housing and urban development to date, little research has looked at the mechanisms whereby the majority of the urban poor manage to provide themselves with shelter, however inadequate, and how they interact within social situations, as well as with the state and the market. This is a necessary first step in understanding both the real demand for housing, and the possible socio-economic mechanisms that can respond to this demand, as well as channeling such mechanisms to permit more effective and beneficial society–state and society–market interaction, within an essentially society-oriented form of development.

For the rapidly growing urban areas of the developing world with a high incidence of poverty to be more sustainable in future, nuanced policies will be required that reflect the demand and capacities of the wider population, and do not become side-tracked into supporting political and economic elites. This, above all else, requires strengthening of civil society, both horizontally and vertically (Jenkins, 2001c). How this can happen in adverse political and economic contexts is a major challenge for activists, intellectuals and professionals.

CHAPTER EIGHT

Community empowerment and social sustainability in Florianópolis, Brazil

Denise Martins Lopes and Carole Rakodi

INTRODUCTION

In the past few decades in most developing countries, community development-oriented activities have been among the major strategies advocated to improve the conditions of their people, especially the less-privileged groups. Community empowerment is identified as an important component of community development, and is an aim of most development agencies working at community level, including support non-governmental organizations (NGOs). However, what is precisely meant by the term 'empowerment' is rarely spelt out. Further, there have been very few attempts to evaluate whether NGO support has, in practice, empowered communities in the short and, especially, the long term.

This chapter attempts to operationalize the concept of empowerment through the development of indicators. In turn, such indicators are the basis for a methodological approach adopted in a longer-term evaluation of the impacts of the work of a local Brazilian NGO, Centro de Apoio e Promoção ao Migrante (Centre for the Support and Promotion of Migrants, CAPROM). This NGO, during the period between 1989 and 1992, had as one of its aims the empowerment of low-income communities, through support to the promotion of organized, but initially illegal, land occupations. Case studies of three communities that were supported and organized by CAPROM were undertaken using the indicators of empowerment developed, for three different periods – before, during and after the intervention of the NGO. A mainly qualitative research approach was adopted for this evaluation.

The findings of the case studies are presented, and suggest that community residents, particularly leaders of the community-based organizations (CBOs), have indeed been empowered by the intervention of the NGO and, most importantly, have developed a long-lasting capacity for organization and action, not only satisfying immediate practical needs, but also meeting the strategic need for empowerment.

CONSIDERATIONS OF POWER AND EMPOWERMENT

To conceptualize the term empowerment is not an easy task. Probably, one of the reasons is because it contains the word 'power'. Like empowerment, power means many things to many different people.

Without entering into any philosophical depth, Batliwala (1994, p. 129) broadly defines power as 'control over material assets, intellectual resources and ideology'. The material assets over which control can be exercised may be physical, such as land and water; financial, such as money and access to it; or human, such as people's bodies and labour. Intellectual resources incorporate knowledge, information and ideas. Control over ideology means the ability to create, spread, sustain and institutionalize certain sets of beliefs, values, attitudes and behaviour, determining how people understand and act within given political and socio-economic circumstances.

In this sense, it could be said that a person is more or less powerful depending on the extent to which he or she is able to control available resources. The ability to control such resources confers on the person the power to take decisions by him or herself – having autonomy or shared responsibilities in decision-making.

Friedmann (1992), in his study of alternative development, identifies three different kinds of power which civil society – represented here by its nucleus, the household – disposes in its search for life and livelihood: social, political and psychological power. Social power is concerned with access to certain bases of household production, and can be measured by the differential access households have to them. He considers defensible life space, surplus time, social organization and social networks as being the bases of social power and fundamental to households' struggle to improve their situation. Once these bases are minimally guaranteed, households can dedicate their efforts to the remaining dimensions of social power: knowledge, skills and information, tools of production and financial resources. Political power concerns the access of individual household members to the process of decision-making, especially decisions related to their own future. Like the power of voting, political power implies the power of voice and of collective action. Finally, psychological power is best described as an individual sense of potency and, where present, is demonstrated in self-confident behaviour. An increased sense of personal potency will have positive and continuous effects on a household's struggle to increase its effective social and political power.

Control over power is a dynamic process. It may favour different actors at different times, depending on who has more and who has less power in that specific context. Certain groups of individuals will have more scope than others to influence the decision-making process. When a process of redistribution of power is intended, challenging existing basic power relations, and aiming at providing greater control over the sources of power for one person or for a group of people, this process could be termed empower-ment (Batliwala, 1994).

Most authors of the literature reviewed agree that any initiative to empower a group of people should be directed at enabling them to make their own decisions about their surroundings and to take more control over their day-to-day lives. This implies assessing their own needs and priorities, setting targets and objectives, planning and implementing their strategies to achieve those objectives, and being able to evaluate the whole process. Gajanayake and Gajanayake (1993) understand that empowerment pre-supposes enabling people to perceive the reality of their environment, to reflect on the factors shaping that environment, and to take steps to bring about changes to improve the situation.

However, the demand for change does not usually emerge spontaneously from a condition of subjection. On the contrary, empowerment normally needs to be externally induced by outside forces working with a more egali-tarian notion of society, aiming at encouraging powerless people to organ-ize and take further action by themselves. A key role for external agents lies in giving powerless people access to a new body of ideas and information, and raising their consciousness and awareness that the existing network of relationships is unjust. Hence, one could say that the role of intermediary institutions is of critical importance in any attempt to empower low-income communities, especially the very poor, as self-empowerment is rarely spontaneously developed from within a community.

Through empowerment, low-income people gain access to new worlds of knowledge and can begin to make new personal and collective choices for their lives. A feeling of being able to do what is needed to reach the desired outcome is very important for residents (Holmes, 1992) and brings about significant benefits, such as raising people's self-esteem, making them more aware of the reality shaping their lives, lessening the likelihood of poverty, opening new spaces for collective participation and discussion, liberating people from mental and physical dependence, employment training, etc.

It is recognized, though, that a community should not be assumed to be a unity, but a group of people with varying interests and socio-economic char-acteristics. In this sense, for the purpose of this study, 'community' is defined as a dynamic group of people who share, to a certain extent, their socio-economic characteristics, resources, values and problems. They live in the same vicinity and have developed social and political relations among them-selves, and between themselves and other people or groups of people from outside their area. Such relationships may be influenced by their internal dynamics, organizational and social structures and gender relations, and by their individual members' differentiated access to sources of power.

A set of indicators of empowerment was developed, based on these con-siderations. These indicators were the basis for an evaluation of the work of the NGO CAPROM in its attempt to empower three communities in the city of Florianópolis, Brazil.

INDICATORS OF EMPOWERMENT

Due to the fact that social development projects often have non-measurable and non-material objectives, and their outcomes are not always pre-dictable, a methodology for their evaluation needs to go further than the usual verification of presumed effects, which is entirely based on quantita-tive data. According to Garaycochea (1990), appropriate indicators for the evaluation of qualitative aspects need to be chosen through the selection of an element or components within the social process that can best describe it. Such qualitative aspects cannot be measured by collecting and analysing numerical data, so an indicator or a set of indicators is needed to describe and explain phenomena taking place during the process.

As this piece of work is concerned with an evaluation of the process of empowerment intended for some low-income families that participated in illegal land occupations promoted by the NGO CAPROM, during the time it worked in Florianópolis, and based on the assumption that qualitative research is basically concerned with social processes, the approach adopted for this research was essentially qualitative. Bearing this in mind, and based on the aspects of power and community empowerment reviewed above, a series of nine indicators of empowerment were identified:

- self-confidence among a community's residents
- ability of the community to organize itself
- residents' ability to understand and reflect about the reality of the environment in which the community is living
- ability of the community to set goals for the future
- ability of the community to develop plans
- ability of the community to put its plans into practice
- ability to build networks
- ability to communicate effectively
- capacity of the community to evaluate the outcomes of its activities.

THE PROCESS OF ORGANIZED LAND OCCUPATION AS A MEANS OF COMMUNITY EMPOWERMENT

Having passed through earlier stages of promoting welfare-oriented activ-ities and assisting already established low-income illegal settlements to fight government attempts to evict them, the NGO CAPROM later focused on empowering low-income people so that they would be able to fight to meet their needs regarding land, housing, and housing-related services and infrastructure. Its work, during the period between 1989 and 1992,[1] was aimed at developing and supporting community organizations that would be able to organize and carry out collective land occupations, put pressure on the government to gain access to secure tenure, make demands for public services and infrastructure, participate in the implementation of services and infrastructure programmes, and influence official land and housing practices, through the presentation of alternative policies for low-income settlements.

A series of factors contributed to CAPROM's decision to adopt a strategy of organized land occupations. First, in the late 1980s no official policy was planned for the near future to facilitate access to land by the low-income population by local, state or national government levels. Second, because of clashes between local government and representatives of social movements in the city, caused by the government's early attempts to evict settlers from illegally occupied land, there was no hope of amicably negotiating a solution to the housing problems of those who were still waiting to be housed. Third, because of such eviction orders against low-income communities, a series of groups opposing the government's actions appeared in civil society and started giving support to the work of CAPROM. Valuable support also came from some sectors of the Catholic Church, support which was a helpful source of influence on some political forces in the city. In addition to the help received from outsiders, the low-income communities also created a solidarity network among themselves. This was considered a great asset in their struggle, and was of invaluable help in the implementation of land occupations and in the defence of the new communities in the face of police reaction.

However, despite the strength drawn from this favourable situation, CAPROM was still in a reactive position in relation to the government's actions towards the low-income communities, especially as far as threats of eviction were concerned. So, in order to improve on its 'fire-fighting' role, and taking advantage of all the support it was receiving, CAPROM decided to promote organized land occupations, moving from a reactive to a more active position in the local scene (Franzoni, 1993).

Box 8.1   Case studies

Santa Terezinha II is a community of 55 families, the result of the very first organized land occupation in Florianópolis, which took place on 28 July 1990. The land on which part of the community of Santa Terezinha II is located today already had around 40 families illegally living on it prior to the organized occupation promoted by CAPROM. These families occupied the land gradually and spontaneously, with no formal spatial arrangements. Their first contact with CAPROM came with the need to organize themselves after a threat of eviction posed by the municipality. They were joined by some other families from outside the settlement who had already participated in CAPROM's meetings, and decided to occupy a new site adjacent to the original one. The groups decided to (re)-arrange their houses on regular plots on both sites. The original settlers simply transferred their shacks to the building plots they had previously demarcated, and built new ones to accommodate the newcomers.

By 1997 the whole community had legal access to piped water and electricity. It also had access to some paved roads, a sewerage system, a crèche, a public doctor's surgery, public telephones and rubbish collection. Their Communal House was built by mutual help, with building materials acquired with funds raised from parties, raffles and bingo sessions organized by the residents themselves. Residents have also made good progress in upgrading their houses.

Nova Esperança is a community formed by 50 families from a variety of different backgrounds: people living in overcrowded accommodation, people on the verge of being evicted from their rented houses, people who had been on the waiting list for an official popular house for more than 10 years, and so on. In contrast to Santa Terezinha II, neighbourhood bonds in Nova Esperança were formed in the meetings that preceded the occupation itself, which took place on 2 November 1990, and followed the pattern described above.

The publicly owned site occupied by the participants had to undergo an intensive process of cleaning before the occupation, because it was full of bushes, rubbish and mice. For 17 months the settlers lived in temporary accommodation with only three water taps, illegal electricity connections, and no sewerage system. Negotiations with the municipal authorities were undertaken during this time, with a view to building houses in a new settlement and relocating the families to it. The settlers were to be responsible for building their two-bedroom houses through mutual help, and the municipality was to provide the building materials and technical advice with respect to the use of interlocking concrete blocks and water and electricity connections.

In 1997, the community of Nova Esperança was served by some paved roads and a sewerage system. Most of the residents had surrounded their plots by a wall, and some had made modifications to some of the original features of their houses.

Novo Horizonte community, during the time of the organized land occupation which took place in September 1990, was formed by 96 families. These people used to live with parents, other relatives or employers, and were facing threats of eviction or were already living in an illegal situation. Most were migrants who originally came from the western part of the state, an essentially agricultural region. The site they occupied was originally destined to house a low-income housing project. As no formal plans for that purpose had been implemented in the state for a long period, the site was idle and very badly maintained. The settlers obtained water from a tap outside a neighbouring school's wall with the permission of its headmistress. Light was obtained from candles, torches and lanterns.

In 1997, the community was served by piped water, electricity, some paved roads, a sewerage system, a crèche, a public health clinic, and rubbish collection. A Communal House was built about two years after the occupation took place, through mutual help. Most of the individual houses now have more permanent features. Community leaders believed in 1997 that there were more than 200 families living in the settlement, because of subdivision of plots.

The three communities analysed in this study have the common characteristic of having started their organization through the fight to gain access to land (Box 8.1). They all had the support of the NGO CAPROM for the process of organization, which started well before the land occupations took place. Those families who wanted to take part in an organized land occupation participated in regular meetings promoted by CAPROM, during which their community associations were formed. It took an average of six months of meetings prior to the occupations themselves and, during that time, future neighbours started to interact with each other. It was in such meetings that settlers and CAPROM members carefully planned the occupations, strategically choosing the site and date so as to maximize the possibility of them remaining on the land. Already during this time the whole process of participation, discussion and decision-making for the land occupations put the settlers into contact with the means necessary to develop many of the abilities identified above as indicators of empowerment.

The occupations themselves were carried out under great tension, especially because the police always appeared to try to disperse the settlers. On the night of the occupation itself, the first job was for the demarcation committee to enter the site and subdivide the plots, while the others, silent and hidden, waited patiently in the surrounding area. Once the site had been subdivided and demarcated, the rest of the committees started doing their jobs: carrying tools, putting up tents, keeping guard, and so on. The early constructions were temporary and fragile, usually made of canvas or strong black plastic. Later on, more substantial buildings were erected, but only after the initial tension had passed, the occupants had started feeling safer and the occupation appeared to have been successful.

The first days in the settlements were the most critical, when settlers had to meet their basic needs, such as cooking, eating, washing, bathing and sleeping, in very precarious conditions. They also had to live surrounded by a police cordon, and to face their neighbours' anger. Usually the first deliberations of residents were concerned with finding ways of tackling criticisms from neighbours and the media, and trying to portray their actions in a positive light to the rest of the city. Afterwards, they started exerting pressure on the public authorities for infrastructure and services, legal tenure, or both. Community meetings during this time usually happened either on the open spaces that had been reserved for communal use, in someone's tent, or in some neighbouring parish. In every case, at least one settler was posted to keep guard in the settlement, to prevent any undesirable visitors.

The provision of legal infrastructure – basically, water and electricity – for the settlements usually happened during constant clashes between the local-level institutions that were responsible for solving the land question, and state-level institutions that were responsible for providing water and electricity. In providing legal infrastructure for the settlements, the state institutions were, in a sense, legitimizing the illegal land occupation, which the local government was still trying to resolve. The settlers, once the legal infrastructure had been installed, besides having their most immediate needs attended to, also had a strong point to count in their favour in the forthcoming legal battle to stay on the land.

METHODOLOGICAL APPROACH FOR EVALUATION OF COMMUNITY EMPOWERMENT

Table 8.1 summarizes the methodological approach adopted to evaluate the process of empowerment of the selected communities. Each numbered line represents one indicator of empowerment. As some of the indicators of empowerment are complex to assess, and it was recognized that it would not be easy to identify them straight away or directly to ask residents about them, some aspects of the community's daily life that could give clues about their situation regarding each indicator were identified. These are listed beneath each indicator. The blank cells in the table were used to record the information collected.

Table 8.1   Empowerment indicators

Indicators	NGO involvement		
	Before	During	After
1 Self-confidence among a community's residents			
Sense of being in control of their own lives			
Confidence to make demands			
Courage to act on their own behalf			
Feeling of being respected			
2 Ability of the community to organize itself			
Existence of organized groups			
Existence of local leaders			
Acceptance by community of organization as a way of mobilization			
Access to physical resources: places of meetings, stationery, fax, etc.			
3 Residents' ability to understand and reflect about the reality of the environment in which the community is living			
Awareness of problems			
Awareness of local needs			
Existence of discussion meetings			
4 Ability of the community to set goals for the future			
Ability to define goals for the future			
Who defined goals?			

Table 8.1   Empowerment indicators *contd.*

Indicators	NGO involvement		
	Before	**During**	**After**
5 Ability of the community to develop plans			
Ability to pursue goals by themselves			
Preparation of alternative plans			
Access to physical resources			
Access to human resources			
Level of acceptance by official bodies			
6 Ability of the community to put its plans into practice			
Ability to gather forces to:			
– implement self/mutual-help projects			
– make demands for improvements			
7 Ability to build networks			
Involvement with other communities			
– in the neighbourhood			
– in the city			
– in the region			
– in the country			
Involvement with other groups			
8 Ability to communicate effectively			
Ease of expression			
Understanding of outsiders' speech			
Feeling confident to speak in public			
9 Capacity of the community to evaluate the outcomes of its activities			
Promotion of evaluation meetings			

In view of the methodological requirements of this study, in addition to collecting secondary data, in-depth interviews were used in the collection of primary data. This type of interview is suitable in cases where the data required are mainly qualitative. A decision was taken to interview both CAPROM staff members, and past and present community leaders.

Although the land occupations had occurred about six years before the evaluation was carried out in 1997, and CAPROM had been active for only a limited period, it was possible to identify informants from the communities and the NGO who were involved at that time and who could give accurate accounts of both the work of the institution, and the changes and longer-term results since the beginning of the 1990s. Using the NGO CEDEP[1] as an entry point, former members of CAPROM staff were identified, using a snowball sampling technique and selecting those whose names were mentioned more than once. In the end, four ex-members of CAPROM were interviewed.

The choice to interview community leaders, despite the risk that they might not represent different interests in communities which are non-homogeneous groups of people, was based on the assumption that the leaders would be more aware of the communities' situation than ordinary residents. Also, all the leaders selected for interview were community residents themselves, and had been democratically elected by the residents of the communities they represented. It was assumed that, besides being able to speak about community organization on behalf of the residents in general, they were reliable sources of information as far as representing the views of other residents was concerned. In all, four persons were interviewed in Santa Terezinha II Community, three in Nova Esperança, and five in Novo Horizonte. These communities, since the beginning of their organization for the land occupations, have had a significant number of women in leadership roles. Because of the predominance of women leaders, most of those interviewed were women.[2]

FINDINGS

Community empowerment is a complex issue. There is no ready-made model that can be applied in each and every particular situation. Every community has unique features and is characterized by complex social, cultural, political and gender relations. Here, conclusions are drawn about whether CAPROM's attempt at community empowerment was successful according to the nine indicators of empowerment (above), and with regard to Batliwala's (1994) and Friedmann's (1992) concepts of power.

Indicators of empowerment

A summary of the results of the case studies with respect to each of the indicators of empowerment is given below.

Self-confidence of community residents

It is evident from the case studies that some of the residents in all three communities had experienced an increase in their sense of self-confidence. As demonstrated by the interviewees' testimonies (Lopes, 1998), they moved from a condition of subjection and lack of initiative before their involvement with the NGO CAPROM, to a condition in which they felt confident enough to take on leadership roles, start making demands, negotiate with public institutions, participate in the city-wide process of decision-making, and much more.

Despite increased gender equality not being a direct objective of CAPROM's work, nor the prime subject of this study, it is important to stress the perceptible change in women's attitudes regarding their roles in community life. From the case studies, it is clear that women have experienced a considerable increase in their sense of self-confidence. This may be due to the fact that, with collective organization, women passed through a learning process that provided them with an unprecedented opportunity for self-discovery. In many instances, this transformation was evidenced in their statements, as shown by Lopes (1998). In the same way, women were introduced to new spaces for discussion and action, and felt confident enough to take on leadership roles.

Ability of the community to organize itself

According to Colenutt and Cutten (1994), an important aspect in any process of empowerment is the organizational structure of the communities involved, as community empowerment can be achieved only through community organization and participation. From the case studies, it is clear that, since the beginning, one of the main concerns of CAPROM was the formation of community associations among the families with which it was involved. Having the status of an organized community proved to be effective in bringing a series of benefits for residents during the time they were involved with CAPROM. Because of their organization, residents were able to gain access to a piece of land through organized land occupation, resist eviction, and negotiate with public institutions to obtain access to basic infrastructure for their settlements, among others. In 1997, five years after CAPROM's withdrawal, each community retained the organizational structure formed during the time of CAPROM's support.

Residents' ability to understand and reflect about the reality of the environment in which the community is living

It has already been concluded that communities' access to intellectual resources increased during their involvement with CAPROM. This certainly contributed to making residents more aware of their situation, and changing their attitudes regarding the way they sought solutions for their problems. However, after CAPROM's intervention ceased, community leaders felt that the communities' ability to reflect on their reality had diminished. Assuming that people cannot 'lose' a developed capacity to understand and reflect about the reality of the environment in which they are living, it cannot be unequivocally asserted here that, as a consequence of the work of the NGO CAPROM, all the residents of the communities studied had increased their level of understanding. Some clearly had, and these are people who still demonstrated a certain concern regarding their situation and who were trying to take steps to change it. It could almost certainly be said that the way these residents saw their situation in 1997 was a direct legacy of the learning process through which they passed during the time CAPROM was working with them. But this assertion cannot be generalized for all the residents in the communities, some of whom were not involved, and some of whom took up residence more recently.

Ability of the community to set goals for the future

The families' understanding of their immediate needs – land, shelter, basic infrastructure – as their legitimate right has certainly made a difference to the way they started to assess their priorities and, subsequently, to the way they targeted the objectives to be pursued. Some of the residents have kept working in this direction, and have perfected the ability to set objectives acquired during the time of CAPROM's support, through their integration into the Municipal Participatory Budget process. Their ability to participate fully in this process was the main legacy from CAPROM's time, as far as setting goals for the future is concerned.

Ability of the community to develop plans

Before the families' involvement with CAPROM, although they had the capacity to decide on what they wished to achieve for the future, their ability to develop a successful strategy or plan was virtually non-existent. However, both during the period CAPROM was working with the communities and after it ceased its activities, community organizations were able to develop the plans and strategies needed to pursue their previously defined objectives.

Ability of the community to put its plans into practice

Here it seems that success is directly linked to a community's access to certain resources. Prior to the communities' involvement with CAPROM, their limited access to professional assistance, information, social organizations and networks, financial inputs, political power and other factors, clearly constrained their ability to put into practice any plans or strategies they might have had. Through their involvement with CAPROM, not only did they have considerably increased access to the resources mentioned above, but they also experienced an increase in self-confidence, knowledge and skills. This provided them with real opportunities not just to develop plans and strategies, as mentioned above, but also to implement them.

Ability to build networks

It is evident from the case studies that the families in the three communities had progressed from a situation of relative isolation and lack of collective work, to a situation in which they were able to be associated with the work of other communities and groups. One of the most important features of CAPROM's work was its ability to unite the low-income communities of the region around common issues and promote their joint participation in a range of events, from weekly meetings and training courses, to protest marches, sit-ins and the implementation of organized land occupations. As shown by Lopes (1998), acting collectively through organization and networking tends to reinforce the process of community empowerment.

It is clear that, both during the time the communities were involved with the work of CAPROM and in the late 1990s, when they were involved in the network of communities which were integrated into the Participatory Budget, the capacity to build networks cannot be solely attributed to the communities themselves. Nevertheless, based on the interviewees' accounts, it is believed that some community residents, if there was a need to confront a common adversary, would be able to build another solid network.

Ability to communicate effectively

It was clear from the interviews that community leaders felt that their ability to communicate had received a considerable boost since their involvement with CAPROM. According to their own perceptions, some of the other residents had also been able to benefit from an increased ability to communicate. Such a new skill has produced important outcomes regarding the way residents, especially women leaders, relate to outsiders, make demands on and negotiate with public institutions, and participate in the public life of the city. Such a sense of being able to communicate better may be a natural consequence of the increase in residents' self-confidence and, as stressed by most of the interviewees, the knowledge acquired through their collective involvement and organization during the time CAPROM was working with the communities.

Capacity of a community to evaluate the outcomes of its activities

In none of the three communities studied did interviewees mention any established practices of systematic evaluation of the outcomes of their activities. It is possible that some evaluation meetings were held. However, if they occurred, they were not treated as an important part of the communities' process of development. While informal reflection on their experiences undoubtedly occurred, more formal evaluation processes had not become established, perhaps because of CAPROM's early withdrawal.

Concepts of power

The two concepts of power reviewed above were found to be of value in considering what is involved in community empowerment. The findings from the communities studied are presented with reference to these conceptualizations of power.

Taking into consideration that people can be regarded as being more or less powerful, depending on the extent to which they are able to control available resources, the application of Batliwala's concept of power in the cases of the communities studied can have a twofold interpretation. First, the communities had become more powerful, as they gained control over some resources which they did not have before. On the other hand, the communities' control over some other resources had not changed.

It is clear that community residents gained access to physical resources such as land, legal water and electricity connections, some services and community premises, and that they had gained greater control over them. It is also possible to conclude that access to and control over intellectual resources – knowledge, information and ideas – increased, because the process through which the communities passed provided them with access to a range of means through which they were able to develop a better capacity to understand their condition and the situation in which they were living.

However, as far as ideology is concerned, there is no evidence that the communities were in the past, or are now, capable of creating, spreading, sustaining and institutionalizing beliefs, values, attitudes and behaviour. Rather, it is clear that, for some time, they were subjects of CAPROM's ability to do this, as this institution was their point of reference in determining how they should act within given political and socio-economic circumstances. This study did not investigate in detail the economic situation of each family, so there is no evidence on which one could judge whether their control over financial resources had changed or not.

As far as Friedmann's social, political and psychological dimensions of power are concerned, some conclusions can also be reached regarding the situation of the three communities. Of the four bases of social power which Friedmann considers fundamental to households' struggle to improve their lives and livelihoods – defensible life space, surplus time, social organization and social networks – residents of the communities studied had clearly increased their access to three since the beginning of their involvement with CAPROM – defensible life space, social organization and social networks. Regarding the remaining dimensions of social power, the assertions made above about residents' access to knowledge and skills, information and financial resources also apply here.

Friedmann's political power is concerned with the access of household members to the process of decision-making, through their vote, voice and collective actions. Before their involvement with CAPROM, residents' political power was restricted to the right to vote. It is clear that, because of the way their struggle to access land was carried out, residents became prominent in the local political scene and also increased their political power. Not only did they challenge existing political practices, or the absence of them, regarding the provision of land to low-income populations, but subsequently they moved to positions of negotiation in the political sphere in order to gain access to infrastructure, services and secure tenure.

Finally, it is evident that some community residents were also able to increase their individual sense of potency, which could characterize an increase in psychological power. As suggested by Friedmann, psychological empowerment can be the result of successful actions in the social or political domains. In the case of the communities studied, as previously concluded, they had indeed undertaken successful actions both in the social and political spheres, which adequately explain their residents' increased sense of personal potency.

CONCLUSIONS

Based on the assertions made above regarding the indicators of empowerment and Batliwala's and Friedmann's concepts of power, it can be concluded that the objective of CAPROM's work on community empowerment was met. It is clear that most of the characteristics of a supposedly empowered community were present in the communities studied five years after CAPROM's withdrawal.

Regarding the methodological approach developed to evaluate community empowerment, it is believed that this study makes a valuable contribution to the limited literature devoted to measuring the performance of empowerment strategies. It provides a useful operationalization of the concept of empowerment, through the development of indicators of empowerment. Using such indicators to guide analysis of empowerment processes over the period considered important for the activities in question, it has been demonstrated that it is possible to undertake systematic evaluation, not only of the outcomes of an NGO's work with low-income communities, but also of the lasting effects of that NGO's involvement.

CHAPTER NINE

When the state cannot cope: community self-management? The case of Rincón Grande de Pavas in San José de Costa Rica, Central America

Harry Smith

INTRODUCTION

This chapter shows how the growth of the large, low-income settlement of Rincón Grande de Pavas in San José, Costa Rica, during the last two decades of the twentieth century, reflected national housing policies adopted during the same period. It thus follows, in a limited way, Ramirez et al.'s (1992, p. 101) research approach which combines the search for knowledge at the macro-level of society with identification of conditions on the ground. It suggests that some self-help policies adopted in Costa Rica have actually created new problems, in the short term, of infrastructure and service provision for the poor. This prompted the 1994–98 government to extend self-help beyond housebuilding through self-build and mutual aid, to what is termed 'community self-management' (*autogestión comunitaria*). Finally, the chapter analyses the appraisal and plan-making phases of the 'community self-management' initiative in Rincón Grande de Pavas, and explores the question of whether this new government-led approach opened up a real space for negotiation, as commented on by Fiori and Ramirez (1992), or was simply a new form of co-optation imposed on the community in order to overcome social unrest.

THE GROWTH OF RINCÓN GRANDE DE PAVAS

Rincón Grande de Pavas (RGP) is a large settlement covering 81 hectares and with a population estimated at over 40 000 in 1996. It straddles a long ridge between two deep ravines 8 km west of the centre of San José,[1] the capital of Costa Rica, and has one only point of access (Figure 9.1). Around it are high-income residential areas.

In the early 1980s this isolated strip of land was practically uninhabited. Since then, development has taken place at different moments and under different modes, producing an extremely complex collection of settlement

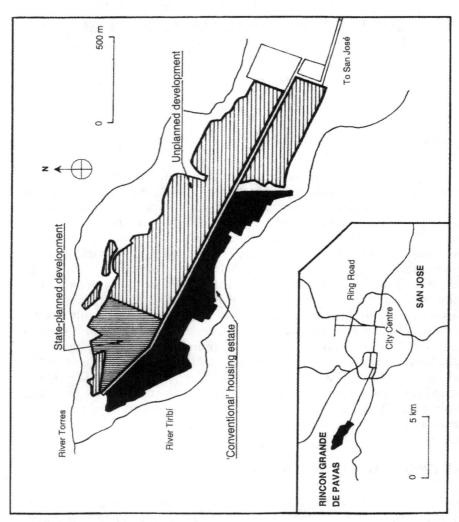

Figure 9.1   Rincon Grande de Pavas, San José, Costa Rica

Source: author

patterns and social structures, like a miniature urban Costa Rica encompassing a broad range of rapid urban growth problems and attempted solutions. The various settlements established during the 1980s and early 1990s, with very different features, fall within the three categories used by Costa Rican sociologists Valverde and Trejos (1993, pp. 141–142) to analyse urban development in this country (Table 9.1).

- 'Conventional' housing estate: built by a private developer and generally lacking a strong political or organizational bond among its inhabitants, who have bought into the estate as individual households. This is the case of Lomas del Río, the first settlement in RGP.
- State-planned development: planned and implemented by the state through the National Institute of Housing and Planning (Instituto Nacional de Vivienda y Urbanismo, INVU). This is the case of Bri-Brí, a sites-and-services scheme implemented under the 1982–86 Monge government.
- Unplanned development (*autourbanización* or *precario*): settlement on unserviced land, usually settled by a well-organized group of households who then build their own houses through self-help. Settlement can take place either without permission from the landowner or backing from public institutions (illegal), or after negotiations between settlers and landowners (agreed – *concertado*). In RGP there are three settlements that were the result of agreements between different groups of households and INVU, who owned the land: Metrópolis and Oscar Felipe, both established in 1986; and San Juan, settled in 1991. There are also squatter settlements in RGP which were established through unauthorized land invasion: Santa Lucía (1989), Loma Linda (1990), Bella Vista (1990), Unidos Pro Vivienda (1990), Precario Metrópolis I (1992) and Colonia Cristo Viene (1996).

The great majority of people living in RGP moved there from other areas within the San José Metropolitan Area. Most of the formal working population is in the service sector (68.6 per cent), followed by industry (29.8 per cent) (Valverde and Trejos, 1993, p. 145). The main problems in terms of work are underemployment and unstable employment. In addition, the average household income is very low. There are many cases of two families living under one roof, as well as a large proportion of female-headed households (30 per cent).

Valverde and Trejos's (1993, p. 151) analysis of the sharp increase in the establishment of settlements such as RGP during the 1980s is that this was due to 'the concatenation of two social processes: the restructuring of Costa Rican society as a result of structural adjustment, and the development of settler movements in the capital city, as a consequence of the impoverishment of broad social sectors'. In response to a combination of donor and lender pressure – for example through World Bank structural adjustment plans – and the sheer growth in numbers of poor households in need of homes, the Costa Rican state, like others with large foreign debt,

Table 9.1 Population of Rincón Grande de Pavas[1]

Settlement category[2]	Settlement type	Settlement name	Settlement population	Category population	Percentage of total population
Conventional housing estate				6,497	18
	Turnkey project	Lomas del Río	6,497		
State planned development				5,000	14
	Sites and services	Bri-Brí	5,000		
Unplanned development				24,753	68
	'Agreed' land invasion followed by central govt. project		13,503		
		Metrópolis	10,514		
		Óscar Felipe	1,500		
		Los Laureles	1,489		
	Squatter relocation on greenfield site		8,000		
		Finca San Juan	8,000		
	Informal settlements		3,250		
		Precario Metrópolis 1	750		
		Loma Linda	710		
		Santa Lucía	710		
		Bella Vista	450		
		Colonia Cristo Viene	430		
		Unidos Pro Vivienda	200		
Total				36,250[3]	100

1. Data for 'turnkey' project, sites and services, and 'agreed' land invasions are from Cordero (1996);
   data for squatter relocation on greenfield site and informal settlements are from the informal
   settlements survey undertaken by MIVAH in 1998.
2. According to Valverde and Trejos's (1993) classification.
3. Other sources indicate that the total population in 1996/97 was probably closer to 40 000 (Cordero,
   1996; Cuevas, 1997) or even 60 000 (Anon., 1997c).
Source: Cordero (1996, p. 4); MIVAH.

has increasingly withdrawn from direct provision of housing and infrastructure. A housing subsidy system has been established to help low-income families provide themselves with homes, but the responsibility for building facilities and infrastructure has often been delegated to the settlers themselves, by default, thus transferring production and maintenance costs to low-income communities. The state has shifted from a 'providing' to a so-called 'enabling' role,[2] but in a way that has given rise to a huge deficit in public services, facilities and infrastructure.

MACRO-ECONOMIC AND POLITICAL REASONS FOR THE INCREASE IN SQUATTER SETTLEMENTS

Costa Rica is the most stable country in Spanish-speaking Central America and, indeed, in Latin America. It has avoided the waves of authoritarian rule and armed conflict that have regularly swept Central America, thus allowing a democratic tradition and highly organized state and civil society to become established. This stability is reflected in Costa Rica's economic and social development. In addition, stable Costa Rica became a bridge-head for US interests in Central America against the perceived threat of the Nicaraguan revolution, and as such received increased US funding during the 1980s.

Costa Rica enjoyed economic and social development from the end of the 1940s through to the end of the 1970s. After the 1948 civil war and the proclamation of the 2nd Republic, the state adopted an interventionist role. Economic development was based on modernization of agricultural cash crop production together with industrialization through import substitution. Industrialization was highly successful, bringing Costa Rica from last to third place in the industrial ranking of Central American countries. In the 1970s the role of the state was expanded to that of an 'entrepreneur state', with the creation of a state enterprise (Corporación Costarricense de Desarrollo, Costa Rican Development Corporation – CODESA).

The social policy of the new 'interventionist state' (post-1948 civil war) built on some advances made in the early 1940s, extending social service coverage to all sectors of the population, with the aim of improving the overall social situation and strengthening the middle class. Social programmes brought about universal health coverage and access to education; improved urban services such as water, electricity and sewerage; agricultural land distribution; and the construction and subsidy of housing for low- and middle-income people. Through this continued focus on social policy, Costa Rica achieved a very high level of human development, as defined by the UN Human Development Index. It was soon to become evident, however, that Costa Rica had developed a political and social structure close to the model in more developed countries, while retaining a productive structure far closer to that of less-developed countries.

As happened elsewhere, import substitution failed. The international external debt crisis, and deterioration in the relations between industrialized and developing countries after 1978, exposed the fragility of the Costa Rican economy and brought about a deep economic and social crisis. The social impact of the crisis was dramatic, with poverty levels returning to around those of 1971. Stabilization became the economic priority of the state during the 1980s. This was achieved with massive funding from the US Agency for International Development, which was part of the USA's strategy to protect its interests in the region in the face of war in Nicaragua and El Salvador. In addition, Costa Rica initiated a process of structural adjustment, financed by World Bank loans.

Despite the comparatively 'soft' implementation of structural adjustment in Costa Rica, the withdrawal of the state, as noted above, was a key element. The 'entrepreneur state' approach was abandoned and the public enterprise CODESA dismantled. The drive was towards a 'more agile, strategic and co-ordinating state' (Quesada, 1997, p. 123). But how did this new role for the state affect the shelter sector?

SHELTER POLICIES AND THEIR EFFECTS ON RINCÓN GRANDE DE PAVAS

Housing has traditionally been one of the lowest priority investment areas of the Costa Rican State, and it was also one of the sectors hardest hit by structural adjustment. Since the 1950s, as part of the state's interventionist approach, central government – rather than local government – had taken on responsibility for providing housing for low and middle income groups, and from 1950 to 1978 it built housing estates adhering to a set of minimum standards. As elsewhere, the number of state-built houses was insufficient to meet demand, and central government estates also showed problems such as a lack of integration with employment centres, lack of public transport, and ineffective pollution control. During the 1978–82 government, when Costa Rica's economic crisis came to a head, a sites-and-services with self-help and mutual aid approach was adopted and put into operation on a national level during the 1982–86 government. Thus the state finally admitted that the previous approach based on building finished houses was incapable of meeting demand, and that this type of housing was too expensive for three-quarters of the population.

The serviced sites provided, however, were insufficient to meet the growing backlog of housing need (71 751 in 1984[3]), and did not quell growing discontent. The institutional crisis of the housing sector, the crisis of Costa Rican society and the deterioration of living conditions brought about the creation of numerous active, independent groups of households, called 'housing committees', formed for the purpose of gaining access to land to build their homes. The proliferation of these 'housing committees' led the main political parties to create umbrella political

organizations – 'housing fronts' – to which the committees became affili-
ated.[4] During the 1982–86 political term these housing fronts gained the
support of 10 per cent of the population in the San José Metropolitan
Area, and undertook a strong lobbying campaign, to the extent of occupying INVU headquarters in order to persuade the government to channel
resources into housing. Housing committees, both independently and as
part of the housing fronts, started invading land as the only immediate
solution that was available.

The strong housing fronts had a notable input to the policy of the incom-
ing government in 1986, which won the elections largely on the basis of its
electoral pledge to build 80 000 new houses during its term.[5] Thus, setting
up a new national housing finance system and allocating more state funding to housing, among other initiatives, were partly a response to pressure
from the fronts. Organized land invasions had been one of the major
instruments used to exert pressure, and were therefore more of a political
instrument employed by the fronts to gain bargaining power than a solution in themselves (Table 9.2). In an attempt to stem the tide, the new Oscar
Arias government reached an agreement with the three housing fronts
whereby funds would be channelled towards the new settlements they controlled, but no further invasions would be endorsed or included in the
80 000 houses programme. However, organized invasions by housing committees increased again after a couple of years, when they realized that
this was the only effective way to gain access to land and put pressure on
government for infrastructure, services and housing.

Table 9.2   New urban informal settlements established in the Gran Área
Metropolitana (including San José) 1970–90

Year	Total new informal settlements	Proportion of informal settlements in period (%)
1970–77	9	6.5
1978–79	4	3.0
1980	1	0.7
1981	6	4.3
1982	2	1.4
1983	11	8.0
1984	7	5.0
1985	19	13.8
1986	41	29.7
1987	8	5.8
1988	3	2.2
1989	16	11.6
1990	11	8.0
Total	138	100.0

Source: Mora and Solano (1994, Table 9).

Oscar Arias' government based its approach to housing on five basic elements: the creation of a national housing finance system funded through a new Housing Credit Bank; a housing subsidy policy based on the final cost of housing units; institutional restructuring of the housing sector (the enabling state); stimulation of the private sector in housing delivery; and the fostering of community organization. The state retained a degree of interventionism, however, and implemented a Slum Eradication Programme through a new Special Housing Commission (Comisión Especial de Vivienda, CEV). This programme served to consolidate what would henceforth become government policy: to provide households with a home according to their capacity to pay. Thus CEV had three levels of provision: a completely finished house for higher-income households; a shell for poorer households; and a serviced site plus building materials for the lowest income bracket (Mora and Solano, 1994, p. 123). Costa Rican researchers (Chavez et al., 1989; Chaves and Alfaro, 1990; Molina, 1990) have seen CEV as an instrument used by the Arias government to prioritize actions addressed to sections of the population that threatened social destabilization, in an attempt to maintain consensus and political and ideological control, but without relinquishing centralized decision-making. Chaves and Alfaro refer to CEV as a strategic element in the government's approach to the housing problem, which could be described as one of co-option. These authors stated that: 'The way the families are treated during project implementation by the interdisciplinary field teams, enabling them to participate in the solution of their own housing problem, has neutralized the initial effervescence shown by some housing organizations' (Chaves and Alfaro, 1990, p. 251). More crucially, the leaders of the three housing fronts were either directly contracted to work for the Ministry of Housing, or allocated housing funds to manage through their fronts. The fronts were considerably weakened and the number of housing committees dwindled.

The national housing finance system set up under the Arias government continues in operation to this day, though subject to alterations. Calderón Fournier's government (1990–94) won the 1990 elections with, among others, the pledge to convert the Family Housing Bond given to households with up to four minimum wages from an interest-free loan to a one-off grant. The pledge was fulfilled, but the amount of the subsidy was lowered and the actual construction of housing units for low-income families decreased. In terms of new squatter settlements in the main urban areas, Calderón's government was faced with a similar situation to that encountered at the outset by the previous one, compounded by densification and lack of infrastructure in public sector housing estates. A relocation policy was implemented, whereby households were taken in groups of 25 to 300 from squatter settlements to greenfield sites with no infrastructure or services (Grynspan, 1997). CEV continued to be the main institution involved in attending to housing demand from low-income groups, but its funding was reduced.[6]

Figueres Olsen's government (1994–98) returned to the concept of linking the housing subsidy with the real cost of housing units, whilst retaining the Family Housing Bond as a one-off grant, thus raising the amount to which households had access. This was complemented with a range of discounts for low-income households, covering fees and taxes related to house building. The state became proactive again by organizing a network of local support centres to identify low-income housing demand. In response to the serious deficit in infrastructure and services created by previous administrations' exclusive focus on housing, a programme of 'integrated community development' was included in the National Plan Against Poverty, representing an attempt to link housing policy with overall social policy.

The evolution of the approach to housing in Costa Rica explained above can be clearly seen in RGP (Table 9.3). After the commencement of the private development of Lomas del Río, in 1984, the government implemented a sites-and-services scheme at the west end of the area in 1986, under the direction of INVU. This scheme comprised 917 serviced plots, was successful in its uptake, and is today completed. However, a survey carried out in 1988 revealed that the state of the housing was bad, that most houses were overcrowded, and that there was a general lack of services (Aguilar and Gutiérrez, 1988, pp. 103–104). The next major expansion of the area took place in 1986, immediately prior to the election of the Arias government, with the 'agreed' invasion of what was then known as San Pedro de Pavas. This was done by the Frente Democrático de Vivienda (FDV) after an agreement was reached between FDV, Frente Costarricense de Vivienda (FCV), and the outgoing government.[7] This land belonged to a wealthy San José developer and its purchase was negotiated by the FDV, although the money was eventually to come from state coffers. San Pedro de Pavas then became one of the target sites of the Slum Eradication Programme, in the form of two separate projects: Metrópolis (1550 housing units) and Óscar Felipe (323 housing units). CEV undertook the building of the new houses in 1988, meeting the target for Oscar Felipe within the political term. Many of those in Metrópolis were also built, though in 1996 some sectors were still not completed (Smith, 1999).

In 1991, as part of Calderón Fournier's government's relocation policy, the last formally endorsed settlement was established in RGP: Finca San Juan. This was a badly managed transfer of squatters from settlements in the centre of San José. The responsibility for transferring the squatters to this greenfield site was handed over to corrupt community leaders. The transfer created great tension between the new settlers and the inhabitants of Metrópolis, whose social facilities and open spaces had originally been planned in Finca San Juan. It was not until 1993 that the government began to lay out streets (G. Huertas, Ministry of Housing coordinator for RGP, July 1994–September 1995: interview held at the Ministry of Housing and Human Settlements, 29 October 1997). The result was an overcrowded informal settlement in San Juan, where 85 per cent of the houses were still shacks in 1996.

Table 9.3   Costa Rican development policies, shelter policies and their effect on Rincón Grande de Pavas between 1978 and 1998

Administration	National development strategy	National shelter strategy	Events in Rincón Grande de Pavas
1978–82 Carazo Odio Partido Unidad	Internal conflict in government between 'Christian Socialists' (who aimed to increase standards of living) and neoliberals (reduce state intervention and promote involvement of the people). Central government tried to force reductions in state budget and public expenditure, especially in non-productive social policies.	Reorganization of government institutions into sectors: Housing and Human Settlements Sector executive Secretariat headed by the Housing Minister. However, centrally coordinated housing policy never developed and all institutions in the sector continued to act independently. Increased development of sites and services with funding from international agencies.	RGP practically uninhabited.
1982–86 Monge Álvarez Partido Liberación Nacional (PLN)	*Let's go back to the land (National Development Plan)* Deep revision of the production structure, aiming at import substitution and export growth. Agricultural development aimed at self-sufficiency in basic foods, production for industry, and a surplus for export. *Structural Adjustment Plan I (1985)*	Land distribution controlled by politically linked organizations, financed through emergency decrees; massive relocations of communities on large areas of state owned land. Institutions continued sites and services, now official central government policy (Progressive Housing Programme). Diversified financial programmes: number of 'solutions' increased while number of houses built by INVU halved.	1984: Private developer started to develop Lomas del Río. 1984: Brí-Brí sites and services scheme commenced.

1986–90 Árias Sánchez PLN	*National Development Plan* Aimed to: – recover sustainable high GNP growth – increase equity in access to resources for production – reduce extreme poverty – achieve high social mobility. *Structural Adjustment Plan II (1989)*	Main aims: – increase number of housing solutions (pledge to build 80 000 houses). – give greater priority to low-income sectors – attempt to control housing sector institutions Created: – Ministry of Housing (MIVAH) – National Housing Finance System, Housing Credit Bank and Family Housing Bond – Special Housing Commission (CEV) with remit to implement Slum Eradication Programme (emergency funds)	1986: 'Agreed' invasion of San Pedro de Pavas by Democratic Housing Front (FDV). 1988: Building of houses in San Pedro by CEV commenced as part of Slum Eradication Programme – two projects: Metrópolis and Óscar Felipe. 1989: Land invasion on edge of Bri-Brí sites and services scheme, establishing Santa Lucía informal settlement.
1990–94 Calderón Fournier Partido Unidad Social Cristiana	*Sustainable development with social justice (National Development Plan)* Aims: – sustained growth through opening up the economy – social and political stability – promotion of socio-economic and cultural processes allowing wide participation in building society – rational use of resources – modernization and rationalization of the state's institutional framework.	Squatter settlement relocation policy. No policies for upgrading of old low-income settlements. Family Housing Bond became a one-off grant (1991), but amount is considerably reduced and access for low-income people diminished.	

Table 9.3 Costa Rican development policies, shelter policies and their effect on Rincón Grande de Pavas between 1978 and 1998. *Contd.*

Administration	National development strategy	National shelter strategy	Events in Rincón Grande de Pavas
1994–98 Figueres Olsen PLN	*Francisco J. Orlich National Development Plan* Aims to change: – an exclusive society divided by poverty into a society integrated by opportunities – unconditional economic openness into intelligent integration with the world – wasteful growth into sustainable development – a weak and inefficient State into a strategic and coordinating State – formal democracy into participatory democracy. *National Plan Against Poverty* Components: childhood and youth; women; work; solidarity; local development; housing and living standards.	Continuation of National Housing Finance System, linking housing subsidy with real cost of housing units and raising amount of individual subsidies. Organization of local support centres network. National Plan Against Poverty: included programme of 'integrated community development', attempting to link housing policy with social policy.	

Sources: Argüello (1992); Céspedes and Jiménez (1995, p. 85); Cuevas (1997); Grynspan (1997); Gutiérrez and Vargas (1997, p. 68); Mora and Solano (1994, p. 68); Anon., 1997e; Quesada (1997, pp. 95, 102–103).

To these officially 'accepted' settlements one must add squatter settlements that occupied the open spaces of Bri-Brí and Metrópolis III. Also, Finca San Juan saw its few open spaces invaded in 1995 by 72 families and more recently, in 1996, a whole new squatter settlement sprang up by the access road to RGP. These invasions are, to a large extent, sited on land unsuitable for development. More crucially, however, they have not been supported initially by any housing front or state institution.

RGP has a continuing role as a settlement area for urban households unable to pay market prices and with no access to official housing programmes, and who see no solution other than land invasion. Low-income people are still seeking their own solutions independently from both the state and the market. In the process, however, RGP is becoming increasingly densely populated while remaining deprived of services and infrastructure, and deprived of sufficient housing of a standard commonly accepted in Costa Rica.

THE GOVERNMENT'S RESPONSE: COMMUNITY SELF-MANAGEMENT

The 1994–98 Figueres' government prepared a National Plan Against Poverty that aimed to address poverty directly, and incorporated the idea of participation of civil society. This Plan identified 16 communities requiring 'priority attention', RGP being one of the largest. In 1995 a Costa Rican government/UNCHS-Habitat project set up in 1991, the Project for the Strengthening of Community Self-Management (Proyecto de Fortalecimiento de la Autogestión Comunitaria – PROFAC),[8] was appointed to lead a local development process in RGP that would complement the physical planning initiative undertaken by the San José local authority earlier that same year.

PROFAC had been established as part of the UNCHS-Habitat/DANIDA (Danish International Development Assistance) Community Management Programme, with a view to it lasting five years initially. The aim of this programme was 'to strengthen the capacity of low-income communities to plan, operate and maintain needed facilities, services and housing improvement' (DANIDA, 1994, p. 1) and through it, community management programmes were set up in Costa Rica, Ecuador, Ghana and Uganda. The agreed funding for the first five years[9] of the Costa Rican project, PROFAC, was to be US$15 034 296 in staff, premises and equipment from the Costa Rican government, US$1 676 133 from DANIDA, and US$100 000 from UNDP (Pichardo and Eslava, 1995, p. 5). The project was originally to be staffed by a National Project Coordinator, a Project Officer, two Local Project Coordinators, and specialized technical staff from the Costa Rican government, plus a Chief Technical Adviser and other advisers to be supplied by UNCHS-Habitat (DANIDA et al., 1991). Staffing eventually grew to a total of six personnel supplied by the Ministry of Housing and Human

Settlements (MIVAH) and 24 staff and external consultants paid by UNCHS-Habitat. PROFAC focused mainly on the training of community members and representatives from institutions, and in its first five years it used seed capital to attract further funds from communities and the government towards capital works and social projects identified through participatory methods in seven targeted low-income settlements.

With the setting up of PROFAC three years earlier, the then government had recognized 'the need to involve the local communities with the aim to ensure an optimal use of public investment . . . [and declared] . . . public participation as the primordial agent of social development policies' (DANIDA et al., 1991, p. 6). In consequence, central government had identified the need to strengthen public servants' and local authorities' faith in community participation. The state was seen as becoming an enabler of local development managed by the communities themselves.

In RGP, PROFAC applied the method already tested in smaller settlements during the early 1990s, albeit this time on a much larger scale. The first step was a rapid appraisal undertaken jointly with the Municipality of San José. An inventory of community and institutional resources and of their organization and operation revealed a high degree of community organization, although there were a lot of different organizations and a considerable amount of conflict. Community leadership was found to be strong but often undemocratic, and there was a vast experience in collective work. As for the institutions, it was established that there were 18 official organizations involved in a large number of programmes, with a very low impact and no coordination. Once this situation was established, PROFAC became the coordinator of a process with the aims of 'strengthening institutional work in relation to the real needs of the population, and enabling the articulation of demand on the basis of the strengthening of community organizations with a self-management outlook' (Cuevas, 1997).

PROFAC adopted a mediating and coordinating role and set up a twin-track process involving two separate representative bodies: an Inter-Institutional Network, which brought together 36 institutions[10] working in RGP, and a Community Representation, which achieved membership of 90 per cent of the representative community organizations. At a meeting of representatives from both community and institutions – the First Community Forum,[11] organized by PROFAC – an agreement was reached to undertake a participatory local development process using PROFAC's method. The Inter-Institutional Network set about working through two large committees, one for infrastructure and housing, led by the Municipality of San José, and the other addressing a wider range of social issues and community organization. Through the Community Representation a participatory appraisal process was initiated, based on workshops that involved around 600 community representatives. During the process PROFAC strove to ensure information flowed between the two collectives, as well as within each of these.[12]

The major outputs in terms of 'product' were a Land Use Plan and a Local Development Plan. The Land Use Plan was prepared by the Municipality of San José, taking the expressed needs of the community into consideration. It was approved after a 15 month impasse – due to legal hurdles, lack of resources and a lack of political will in some circles – which ended with the direct intervention of the Minister for Housing. The Local Development Plan was the result of the participatory appraisal process undertaken with the Community Representation, which culminated in October 1997 with the presentation of the finalized plan to an assembly of representatives from the community and institutions. The plan covered a wide range of issues: economy, employment and income; housing; health; drug addiction and alcoholism; education and training; infrastructure; environment and leisure; community integration, participation and organization; youth and childhood; and others. This later led to the implementation of the designated priority actions jointly by a Local Development Plan Steering Group and Sectoral Committees on behalf of the community, and a new set of Working Committees on behalf of the institutions.

PROFAC's stated perception of the process in RGP in 1997 was positive (Cuevas, 1997). PROFAC considered it a successful local implementation of the guidelines set out in the National Plan Against Poverty, which had benefited from centralization,[13] training, high levels of investment,[14] a favourable political environment, and a high degree of community organization. Perceived achievements were stated as including: that the community sees institutions as allies rather than enemies; that for the first time the Municipality of San José took community organizations' needs on board in a land-use plan; that negotiation had replaced conflict in RGP; and that the communities had accepted institutions' technical criteria and legal mandate. The 'achievements' identified in PROFAC's evaluation suggest that the primary unstated goal of government policy was not community development but rather co-option and the defusing of an explosive urban situation. Indeed, PROFAC boasted that 'discussion at the negotiating table overcame the strikes, barricading and road closures' (Cuevas, 1997).

The community leaders' view of the process at the time was different. Criticism was directed towards PROFAC, the Inter-Institutional Network and the community leaders themselves: PROFAC was described by some leaders as a pawn in the hands of central government ('PROFAC was sent to Rincón Grande to dispel any probability of rebellion'); the relationship between institutions and community were seen by some not to have improved ('. . . we have been at it for two years and we have had no institutional recognition. . .'); community organization itself was seen to be lacking and this was considered crucial for achieving recognition by the institutions ('. . . we need the Community Representation to be recognized, which it never has been'). In addition one of the leaders, with many years of experience, pointed out that the most important skill the community could learn was to negotiate, and PROFAC was providing training in administration, management, etc., but not in how to negotiate with those who are in power.[15]

The community leaders' own self-criticism clearly showed that the process had at the time not been successful in establishing the foundations for a sustainable community development process. In May 1997 PROFAC admitted that the sustainability of the Community Representation and the Inter-Institutional Network could not be guaranteed, and that PROFAC was still the binding agent. A participatory SWOT (strengths, weaknesses, opportunities, threats) analysis undertaken by representatives from the Inter-Institutional Network in September 1997[16] showed that the participants were aware of a range of institutional weaknesses related mainly to the lack of formalization, decision-making power and resources of the network – at the level of government that was directly dealing with the RGP process. In addition, there was concern that the participatory appraisal carried out with the community had raised expectations beyond what the Inter-Institutional Network was able to deliver.

Eventually, the Community Representation used its voice to demand training in negotiation skills from PROFAC, and was able to deal directly with the candidates for the presidency from the two major parties during the general elections in 1998. The community-strengthening initiative appeared therefore to have reached some level of success, though there remained serious issues related to continuing conflicts between community leaders and legitimacy, in the eyes of both the community and the new government that took office in 1998 (Smith and Valverde, 2001). It was less successful at the institutional level, with the Municipality of San José declining to take over PROFAC's leading role, and the Inter-Institutional Network continuing to lack decision-making power. PROFAC was closed down in 1999, when it reached the end of the programme established by the funding bodies.

CONCLUSIONS

The different housing strategies affecting the growth of RGP to date allow us to verify Hans Harms' (1982) observation that when self-help leads to coordinated action, solidarity, land invasions, etc., the state will attempt 'to break down group solidarity, to individualize the problem, to propose reforms with low costs, to get people individually on waiting lists for housing, and to promote individual self-help' (Harms, 1982, p. 49). This can be clearly seen in Costa Rica, and specifically in RGP, in the formation of the housing fronts and the increase in land invasions in the mid-1980s, and in the subsequent housing finance policy based on subsidies to individual households. Government reliance on self-help later peaked with the policy of relocation to virtually greenfield sites.

However, during the 1994–98 administration, and as part of a programme funded by international aid, an alternative approach was attempted, purportedly with the aim of strengthening 'community self-management'. The evidence from the appraisal and plan-making phases of this initiative shows that, beneath this 'community-enabling' approach (UNCHS, 1987), there was an intention to defuse what had become an increasingly explosive and unmanageable situation in a large, low-income settlement on the edge of the capital city of Costa Rica. 'Community self-management' was being used as a means of stabilizing deprived communities and legitimating the state.

In addition, the evolution of RGP allows us to reflect upon Fiori and Ramirez's (1992) assertions that state intervention through self-help housing policies defines a 'space of negotiation', which can lead to a redefinition of decision-making structures and, ultimately, to the transference and redistribution of resources. In the 1986 climate of land invasions, and with the results of a general election at stake, a space of negotiation was created whereby the allocation of state resources for the provision of housing was achieved by the housing fronts. However, the successful break-up of the housing fronts by the Oscar Arias government allowed its successor to deal with low-income settlers with a much smaller transfer of resources, as evidenced in Finca San Juan. Finally, the 1994–98 Figueres government opened up a 'space of negotiation' in RGP through the intervention of PROFAC, accompanied by a large allocation of resources.

The question remains, however, to what extent this was a real space for negotiation. From the evidence presented here it appears that the community in RGP would have a higher chance of ensuring that real negotiation takes place if it transcends its local space and joins forces with similar low-income communities in engaging with the state, as happened in the mid-1980s. The recent mobilizations in Costa Rica against the privatization of utilities might be the stirrings of new social movements that could perhaps lead to similar responses around the issue of housing, although the current government's (1998–2002) 'Triangle of Solidarity' initiative, involving representatives of civil society in district-wide prioritization of public investment, could provide a form of pre-emptive 'soft' co-option.

Returning to our case study and to the title of this chapter, it is suggested that if the resources allocated by central government to RGP were indeed sufficient to quell community discontent, far from the state being unable to cope, it was indeed coping very well with minimal resources.

Finally, this chapter raises issues regarding the social and institutional sustainability of low-income human settlements, in particular regarding the sustainability of processes that are initiated with government or international aid funding. In the case of the process managed in Rincón Grande de Pavas by PROFAC, and given the complexity of the new working relationships that were to be established and the contradictions in the relationships between the government and residents, it is questionable whether a three-year period of support from external agencies could have been sufficient to establish a successful arrangement for the management of the settlement. It remains to be seen how the real interests of the participant organizations unfold, and how the members of the community benefit from this initiative in the long term.

CHAPTER TEN

Cultural continuity: comparing the *fereej* system and modern housing development in Hofuf, Saudi Arabia

Mashary A. Al-Naim

INTRODUCTION

A key contemporary issue is our ability to understand social dynamism and what people think about their home environments, how they organize themselves in these environments, and why. How do traditions work in society? How do people create new traditions? This study argues that every society has continuous traditions. They may change and take different forms, but their existence is essential for social sustainability. As Rapoport (1986) states, for any group to survive it is important that there must be continuity at some level. Saudi Arabians have tried to maintain a certain continuity, which can be linked to the strong impact of their religion (Hamdan, 1990; Al-Soliman, 1991). These traditions can be linked with what Rapoport (1986) named a society's 'cultural core'. He differentiated core from peripheral values, which are modified to suit changes in life circumstances.

Understanding such core values and their impact on the physical and social characteristics of home environments will lead decision makers, planners and designers to understand the cultural frame within which people operate. The future development of home environments may become more compatible with people's cultural needs if there is a realization that home is not merely a place in which to carry out a number of functions, but also a symbol, and a way of interacting with one's community (Dovey, 1985). This chapter aims to examine one of the mechanisms that is used by people to make a place in their home environment: the *fereej* system, or the mechanism of clustering residential settlements based on shared values and habits in the city of Hofuf in the Eastern Region of Saudi Arabia.

Fereej comprises the basic structure of social interrelationships that we might call an extended clan. This concept expresses the intimate relationship between people and their physical environment. It also expresses their collective identity, as well as their individual membership of a specific group and of the whole of society. Being a member in a *fereej* means that a link with both people and place has been developed; the sense of home in this sense stems first from the feeling of being part of this social and physical entity. It implies a sense of the group, and is considered both as a point of reference for individuals and groups, and a link between them and the whole community. In many cases it carries the family name of the group living in it. This system expresses the idea of lineage, whereby many generations from the same clan maintain a certain continuity over time by defining their territory and keeping it as part of the community's shared image. It also embodies the norms, customs and values that people have developed over the centuries to organize themselves in their home environment. When we say 'this is a *fereej*' we mean that a minimum set of shared values, norms and habits already exist and are practised by those who live there, thereby forming a homogeneous residential community.

THE SOCIAL BASIS OF THE *FEREEJ* SYSTEM

The concept of *fereej* was a result of the interaction between different families in a traditional community. It is therefore impossible to understand how the *fereej* system works without understanding the kinship structure in the traditional community of Hofuf. Traditional society consisted of clans, called locally *hamola*. Each clan included a number of extended families living in a distinctive territory, with hidden boundaries dividing the unitary mass of the traditional physical environment into a number of social units of varying size according to the size of the clan living in them. Such a social and territorial unit was called by the local people of Hofuf *fereej*.

The principles of domestic spatial organization can be understood only by grasping the dynamic traditional kinship system, which worked for a long time to mediate between individual and family needs and obligations to the whole community. The kinship system was divided into three levels: primary, intermediate, and communal (Figure 10.1). Each of these levels was associated with specific norms and conventions, ultimately reflected in the way that people interacted at the relevant level. The role of the family was to inform and mobilize the basic norms and conventions throughout the generations. Relationships between different extended families, from either the same or related clans, created the intermediate level of kinship.

The *fereej* system resulted from this level, at which specific groups (a clan or a number of related clans) lived together and interacted with the whole community as one group. Finally, the communal relationship gave the traditional community its identity and consistency, because the communal shared values were found at this level. The other two levels of kinship, therefore, adapted and worked within this frame of community beliefs.

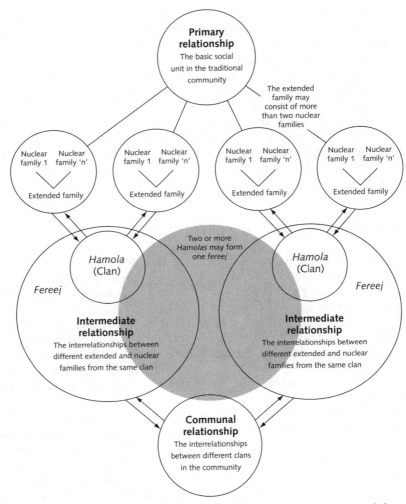

Figure 10.1   The social system in the traditional home environment in Hofuf
Source: author

THE *FEREEJ* SYSTEM: FROM SOCIAL ORGANIZATION TO PLACE-MAKING

Societies, as Hillier and Hanson (1984, pp. 26–27) argue, adopt two ways of establishing definite spatial forms. The first is to arrange people in space by locating them in relation to each other. The second mainly deals with the physical responses to the social arrangements, arranging space itself by means of buildings, boundaries, paths, marks, zones, and so on. By these two arrangements, Hillier and Hanson suggest, a society acquires a definite and recognizable spatial order, which enables us to recognize the ways in which members of any society live out and reproduce their social existence. Rapoport (1977) attributes processes of clustering in the urban environment to the 'selection and choice of particular environmental quality, so that the city becomes a set of areas of different groups which tend to define themselves in terms of "us" and "them". There is a process of inclusion and exclusion, of establishing boundaries and stressing social identity by use of cues and symbols. . .' (Rapoport, 1977, p. 248).

The degree of aggregation or separation in the spatial formation of the traditional home environment in Hofuf, as noted above, was strongly influenced by clan arrangements, shared beliefs, and women's role in society. In Hofuf, the kinship system classified the community and categorized individuals and groups. The residential unit, in many cases, emerged as the physical symbol of a family's origin (Shetty, 1990). We can argue here that families and groups in the traditional home environment in Hofuf developed several symbols and cues to preserve their identity within the local community. Many people in Hofuf attribute the name *fereej* to the Arabic word *furja* (plural *furaj*) which means the small opening in a wall. This small opening was usually found in the party walls between houses, to connect different houses in the *fereej* by roof footpath. Some openings have doors and others do not. This roof footpath was used only by women, because they were not allowed to go outside in the daytime. If a woman wanted to visit her neighbour, she could use the roof footpath. The role of women in society required them to be out of men's sight. This translated into a physical configuration involving houses becoming connected with each other. Moreover, the extent of this footpath network defined the boundary of a *fereej*, both socially and physically. Those houses connected by footpaths formed a *fereej*, which could over time include new members or exclude others (Figure 10.2).

Every extended family lived in a single house. After the death of the head of the family, sons usually divided the house into a number of dwellings. This created another type of extended family, which was usually expressed physically by a small private cluster within the *fereej*, expressing the desire of a family to be distinguished from the surrounding families. This close relationship was then considered more private than other parts of the territory occupied by the same clan. This type of relationship was characterized by more connections by roof footpath, and usually by houses clustered around a cul-de-sac or sometimes an open space called a *baraha* (Vidal, 1955; Figure 10.3). In most cases a *sikka sad* (cul-de-sac) was created during the division of the main house to provide accessibility for the houses located furthest from access to the street. In many cases these clusters formed new *fereejs*. However, it is difficult to attribute the origin of the *fereej* system to this phenomenon alone because, in many cases, groups of people collectively moved from one place to another and created a *fereej*. Still, in traditional Hofuf, division of houses because of the expansion of an extended family was one of the main mechanisms that created this system. Most of the cul-de-sacs had an outer door to enable the inhabitants to act

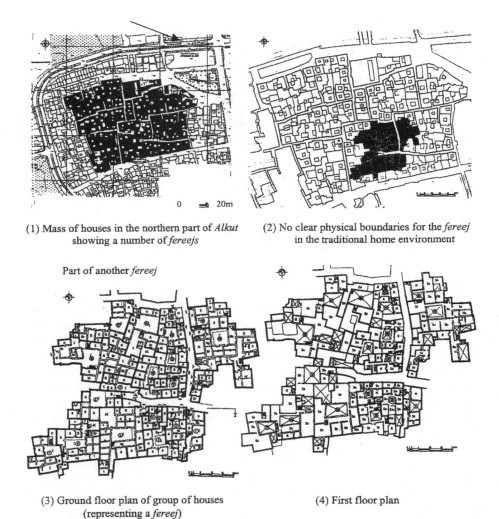

(1) Mass of houses in the northern part of *Alkut* showing a number of *fereejs*

(2) No clear physical boundaries for the *fereej* in the traditional home environment

(3) Ground floor plan of group of houses (representing a *fereej*)

(4) First floor plan

Figure 10.2   Physical characteristics of *fereejs* in the *Alkut* quarter, Hofuf
Source: Al-Musallam (1995, pp. 3–4, 11–12)

freely in the street; for example, women could visit each other without covering their heads or faces. In the absence of men, the front door usually remained closed to provide the women with maximum freedom. This physical representation can be seen as a symbol of identity, saying to other members in the community 'this is our place'.

Thus, the concept of *fereej*, in its physical sense, worked as a mediator between the most private parts of the home environment, the dwelling, and the whole community, while in its social meaning it was employed to define different groups in society and to provide them with a certain level

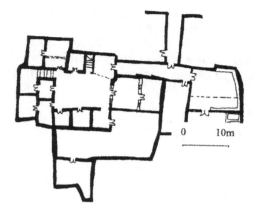

The original layout of a house occupied by an extended
family in *Anna'athil* (according to the description of
the family members)

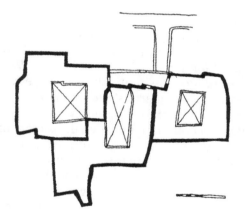

The houses had been divided into three houses after the
death of the head of the family (each son created his
own house)

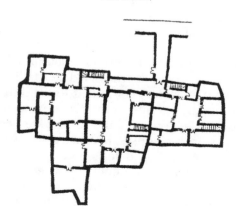

Figure 10.3 Three houses with
a private cul-de-sac

of security by developing a mechanism for defining places and the people who lived in those places. This reflected the need to project clan identity by defining its territory both socially and physically. Territoriality, therefore, can be understood as a 'self–other boundary mechanism that involves personalization or marking of a place or object, and communication that it is "owned" by a person or group' (Altman, 1975, p. 107).

THE *FEREEJ* SYSTEM IN TRANSITION

The Saudi home environment in general has experienced radical changes since the discovery and export of oil in 1938. The socio-economic status of Saudi citizens changed dramatically, changing their way of living and producing a new daily routine. The *fereej* system was one among many cultural and physical targets for such changes. This can be seen as early as the 1940s, when the government started to build new roads inside the old city of Hofuf (Vidal, 1955; Al-Shuaibi, 1976). Later, the traditional home environment faced such severe transformations as to render it uninhabitable (Al-Naim, 1993). It is relevant to this chapter to understand how the *fereej* system responded to these social and physical changes, and how it eventually re-emerged in new developments.

The new roads ignored the social tissues that bound the physical environment together. They divided the traditional quarters into small pieces, each containing parts of different *fereejs*. They broke the hidden social and physical boundaries, because new physical boundaries divided the unitary mass of the traditional quarter. This situation created a chaotic physical and social environment which made the traditional home environment uninhabitable, and so people started moving from it to other places (Figure 10.4).

During this period the government increased its involvement in the physical environment. This first appeared in the physical arrangements in new areas in the city of Hofuf in 1960 (Al-Shuaibi, 1976). Also, a set of building regulations was initiated in the same year. These mainly introduced setbacks for dwelling design and segregated dwellings by applying grid patterns for land subdivision (Al-Hathloul, 1981; Al-Said, 1992).

Those families who were directly affected by the new development moved collectively into new suburbs and constructed small *fereejs*. For example, two small neighbourhoods appeared between 1960 and 1975, each occupied by one clan. However, people who lived in traditional dwellings which were far from the new streets continued to live in their houses until 1975, when the government started to subsidize private housing by establishing the Real Estate Development Fund to provide people with interest-free loans to build new private houses. Because the *fereej* system in the traditional home environment had deteriorated people were ready to move, and so used this opportunity to produce new *fereejs*. This happened through collective migration from traditional areas between 1975 and 1985, and led to the traditional areas falling into decline and ruin.

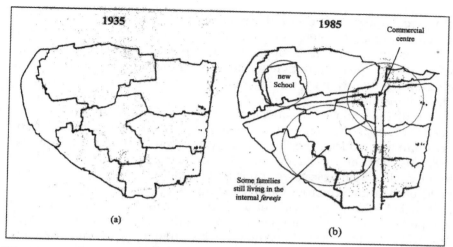

Figure 10.4 New road construction in the traditional quarter of Hofuf
Source: author

Every clan moved and concentrated in one suburb. This is not to say that the whole suburb was occupied by one clan, but that each clan tried to reorganize itself and to define its territory within a new suburb. The direction of migration was, in most cases, according to the location of the clan in the traditional quarters. For example, those who lived in the south-east (southern *Arrif'a*) moved to the south-eastern neighbourhoods. The same was true for the clans who had lived in the north-east (northern *Arrif'a*) and south-west (*Anna'athil*). Those who had lived in the north-west (*Alkut*) moved to the south and south-west because there was a cemetery on the north-western boundary.

CONTEMPORARY FORMS OF THE *FEREEJ* SYSTEM

Economic growth in Saudi Arabia encouraged the government to start implementing a series of five-year development plans, from 1970 onwards, in order to benefit from oil revenues. These plans were intended to develop economic and human resources and to enhance the social sector and physical infrastructure. The oil price boom in 1973 made these plans more effective in transforming the physical characteristics of all Saudi cities.

Several master plans were initiated for Saudi cities between 1967 and 1976. These plans institutionalized the gridiron land subdivision and set-backs as the only way to deal with the home environment at both macro- and micro-levels. The villa has been the only house type for new housing in Saudi Arabia since 1975 (Al-Hathloul and Anis-ur-Rahman, 1985). The process of producing the physical environment shifted from the incremental mechanisms that occurred daily at a micro-level, to a rigid process imposed at the macro-level without real understanding of people's cultural needs. It was a complete contrast to the traditional home environment where communal relationships had maintained the identity and consistency of the home environment at the macro-level and let the family, at the micro-level, modify living arrangements as necessary to adjust to changing life circumstances.

One of the major consequences of the ignorance of people's cultural needs was that the physical characteristics of the contemporary home environment reduced the domain of women and children (Al-Nowaiser, 1983; Al-Olet, 1991; Al-Hussayen, 1996). The *fereej* system in the traditional home environment was very supportive of a lively social life for women and children. Through the roof footpath, women could meet their neighbours and socialize with them without using external spaces. Parents also never stopped their children from playing outside the home because there were no hazards for them. Children knew the *fereej* boundary and practised their activities within the intimate spaces outside their homes. This is not the case in the contemporary home environment, in which women have no outside space to meet their neighbours and children are forced to play inside their homes because people and places have not yet been defined by the inhabitants.

What is really noticeable about the contemporary home environment in Hofuf, however, is that people have striven to maintain their sense of the group, their sense of social homogeneity, in the new suburbs. This has been accomplished by maintaining intermediate kinship relationships and reproducing the *fereej* system. Although the flexibility that existed in the traditional home environment has decreased, due to regulations that have forced people to build individual dwellings and prevented them from making changes to their houses, people have persisted in their way of socializing and have resisted the changes by reorganizing themselves in the new suburbs.

Living as groups is considered by the people of Hofuf to be very important. For example, two clans who used to live as one group in the past moved from the old city into the suburb of *Assalmaniyyah* in 1980 and formed one big *fereej*. The land value of this cluster is almost double that of other land in the same suburb. People in the area call it *bulik Annar* (the fire block) due to the high value of the land.[1] What led people of these two clans to persist in living together, even if the cost was double that for living separately elsewhere, was the social quality of the area. In this contemporary *fereej* people know each other: women visit each other safely and children play outside. The sense of home is very high and a definition of place and people has been established or reproduced.

At the family level, economic independence encouraged young men to separate from their family houses and create nuclear families. For example, average income per capita in Saudi Arabia increased from 600 SR per month in 1970 to 6000 SR in 1990 (Hamdan, 1990). This increased individual expenditure and brought new lifestyles for families. In the past, such changes were difficult because young men worked mainly in their fathers' farms, industries, or trades. They had no private property, which made it difficult for them to separate from the family house even if they wished to do so. This is not to say that every young man would have separated if he was able to, because even in contemporary Hofuf many extended families still live in the same house.

In fact there is some continuity of the old social structure, but it is not as strong and common as in traditional society. Nowadays, newly married couples prefer to have a separate house. To allow for this, people have developed physical solutions by creating one or two apartments on the first floor of their villas. An apartment is usually used as an additional income source by renting it out until the oldest son gets married, then he uses it with his new wife. If there is more than one apartment, the second son can use one, but if there is only one, the oldest son may leave the house and give the opportunity to his younger brothers. This solution has been developed recently by people, to help their young sons economically by providing them with a free house and to guarantee that at least one of their sons will continue to live with them.

This is not the only way that people have tried to maintain the form of the traditional extended family. Some people have tried to reproduce the traditional *fereej* in their new neighbourhoods, by building a group of villas owned by a man and his sons. The main house is considered by all as the family house, while every son has his own house. All these houses are connected by one internal passageway, to allow the women to visit each other without leaving home. All the family members gather in the family house every night and have their dinner together (Figure 10.5). Also, the father sits in his *majlis* (men's reception space) and a number of his sons, grandsons, clan members and males from related clans visit him between *Asr* and *Maghrab* prayers (4–6 pm).

In the above example, all the family members are connected physically and socially. This is a clear attempt to overcome the physical and legal constraints and reproduce a modern form of the *fereej* system. However, it requires a huge budget, and not every family afford it. It is common now to find different clustering forms for extended families in contemporary neighbourhoods. They share one goal: living as a group and providing maximum freedom for women and children. Even if the family members are physically living apart from each other, at least one day a week they gather in the family house and have lunch or dinner together. The family house in this situation becomes a symbol for the extended family.

Clustering in contemporary Hofuf is not limited to certain clans or restricted to one area. It exists in every new neighbourhood. We can say that the traditional community system has continued, despite all the constraints of regulations and physical planning during the past four decades. The traditional clans are now redistributed in the new neighbourhoods, but with clear physical boundaries and less physical connectedness.

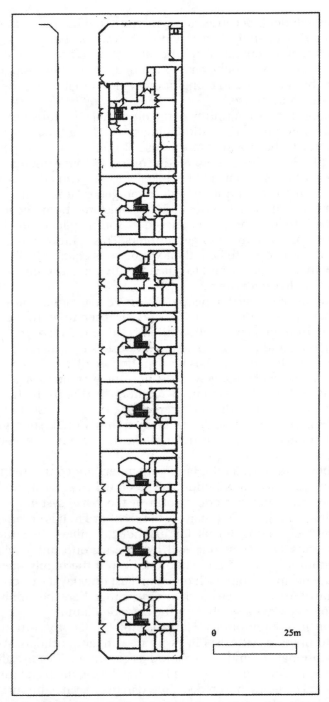

Figure 10.5   Reproducing a traditional *fereej* in the contemporary home environment in Hofuf: a group of villas in *Almazrou'* neighbourhood

CONCLUSIONS

The contemporary physical environment of Hofuf assumes a Western model of the nuclear family. The physical characteristics of this environment ignored traditional social structures and encouraged the nuclear family. Yet the *fereej* system continued, and people found a way of expressing their shared values by reproducing the concept in different forms and in a variety of ways. This is because the *fereej* is not simply a family grouping, but also serves as a vehicle for social values. It is, at the same time, deeply established in people's minds as providing patterns of appropriate social behaviour; and resilient because of its ability to adjust its original shape or position over time.

A distinguishing feature that people of Hofuf still display is the desire to reproduce the concept of *fereej* in their contemporary home environment. This desire stems from particular needs: communality as an attractive social quality connected with people's way of life; the acceptance of living as an extended group (intermediate relationships); and extended family bonds (primary relationships). Therefore, despite the physical changes in neighbourhood organization, these features have contributed to the survival and continuity of the *fereej* as a concept with which common people can identify, and which they try to reproduce. The process of modernization, which affected the physical appearance of the home environment in Hofuf, has had a much smaller impact on its cultural aspects. Inter-family relationships, private and communal behaviour, and a sense of identity and social status remain distinctive characteristics of contemporary society in Hofuf. The primary relationships may have been weakened due to the economic independence of the younger generations. However, symbolically the family house remains a reference point that every member of a family (even those sons and daughters who have left the family house) regards as a common place.

The implementation of insensitive development actions in the traditional areas of Hofuf led to a decline. Ignoring the hidden boundaries of the *fereej* system reduced the quality of the living environment, and forced people to move to places where they could reproduce their *fereejs*. Planners, then, may destroy existing home environments if they work without considering existing social and physical determinants. Planning for any existing residential settlement should work within the systems that exist, including not only the settlement's physical configuration but also, and more importantly, its social characteristics, which need more research and sensitive treatment. Planning for a conservative society such as the one in Hofuf needs to consider the major cultural constituents of the belief system and ways of living. It is clear that the efforts to modernize Hofuf concentrated mainly on physical appearance and the application of foreign models, without considering or realizing the consequences for people's daily lives. Future home environments should reflect different planning attitudes, in order to meet people's social and cultural needs. One approach would be to let people create their own *fereejs*. To do that, planners first need to understand both that this system is a deep expression of social behaviour, and that its physical representation is not fixed, which means that people may reproduce their *fereejs* in different forms. Second, planning for the physical environment should recognize this by developing flexible mechanisms and techniques at the micro-scale, allowing dwelling arrangements and design to be modified to fit changing life circumstances.

PART III

SUSTAINABLE URBAN DEVELOPMENT PROCESSES

CHAPTER ELEVEN

Incremental transformations for sustainable urban settlements

Sam Romaya[1]

INTRODUCTION

Sustainable development is development that meets the needs of the present without compromising the ability of future generations to meet their own needs.

(WCED, 1987, p. 43).

This statement succinctly describes what sustainability aims to achieve, but does not identify the means by which sustainability goals might be achieved. To translate this general definition into meaningful objectives for sustainable urban development is complicated and subject to a variety of interpretations. Rogers and Gumuchdjian (1997), for example, identify seven basic attributes or policy objectives, three of which may be generally applied: *a just city*; *a city of easy contact*; and *a compact and polycentric city*. The remaining four are desirable attributes: *beautiful, creative, ecological* and *diverse*. Such terms may be used as marketing slogans but they also describe planning objectives – to achieve them requires both appropriate planning approaches at city and local levels, and means for assessing the sustainability of proposed development and renewal. Much of the current debate on sustainability is focused on the global dimension and addresses carbon dioxide emissions, damage to the ozone layer and global warming. These are vital issues. However, local planning issues are equally important: the urban fabric must be transformed to achieve more efficient use of a whole range of resources which are finite or vulnerable to depletion or degradation.

As living organisms, urban settlements evolve gradually and develop incrementally. Many actors are involved in the development process: architects, planners, estate agents, politicians and financial institutions (Potter and Lloyd-Evans, 1998). Both the individual components of urban settlements and the overall urban fabric are dynamic. A quality building is assumed to have a life expectancy of 50–60 years, yet its use may change every 10–20 years. This implies transformation: a change of use, refurbishment, or even demolition for renewal. The urban fabric grows and changes in response to population increase, the changing needs of residents and employers, technological advances, or new requirements for infrastructure, such as new roads and public transport routes (Stewart, 1999). Land is a scarce resource which should be used efficiently: greenfield sites are valuable as agricultural land, while plots in central areas, brownfield sites, are often underused or abandoned. Expansion into surrounding areas, high-rise development or densification of use is the normal response to increased demand for central area uses, but the process of densification and expansion, left to the market, may involve demolition, waste and blight. Neglected properties become derelict and attract vandalism. The cost of conserving buildings of historic value may deter private owners, leading to a loss of the architectural and historic heritage.

The requirements of users of buildings and the urban environment also change over time. For example, within traditional social systems in developing countries, housing arrangements were flexible, with additional rooms added to accommodate the extended family, but in contemporary society this is more difficult and lack of adaptability in housing may lead to social disruption, with over- or underoccupation, and to physical decay.

Constant change in the urban fabric is required to meet the aspirations of communities for better housing, employment opportunities and leisure facilities. Planners can perform a central role in managing change. The bulk of the urban fabric, even in rapidly growing settlements, is inherited: planners have responsibility for the management of this inheritance by conservation, conversion or renewal, as well as planning for the accommodation of new development. They should manage, guide or direct urban transformations and integrate them with the existing fabric.

This chapter is concerned mainly with the ongoing renewal of the built environment, although also with urban expansion. One of the neglected aspects of urban renewal is attention to improved environmental sustainability. The sections that follow focus first on selected issues and potential solutions to be considered in this context; and second on the manifestation of these issues and attempts to deal with them in Cairo. Finally, an approach is suggested for incorporating a systematic consideration of sustainability objectives into planning for development and regeneration.

IMPROVING THE SUSTAINABILITY OF URBAN SETTLEMENTS: ISSUES AND POTENTIAL SOLUTIONS

Key issues relevant to improving sustainability with respect to the urban environment are identified and discussed in this section: land-use patterns, traffic and transportation, environmental pollution, housing, urban renewal, urban conservation, and environmentally sensitive design and construction. Although the discussion generally refers to developing countries, experience from developed countries is referred to where appropriate.

Land-use patterns at metropolitan and local levels

As cities grow, problems of congestion and sprawl intensify. Failure to develop strategic objectives and infrastructure investment policies at the metropolitan level results in wasteful patterns of land use. Development occurs usually along radial arteries, with adverse effects on agricultural productivity in the areas in between, inadequate waste disposal, increased traffic congestion and inefficient use of land within the built-up and peri-urban areas. To improve the management of urban growth, a metropolitan development strategy is needed to formulate flexible policies for the use of strategic investment, especially in infrastructure, to identify and improve the pattern of development for the metropolitan region and reduce sprawl, congestion and environmental impacts.

In early urban planning approaches, standard uses were identified relating to three basic activities: housing, shopping and work (offices or factories). These were separated because they were deemed to be incompatible with each other. Residents require safe, pleasant and sociable environments and it was assumed that these could be ensured only by reserving areas solely for residential use. Retailing, from the corner shop to the department store, is vital to any community, but it may generate pedestrian and vehicular congestion and so was mostly limited to areas specifically designated as shopping centres. Work areas were concentrated in industrial estates or central business districts.

However, in developing countries, mixed land use, in the same building or in a group of buildings, is often normal, with houses being used not only as homes, but also as shops or the base for enterprises. Today, the benefits of mixed uses are increasingly recognized, and the relaxation of land-use zoning control makes it possible to plan communities where the bulk of travel can be undertaken on foot, by bicycle or using public transport, lessening environmental impacts by reducing the number and length of trips by motorized transport.

Traffic and transportation

In developing countries the most common means of travel is walking. The mosque, church, corner shop or primary school is usually within walking distance. However, sometimes the journey to work and back may take an hour or more. Pedestrian routes may be alleyways, shared with donkeys or wheeled transport, badly lit and muddy when it rains.

After walking, the main means of travel in large urban areas is public transport, usually in buses and taxis operating like minibuses. These accommodate the bulk of trips but are often uncomfortable, overcrowded, unreliable and restricted to the wider urban roads. Such roads have triple functions as routes for cars and pedestrians and also as areas for trading, which provides a valuable source of employment but leads to congested environments (Southworth and Ben-Joseph, 1997). Other forms of informal transport include cycle and motorized rickshaws, which are cheap but add to congestion and slow traffic speeds, leading some local authorities to ban them from main roads or central areas. Rail transport is used less frequently. Mega-cities need rail transport, but it is not easy to introduce.

Water transport is another option: Istanbul's ferry services, for example, are well developed and used.

The private car is not only a means of transport, but also a prestige symbol. Professional groups and the emerging bourgeoisie use the private car extensively. Affluent families may employ a driver for commuting, shopping and visiting. With road improvement, urban development spreads along major routes, causing suburban sprawl, inefficient use of land and resources, and environmental pollution (Rogers and Power, 2000). However, electronic communication technologies facilitate the decentralization of business activities, enabling land-use policies to reduce the inefficient and energy-wasting use of the private car for commuting to work.

Environmental pollution

Environmental pollution dominated the proceedings of the 1972 Stockholm Conference. It became clear that the interests of developing countries were incompatible with those of developed countries. The former prioritized development, even if environmental pollution was the result, while reducing pollution was the primary concern of the developed countries. Subsequent discussions and reports have attempted to reconcile the need for international agreement on reducing pollution and tackling environmental degradation with the desire of poorer countries to increase their levels of economic development. The Brandt Commission was primarily concerned with development. In his introduction to its 1983 report, Willy Brandt warned that 'Deteriorating economic conditions already threaten the political stability of developing countries. Further decline is likely to cause the disintegration of societies and create conditions of anarchy in many parts of the world' (Brandt Commission, 1983). The World Commission on Environment and Development attempted to reconcile environmental and development objectives (WCED, 1987). The 1992 Earth Summit in Rio de Janeiro focused on comprehensive environmental controls. Despite international recognition of deteriorating environmental conditions, and eight UN- and four European-sponsored conferences on the global environment since 1972, there is no agreement on a universal policy.

Meanwhile, levels of pollution in the cities of developing countries have increased dramatically, with major impacts on health. While in some countries, such as China, the main source of air pollution is industrial or domestic fuel (usually coal) or suspended particulates from construction operations, in many others vehicles, which change the composition of air pollutants, are the main source. Where wood and charcoal are still used as domestic fuel, levels of indoor pollution are high. Industrialization and the spread of informal settlements with inadequate sanitation systems have contributed to increased water pollution, affecting those dependent on surface or ground sources of water supply and downstream communities (WHO/UNEP, 1992).

Housing

In the 1960s, after initial problems with land acquisition and water and sanitation provision, legislation and procedures supported self-help in many developing countries. Shanty towns may be improved by the regularization of tenure and provision of water supply, vehicular access and drainage. Some low-income housing may become available through sites and services schemes, with or without core houses. But these are generally away from city centres, although the preference of many low-income households is for a central location near work opportunities, despite overcrowding in high-density development. Middle-income group housing tends to be either built by the authorities and sold to special groups with varying degrees of subsidy or, sometimes, built speculatively. The demand for high-income housing is met by the private sector, typically in the suburbs with good road links with the city centre. However, public sector agencies need to husband the use of their limited resources and wherever possible they should adopt an enabling role, so that individuals take responsibility for their shelter, and communities for the management of infrastructure and facilities.

Urban renewal and conservation of historic areas

In the inner city, adaptation to meet the needs of contemporary society is complex because of the varied mix of buildings and uses. Appropriate actions may include regeneration, redevelopment and refurbishment. Where there are historic buildings that need to be conserved, changes of use are further complicated and may require robust legislation and financing. Individual housing units can hardly be renewed separately and a process of cellular renewal, in which groups of sites are successively renewed, is generally more appropriate. For renewal to be satisfactory, planning may need to cover a neighbourhood-sized area, with facilities for commerce, industry, recreation and residence.

Land consolidation for this purpose involves extinguishing all existing servicing arrangements for water supply, sewerage, etc., and providing new services for newly demarcated parcels of land. Even when the value of brownfield sites is recognized, it is unlikely that private developers will take the risks involved in such a complex process, so public support is needed to take a lead and bear the initial costs of infrastructure renewal. Publicly supported approaches to regeneration for cities in developed countries (Rogers, 1999) need to be adapted to the prevailing circumstances in developing countries.

The management of these processes of change provides opportunities for the reduction of environmental pollution by improving provision for public transport and pedestrian movement, and for sensitivity to the needs of existing residents in the design of renewal and relocation programmes.

Although the retention of historic buildings may be perceived as an extravagance in terms of the costs of conservation and maintenance, they are part of the cultural heritage of a town or city. Historic individual buildings are generally protected by a listing procedure. Local authorities have legislation and procedures to deal adequately with the historic urban heritage, albeit with limited funding. In some cases whole villages or cities (e.g. Lamu, Kenya) have been designated as conservation areas or UNESCO World Heritage Sites. A distinction should be made between conservation and preservation. The former is mainly concerned, through the recycling of buildings, with their continuing use. The primary objective of preservation, however, is to protect a building to maintain its architectural integrity, sometimes with no clear idea of what its future role might be. An economic rationale for preservation or conservation may be found in the attractiveness to tourists of historically and architecturally important buildings and areas, in developed and developing countries alike. Apart from its economic benefits, tourism promotes the local cultural traditions (Parfect and Power, 1997).

However, historically or architecturally significant buildings or groups of buildings should not be considered in isolation from their surroundings. The conservation and recycling of such historic monuments maintains interest, legibility and variety in the fabric of urban centres. In urban design terms, the availability of sites for redevelopment provides an opportunity to introduce good modern architectural landmarks alongside more traditional and historic structures. Such a mixture of styles can create a museum of architecture to be enjoyed by tourists and residents alike. Planning for improved environments in new and renewed areas implies that as much attention should be given to public as to private spaces.

Environmentally sensitive design and building

The design of both individual buildings and the spaces between them must be sensitive to local climatic conditions. Sensitive climatic design considers orientation and prevailing wind direction, with recourse to double glazing, wall insulation or cross-ventilation, as appropriate. We know from vernacular architecture (Fathy, 1973; Steele, 1997) that a reasonable degree of comfort in our buildings (including thermal comfort, daylight and ventilation) can be achieved for the main part of the year (Yeang, 1984). Only where climatic design is insufficient to achieve adequate standards of comfort should it be supplemented by mechanical and electrical means of air conditioning, ventilation or lighting.

Climatic design for the external environment is more complex than the treatment of building interiors. It is affected, with daily and seasonal variations, by sunshine, rain, snow and wind, elements that are difficult to control. City centres, in particular, must provide good and bad weather alternatives to attract visitors in all seasons. Wind-tunnel tests and careful orientation of buildings can help designers to create comfortable open spaces. Design of external space depends on complex site analysis to achieve quality and efficiency.

The extraction and processing of building materials can be environmentally destructive, and construction processes are significant contributors to environmental pollution. Society has acquired profligate habits. Scarce resources are often unappreciated, discarded and neglected. Wider issues cannot be discussed here, but the potential during the management of urban change to minimize these effects by reusing materials can be noted. Recycling of glass, metal, paper and clothes has become increasingly acceptable in Northern cities, and is normal in poor cities. However, the recycling of building materials is less well organized, and many redundant buildings are bulldozed or blown up in the course of urban renewal.

Aspects of urban development relevant to the achievement of increased sustainability have been reviewed above, and some solutions suggested. Clearly there is no panacea that can be applied in every context. Much depends on the prevailing geographic, demographic, social and economic circumstances. Although it is useful to learn from the planning experiments of developed countries, they must be adapted and used with policies and strategies prepared specifically for developing countries. In the following section, a case study of Cairo is used to examine these sustainability considerations and to review some attempted solutions.

APPROACHES TO PLANNING FOR SUSTAINABILITY AT CITY AND LOCAL LEVELS

A sequence of planning activities may be envisaged for a city, with sustainability considerations integrated into each. The need for a vision of a city's future, a sustainability strategy and a tool for assessing the sustainability impact of specific developments is argued for below.

In the following part of the chapter the six sustainability issues identified and discussed above are appraised and evaluated with reference to the case study, as part of a systematic approach to assessing sustainability using a sustainability matrix, as described in a later section.

ENVIRONMENTAL SUSTAINABILITY AND PLANNING IN CAIRO

Traditionally the majority of Egyptians are urbanites (Lapidus, 1969), preferring the city to the *Rif* (countryside). The word *Misr* (Egypt) is synonymous with Cairo, underlining its importance as the principal city. Since its foundation at al-Fustat in 641 AD, the urban centre has moved many times, its progress marked by the great congregational mosques of successive rulers (from Amr, 642 and Ibn Tuloun, 877, to Mohammed Ali Pasha in the nineteenth century). In 2000, the population of Greater Cairo

Region was estimated at 10.6 million, with an annual growth rate of 4 per cent (UNCHS, 2001).

In 1985 a symposium, sponsored by the Aga Khan Award for Architecture, was held, entitled 'The Expanding Metropolis – Coping with the Urban Growth of Cairo'. This produced a vision for the city which was shared by many of the stakeholders present, and has continued to inform subsequent planning and development. The goals for the city were agreed as (Evin, 1985):

- to maintain its position as a regional centre, global city and major tourist venue
- to improve living conditions for the poor
- to preserve the cultural heritage.

Of the over 30 papers presented at the symposium, none addressed the issue of 'sustainability' directly. But there was an awareness of its relevance when the then Prime Minister stated in his inaugural address a commitment to 'hasten the implementation of immediate solutions to control pollution and improve the environment.'

Managing a megapolitan area

Planning for an agglomeration the size of Cairo is a major challenge. Greater Cairo megalopolis is a collection of cities: cities of industry, business, culture, sport, shopping, restaurants and night clubs. It functions at a global level. Recently, the dramatic expansion of Greater Cairo has absorbed Giza, Qalyubiya and Heliopolis. In the mid-1980s Egypt's Prime Minister identified the main problem as preserving from encroachment both public housing districts and agricultural land (Evin, 1985). The government has pursued a policy of establishing new cities, satellite towns and other settlements in the desert, each with its own centres for shopping, employment and housing (Figure 11.1).

Pressure on land is intense in the central area, along the radial routes and in areas accessible from major roads. The authorities have reserved land to the south of the city, on the way to Helwan, to be preserved as a rural 'patch'. They are under great pressure to develop at very high density. Each development is assessed on its merits. Currently the height of buildings is limited to 1.5 times the width of the adjoining road, and to a maximum of 12 storeys for the whole of Greater Cairo.

Land use at the local level

As a result of growth by the absorption of adjoining settlements, mixed land use, including residential, employment and infrastructure, can be found in most parts of the conurbation. Metropolitan Cairo is composed of a series of congested residential quarters. Traditionally these areas contain local baths, schools, work and shopping units (*dakakin*) and other facilities,

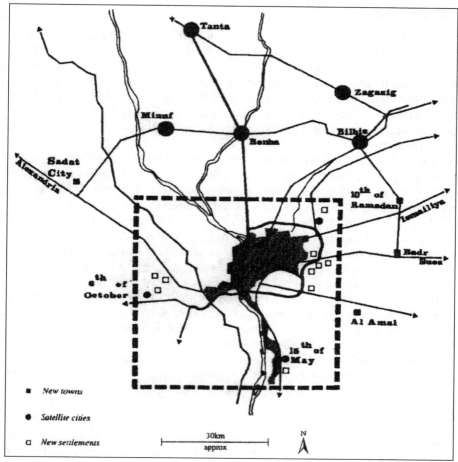

Figure 11.1   Planning for the Greater Cairo Region
Source: The Aga Khan Award for Architecture

while the neighbourhoods (*haras*) of the professional classes, who aspire to car ownership, live in apartments, and have holiday homes by the sea, also include larger stores and petrol stations. Neighbourhoods and communities form self-contained areas in which pedestrians have priority. There was originally no specific land-use zoning designation, but generally the first two to four floors were used for infrastructural services, shopping, offices etc.; beyond that anything from nine to 40 floors were used for middle- to upper-income housing. Despite the variety of urban environments, local management arrangements for these communities seem to work remarkably well, although greater attention needs to be paid to planning for environmental improvements.

Transportation

There is comparatively high car ownership and much long-distance commuting to work, so traffic congestion has become a major problem for both vehicular traffic and pedestrians (Figure 11.2). With limited road improvements, public transport is stretched to meet the demand. Car parking is a major problem. Because of the lack of multi-storey car parks, it is restricted to on-street parking, which causes congestion and gridlock situations at peak hours. Currently 2000 parking spaces are under construction in three central locations.

Proposals for a Metro system were first considered in the mid-1950s, comprising 30 km of underground and 142 km of ground-level track, to serve most parts of the city and, controversially, to connect it with the proposed new towns. Two lines have recently been completed: North–South from New El Marg to Helwan (approximately 15 km, with 35 stations), and East–West from Shubra El Kheima to Giza Suburban (12 km, with 26 stations) (Figure 11.3). There are four interchanges in the central area, and the lines terminate at the ring road, with axes that link to the satellite and new towns by overland suburban railway. Some preparations are under way for the first link with 6th October New Town, which has attracted much development including a 'Dreamland' housing and entertainment complex, Sheraton and Hilton hotels, film production sites and luxurious villas. A third Metro line is in the final stages of planning: it will run North-East to South-West, with 10 stations, and provide a link with the Airport which has a new second terminal.

Cairo now has a rail-based public transport system which includes Giza and Helwan and is expected to be extended to four new towns, three satellite cities, 10 new settlements and three development corridors (to Ismailiyah, Suez and Alexandria). An efficient public transport system is seen as the key to accommodating growth and the creation of an efficient and manageable megalopolitan structure. However, the provision of water transport could be enhanced.

Environmental pollution

In 1985 the Prime Minister identified a high-priority challenge, 'How can we improve over the next twenty years the overall living conditions in the city of Cairo by providing for a smoother flowing traffic, more green spaces and a more orderly and peaceful environment?' (Ali, 1985). As we approach the end of the 20 years, there has been some progress with the completion of the two Metro lines, remodelling of some public squares, and the opening up of leisure-oriented riverside linear parks. However, with rapid population growth, traffic and pedestrian congestion are as critical and the peaceful environment is as elusive as ever.

Great efforts were devoted to cleaning up air pollution, but vehicular emissions control and the banning of leaded petrol were difficult to implement, and although levels of pollutants are decreasing they still exceed

Figure 11.2   Growing problems caused by increasing vehicular traffic in otherwise sustainability-friendly urban environments – Bab Zuwaila, Cairo
Source: The Aga Khan Award for Architecture

WHO guidelines (Anon., 2002a). Similarly, efforts to protect the sources of water supplies depend on adequate treatment of sewage. Although three-quarters of households are connected to the system, only 15 per cent of wastewater is treated, 25 per cent is partially treated, and untreated

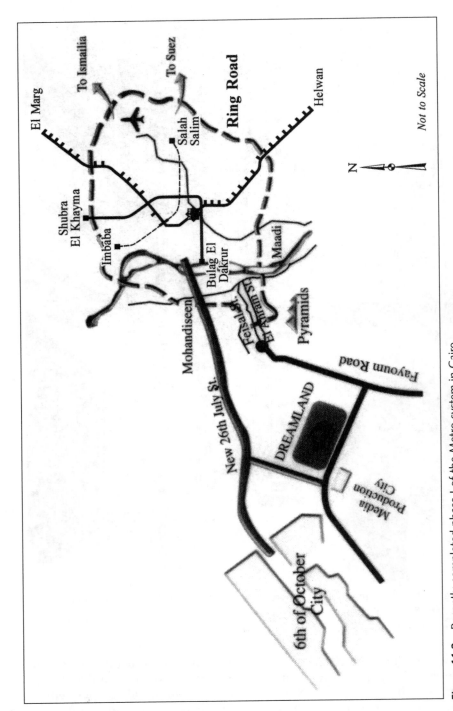

Figure 11.3   Recently completed phase I of the Metro system in Cairo
Source: Cairo Metro, 2002, Dreamland, Bhagat Group

domestic sewage and highly polluted industrial effluents are often dumped into old irrigation canals.

Housing

In 1950 the population growth of Egypt dropped to 1 per cent, while Cairo was growing at 4.1 per cent (Yousry and Atta, 1997). The trends continued so that by 1986 Cairo's population was estimated at 9.5 million. This led to a considerable expansion of the industrial base through new settlements and ambitious public housing. Progress with the new settlements was, on the whole, sluggish and the Greater Cairo Region, with its established services, employment opportunities and ready access to the decision makers proved to be more attractive. As a result, its growth was considerably faster than the national average. Squatters were given rights to the land on which they had settled, services were extended to squatter areas and there was great demand for housing (Myllyla, 1995).

In response to the preference of the low-income population for a central location, tall blocks of flats were constructed, often hastily, poorly and in danger of collapsing. By contrast, the upper-income groups commute long distances to work along motorways from luxury flats with attractive views across the Nile. In both cases there is a degree of speculation; poor housing may be rented by the room, and the Cairo bourgeoisie tend to invest in second homes, used mainly during the school holidays, in the tourist new towns of the littoral zone of the Mediterranean.

Historic conservation and urban renewal

An assessment of historic conservation in the early 1990s concluded that most individual buildings of historic importance were adequately maintained, and mosques fared well under the *Waqf* (charitable endowment) system, but the public realm needed much investment, particularly to promote the tourist industry (Bacharach, 1995). Three special programmes were identified: conservation of Islamic Cairo; rehabilitation and upgrading of historic Cairo; and conservation of the Old City of Cairo (Figure 11.4). They involved various ministries, UNESCO and Western consultants. The programmes covered large areas, subdivided into manageable zones, and included the restoration and preservation of traditional Islamic houses, such as al-Suhaimi house at Darb al-Asfar (Figure 11.5). The conservation officer had to deal with poverty, displacement and demolition orders, and the need to secure the support of the Cairo Governor (Anon., 2002b); there was little time to think of sustainability.

Distinctive aspects to consider in the course of historical conservation and urban renewal are the minarets, which dominate the skyline and aid legibility of the urban fabric, and the orientation of the mosques, which must face Mecca and so pose a challenge to the urban designer while providing variety in the architectural fabric and public urban spaces (Germen,

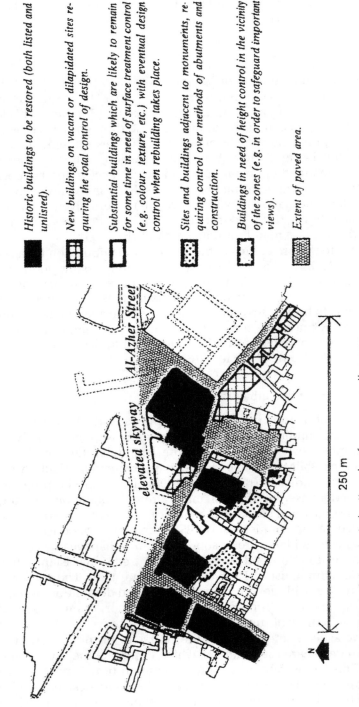

Historic buildings to be restored (both listed and unlisted).

New buildings on vacant or dilapidated sites requiring the total control of design.

Substantial buildings which are likely to remain for some time in need of surface treatment control (e.g. colour, texture, etc.) with eventual design control when rebuilding takes place.

Sites and buildings adjacent to monuments, requiring control over methods of abutments and construction.

Buildings in need of height control in the vicinity of the zones (e.g. in order to safeguard important views).

Extent of paved area.

Al-Azher Street

elevated skyway

250 m

N

Figure 11.4   Historic Cairo: a typical action plan for a conservation area
Source: The Aga Khan Award for Architecture

Figure 11.5 Al-Suhaimi House in El-Ghouri quarter in old Cairo
Photo: S. Romaya

1983). The larger public open spaces, however, are heavily congested with vehicular traffic, and pedestrian crossings are sometimes accommodated on overhead bridges. This is not conducive to a pleasant stroll through the city, so tourists generally use taxis. Recently there have been programmes to improve public open space provision in conservation areas and squares such as Tahrir Square and Ramses Square, which are being remodelled as part of the construction of the new underground system (Figure 11.6).

Most contemporary planning efforts in Cairo are focused on improving the attractiveness of the city for tourism. When traffic congestion became acute, the authorities provided increased capacity. In places this was achieved with the introduction of tunnels, overhead pedestrian crossings and 'skyway' roads, but in practice these roads and bridges exacerbated environmental, visual and noise pollution to such an extent that they have been largely dismantled. In particular the area of Khan al-Khalili and al-Azhar mosque is being pedestrianized as an open public realm for relaxation and leisure activities (Figure 11.7). It is bounded by two famous landmarks opposite each other, the al-Husain and al-Azhar mosques, with a

Figure 11.6   Remodelling of Maidan El-Tahrir, the modern centre of Cairo
Photo: Valerie M. Romaya

Figure 11.7   Extending the public realm, El-Azhar Street
Photo: S. Romaya

vital node in between – the Khan al-Khalili bazaar. Three gigantic umbrellas have been installed for weather protection. Although tourism is vulnerable to global trends and regional politics, it is amongst the top five foreign currency-earning sectors, and is vital for the country's economy. Tourism is affected by a wide range of planning policies, within which priority should be given to sustaining an attractive environment by reducing traffic congestion and taking measures against the negative impact of environmental and visual pollution.

Environmentally sensitive design and buildings

The technology for sustainable developments and services is well established; however its use may be restricted by established practices or commercial preferences.

In the Egyptian context, environmentally sensitive design and building was heralded by Fathy (1973), and his principles were adopted first at Qurna and then for other housing developments. Much can still be done, however, to improve sustainability in housing design and site planning, and to reduce the heavy dependence on air conditioning or excessive use of the private car. Housing and urban development in Egypt depend on the private sector or on attracting foreign investment, so management of development needs to be flexible but effective and sustainable.

Aspects of sustainability within the urban fabric that affect our daily lives are many and varied, but they have one main aim – a more efficient use of resources – a goal that is achievable only with the right tools or procedures. These involve the creation of sustainable urban spaces with appropriate microclimates, and consideration of easily accessible locations, building materials, land-use layouts and orientation of buildings for thermal comfort and good ventilation. However, the bulk of the inherited urban fabric is not efficient; it needs to be transformed in the light of current knowledge and technology. Hence sustainability cannot be achieved overnight, but implies a slow and gradual improvement in the way we use resources, requiring a fundamental change in established practices. To achieve sustainability, development needs to be guided or controlled based on an appraisal of its sustainability.

CITY DEVELOPMENT PLANNING

City Vision

In Sir Christopher Wren's vision for the development of London the skyline was dominated by a variety of church spires; from a good vantage point one might identify landmark buildings and form a mental map of the area. At ground level, monuments were located in public squares which were linked with main roads and vistas. Earlier, Thomas Moore had revealed his visions in Utopia; later, Ebenezer Howard envisaged the Garden City. Richard Rogers, in his televised lectures on London, presented the city from the vantage point of a double-decker bus.

Planners, urban designers, architects and other professionals develop visions of a city for the future. These visions need to be flexible to accommodate changing circumstances. A general appraisal of the historical development of a settlement, its physical and economic features, transportation arrangements and planning can be discussed with residents and other professional and lay actors to assess the desired future of the city and form the basis for developing an overall vision. For example, Doxiadis (1968) saw the need for identifying a new urban structure, the megalopolis, a multi-million population settlement. His vision included the latest developments in communication, transportation, food production and manufacturing (Eldredge, 1967).

A variety of studies are needed to develop such a vision, which in turn can be the basis for preparation of a strategic development plan and sustainability strategy.

Sustainability strategy

As part of a development plan, a strategy for attaining sustainability objectives should be developed to cover a range of topics, including environmental pollution, accessibility and transportation, land-use patterns and site layouts, approaches to urban renewal, energy conservation, and waste management and recycling. It should include a statement of the current position on environmental sustainability objectives and a list of indicators related to the policies and strategies being adopted; these can be used as a basis for evaluating the way development changes affect sustainability – positively or negatively. It should also set out a procedure for evaluating the sustainability of proposed developments to provide a guide for assessing the sustainability statement which should accompany planning applications or environmental impact statements.

Local area planning

At the local level, development briefs should be prepared to accommodate issues of sustainability. These should be set in context, through survey and analysis of relevant issues. Matters of sustainability should be considered systematically, with use of a sustainability statement based on planning guidance.

Neighbourhoods are convenient planning units socially, functionally and from a sustainability point of view; they are flexible and manageable. They vary in size and in the services they provide to meet the socio-economic needs of their inhabitants.

Traditional villages and cities have been much researched (Correa, 1989). Their quality of design stems from the designers' understanding of the inhabitants, structures and materials, and has important lessons for contemporary attempts to build or renew local urban environments in a vernacular style.

Five necessary steps can, therefore, be identified:

- preparing a vision for the future development of a city, using inputs from a survey of citizens and professionals
- preparing a profile of the city, for example by using a SWOT (strengths, weaknesses, opportunities, threats) analysis
- preparing a sustainability strategy as part of a strategic urban development plan, including the identification and weighting of appropriate indicators
- comparing the before and after situation for each indicator, to assess the negative and positive impacts of past or proposed development on sustainability objectives
- adopting a flexible strategy for development.

Sustainability indicators need to be carefully chosen, widely discussed and updated on a rolling programme every three to four years. Indicators used in developed countries could be adapted and adopted by developing countries. In the final part of this chapter, a tool based on the use of indicators, the sustainability matrix, is described in more detail.

TOOL FOR ASSESSING SUSTAINABILITY

As suggested above, sustainability may be assessed by the use of indicators. There are international guidelines on acceptable or desirable levels for some indicators, for example, for air or water pollution. In the UK, guidance has been issued on indicators which could be used for the evaluation of urban development proposals (Redclift and Sage, 1994; DoE, 1996b). Edwards and Hyett (2001) provide a sustainability toolkit with six main themes related to urban settlements. For projects and developments, indicators can be used to measure debits and credits of factors relevant to environmental sustainability, such as the use of land or water, transportation and movement, energy (heating and ventilation), and the choice and use of building materials. The precise levels of consumption of resources that are deemed acceptable or desirable are likely to vary from place to place, depending on existing levels of development, consumption or pollution. For example, Edwards and Hyett (2001) estimate that 87 per cent of extracted water in Africa is used for agriculture, whereas in the UK water is used mainly for domestic purposes (56 per cent), including toilet flushing (33 per cent), bathing and showering (20 per cent) and drinking and cooking (3 per cent). Where water is in short supply, as in Egypt, its conservation is a higher priority sustainability objective than where it is abundant.

The impacts of past or potential development on specific aspects of sustainability can therefore be estimated or measured. However, there is no common denominator of sustainability to use for an overall assessment of the effect on the environment of proposed or actual development. This shortcoming can be overcome by the use of a sustainability matrix (Romaya, 1987; Edwards and Hyett, 2001). The first step is to identify key themes or natural resources such as land, water, air and energy. For example, in the case of Cairo, there is plenty of land, but it is mainly desert land which requires water to sustain it and good transportation links. A new town built in the desert without consideration of environmental issues may be unsustainable, inhibiting the growth of its population. Associated with each of the themes, relevant indicators of aspects of sustainability are identified, such as energy consumption or air pollution. For each, the change likely to be caused by a proposed development can be assessed.

In Table 11.1, to illustrate the approach, the key themes or natural resources needed have been identified as energy, land and water (column 1). For each, the main factors (existing or proposed uses) that place demands on the resource are identified (column 2). An assessment is then made of the extent to which the existing or proposed development satisfies sustainability requirements with respect to each indicator. Specific indicators are used in this stage, but in order to derive comparable evaluation scores a more subjective approach is needed, based on a ranking from 1 to 5. Each is weighted according to its perceived importance (column 4). The scores for each weighted indicator (column 5) can be totalled to provide an overall estimate of the impact or likely impact of a proposed development

Table 11.1   Evaluation matrix for assessing the impact of a development on sustainability

Theme	Factor	Evaluation*	Weight**	Sustainability score
Energy	Heating	Very good (5)	Important (5)	$5 \times 5 = 25$
	Construction	Average (3)	Important (5)	$3 \times 5 = 15$
	Transport	Poor (2)	Very important (6)	$2 \times 6 = 12$
Land	Agriculture	Average (3)	Very important (6)	$3 \times 6 = 18$
	Housing	Average (3)	Ambivalent (3)	$3 \times 3 = 9$
Water	Industry	Good (4)	Essential (7)	$4 \times 7 = 28$
Total sustainability score				**107**

*Evaluation on 5-point scale: very good (5), good (4), average (3), poor (2), very poor (1).

**Weighted on 7-point scale: essential (7), very important (6), important (5), significant (4), ambivalent (3), limited significance (2), insignificant (1).

on the achievement of environmental sustainability, and to provide a basis for comparing alternative proposals. In the example shown in Table 11.1, the particular development proposals being evaluated score well in terms of energy consumption for heating and use of water by industry, but poorly with respect to energy consumption for transport. The most important sustainability indicator in this case is water consumption by industry, perceived as an economic priority, followed by energy consumption for transport and the consumption of agricultural land, with housing provision considered of least importance. Each of the weighted indicators then contributes to an overall sustainability score.

The second stage in evaluating the impact of development is based on before and after studies using a sustainability matrix. Two tables, similar to Table 11.1, are prepared to establish the degree of change. In Table 11.2, the results of the illustrative example in Table 11.1 are transferred to column 2; a similar analysis is carried out for the post-development situation (column 3); and the percentage change in each individual factor is shown in columns 4 and 5. An increase in the post-development score indicates

Table 11.2   Analysis of the effect of development on sustainability (notional values)

Factor	Evaluation		Percentage	
	Before Development	After Development	Enhancement	Degradation
Heating	25	20	–	20
Construction	15	20	33	–
Transport	12	15	25	–
Agriculture	18	18	–	–
Housing	9	12	33	–
Industry	28	24	–	14
Total	**107**	**109**	**2**	

enhanced sustainability, whereas a decrease shows degradation in sustainability terms. Columns 1 and 2 are then totalled to give an overall notional value for the impact of a proposed development on sustainability. In the example, the post-development situation shows approximately 2 per cent improvement.

This demonstrates how a proposed development may enhance or degrade the environment, and provides an overall assessment which should be positive for the development to proceed. It provides a tool for better-informed decision-making and a basis for dialogue on further enhancing the positive or reducing the negative effects of a proposed development.

Although some indicators are relatively easy to quantify, assessment of others involves subjective judgements, as does the weighting process. Further research is needed on the selection and means of quantifying appropriate indicators. Such an assessment can be used as a basis for negotiating more environmentally sustainable approaches to planning and design, increasing the potential for developments to contribute to enhanced sustainability. It can also be used for assessing the impact of developments and monitoring their collective contribution to the achievement of individual and overall sustainability objectives.

CONCLUSIONS

Urban planning can make an important contribution to the process of managing change, to the incorporation of sustainability as a fundamental criterion by which development proposals should be judged, and to the achievement of improved environmental sustainability. However, sustainability assessment needs to be integrated into all stages and levels of the planning process. In this chapter, some of the issues that need to be considered have been identified, based on the experience of developed countries and the needs of developing countries, and with reference to the city of Cairo.

The key points in the appraisal may be summarized as follows:

- recent development practices have caused much damage to the environment in general, and to urban centres in particular
- remedial action is a long-term process, while in the interim, damage to the environment is escalating
- concerted policies need to be adopted to halt and then reverse current environmentally damaging practices
- even in the rapidly growing cities of developing countries, much of the built environment is inherited; change is slow and often difficult
- a systematic procedure for assessing sustainability of medium- and large-scale projects should be introduced based on a 'sustainability statement' to accompany each planning application

■ introduction of supplementary planning guidance, which sets out a sustainability analysis procedure such as that portrayed in the sustainability matrix, as well as providing a basis for the identification of sustainability indicators, is desirable.

To summarize, attention should be given to the management of change in existing urban areas as well as to the planning of new developments. Any development introduces change to the urban environment, with some positive and some negative impacts. If sustainability objectives are taken into account, for example in the design of buildings for refurbishment and reuse, then environmental degradation can and should be minimized. An adaptable evaluation tool for assessing the impact of development proposals on the achievement of environmental sustainability has been outlined.

Sustainability can be achieved using one or more of the following procedures:

■ global level – international control
■ national level – human settlements policy
■ local level – planning guidance and design guidance
■ site-specific development – planning and development briefs.

CHAPTER TWELVE

Good practice in core area development: combating poverty through a participatory approach

Tony Lloyd-Jones and Sarah Carmona

INTRODUCTION

As the Introduction to this book notes, sustainability within urban development is a concept that embraces socio-economic issues alongside physical, environmental and political factors. Barton (2000) suggests that the phrase 'sustainable development' may itself be a paradox, seeking to conjoin two seemingly irreconcilable principles, those of environmental sustainability and economic development. This apparent paradox has led to the development of different uses of the term: an ecology-centred use, and a people-centred use (Barton, 2000). The latter emphasizes the principle of equity (Elkin et al., 1991). Ensuring that development is equitable (for existing and future generations) involves enabling all sections of society to gain access to resources and opportunities for employment, shelter and recreation. Inequity is not just a major concern in its own right, it also implies inefficient use of resources, particularly human resources, and can lead to environmental degradation and resource depletion (Elkin et al., 1991).

The livelihoods of people living in poverty in informal settlements in the centrally located areas of cities in developing countries depend, more often than not, on commercial activities and employment opportunities occurring within the immediate vicinity. Such settlements are continuously vulnerable to commercial development pressures and their inhabitants face eviction, relocation or pressures to move to peripheral areas, limiting the capacity of the poorest households to maintain a livelihood.

This chapter explores an equitable approach to urban development that aims to secure and improve the lives and livelihoods of these particularly vulnerable households and the communities of which they are part. Equity within the development process, in this context, can be achieved through a partnership between the different stakeholders and empowerment of local communities (frequently the weakest stakeholders) to enable their members to engage and participate in processes of urban renewal. The approach is based on making use of the high land values in the central and strategically located areas of cities to help generate economically viable development or redevelopment of low-income communities, including housing and space for employment-generating activities. City centre redevelopment of this kind can contribute to reduced energy use, building an inclusive society and maintaining the social and economic fabric that keeps urban centres alive, self-sustaining, stimulating and prosperous.

The text is based on the findings of extensive research and fieldwork undertaken in Delhi, Jakarta and Recife between June 1997 and March 2001 (Max Lock Centre, 2002a).[1] The research identified relevant core area locations within each city and surveyed the resident low-income population to investigate their living conditions and social and economic circumstances. The feasibility of different options for the redevelopment of the identified core area sites, using varying levels of cross-subsidization of low-income development by commercial development, was explored with the aid of computer-based tools developed as part of the research.[2] The outputs of these studies were discussed with local stakeholders in a series of associated workshops.

The chapter first briefly describes the nature of the core areas of cities. Second, it identifies some of the key development issues arising from these characteristics. Third, the characteristics of the case study communities are described and the research process outlined. A possible means of supporting the livelihoods of poor residents in core areas through a sustainable approach to development is outlined and discussed, leading to the formulation of a number of principles on which such an approach could be based. The process of achieving sustainable core area development is outlined, and some of the barriers to a successful outcome which were identified in the feasibility studies are discussed, leading to identification of the conditions in which the approach advocated would be appropriate.

UNDERSTANDING THE CONTEXT: CORE AREAS AND THE LIVELIHOODS OF THE URBAN POOR

Most cities and their administrations face a fundamental dilemma arising out of the intrinsic nature of urban development. Where large numbers of people congregate to live and work, land becomes an increasingly scarce and expensive resource that commands very high and – over time – everrising prices. At the same time, cities must also accommodate many poor or less-well-off people, who are unable to afford the costs associated with high and rising land values. Cities are concentrations of wealth and centres of investment. Of necessity, they must also export goods and services to surrounding regions and to more distant trading partners to pay for the imports of food, fuel and other resources needed to provide for the needs of their inhabitants. Around such export activities – typically manufacturing and commerce, transhipment and warehousing, legal, financial and other producer services, government, higher education and other public services – grow activities geared towards the needs of urban inhabitants themselves: retail, food and leisure, housing and real estate, transportation and local public services.

With this range of economic activity comes a diversity of employment, wealth and social status. In particular, in the fast-growing cities of developing countries there are growing numbers of low-income inhabitants who act as providers of cheap labour and low-cost services to their fellows and to better-off residents. Most of their economic activity is characterized as 'informal' – unregulated street selling or small-scale manufacture in homes or workshops, domestic service work, and the like. Yet for the well off and not so well off, much of this activity provides an essential basis for life in the city (Max Lock Centre, 2002a). While rapid population growth and in-migration can contribute to unemployment or 'underemployment', the importance of the livelihood activities of low-income inhabitants to the urban economy frequently goes unrecognized. For example, the *Favela do Rato* is a small informal settlement on the *Ilha de Recife*, the old colonial port area on the coastal tip of downtown Recife in the north-east of Brazil. The major port activity is now concentrated in a new container installation outside the city, but the old port, although run down, is still active. The settlement consists of some overcrowded, illegally occupied, derelict port buildings, and numerous small shacks, one deep, that line a few back streets of the port. This pocket of extreme deprivation provides an important service function, with the shacks serving as cheap food outlets for low-paid stevedores.

The concentration of livelihood opportunities in central locations is seldom matched by affordable housing of a decent standard. The result is the mushrooming of overcrowded slums, illegal settlements on waste land and sites considered inappropriate for 'normal' occupation or development, or rented accommodation in legally developed but equally overcrowded and health-threatening conditions.

ISSUES IN PLANNING FOR CORE AREA (RE-)DEVELOPMENT

The term 'core area' is used in the context of this chapter to cover those central and most accessible locations where the livelihood opportunities of the urban poor are often concentrated, where their living conditions are harsh, and where the potential for urban authorities to capture land value to finance social benefit is greatest.

Economic pressures on the central areas of cities give rise to large-scale commercial developments (Bairoch, 1988) that displace or fail to accommodate the low-income households whose livelihoods are based on central service employment. Core area commercial redevelopment too often causes an exodus of residents to the outlying areas of the city, in areas often remote from the source of their livelihoods. In many cases, this process is facilitated by public authorities, who promote planned relocation of low-income core area populations in peripheral housing estates or satellite settlements. Often little thought is given to the relationship between home and work or the implications for the communities affected. In addition, the regional environmental impacts are seldom recognized (Lloyd-Jones, 2000).

The approach outlined in this chapter focuses on the redevelopment of core area sites to release potential commercial land value, part of which can be used to improve the living conditions of the resident community. Any core area site that is currently used at or below its potential land value could be redeveloped for high-value uses and/or social benefit of this kind. Generally, most core area sites have been used, and renewal will involve redevelopment and change of use, rather than new development. In planning for such renewal, a number of key issues need to be considered: appropriate land-use patterns; the locational requirements of small-scale enterprise; land tenure and property rights; and whose interests need to be taken into account. Each of these is briefly discussed, before the approach advocated in this chapter is described.

Mixing uses

The approach to development advocated here requires a careful mix of uses and the provision of community buildings and amenities, to ensure that the sensitive balance between activities, livelihoods and social capital is maintained. Planning legislation and regulations are of crucial importance in this respect. Existing legislation may severely hinder the process if development is regulated according to master plans that zone cities into mono-use areas, and do not accommodate mixed uses. In the context of this chapter, we refer to mixed use, broadly, as development comprising more than one use and value on a single plot or within a single building, or an area where sites and buildings of different uses and values are grouped together, as illustrated in Figure 12.1.

Figure 12.1 Appropriate fine-grained mixed-use development in Old Delhi
Photo: Tony Lloyd-Jones

A conventional zoning approach to planning seeks to minimize the potential functional and environmental conflicts that may arise out of the location of different uses together. Both the short-term profit-maximizing motives of developers and the preference of property managers and investors for a single type of occupier ensure that commercial redevelopments tend to focus on a single use, selected according to the location (Marsh, 1997).

Typically 'mixed-use development' is seen in areas with modestly sized sites and buildings that have grown incrementally, with flexibility to meet the changing needs of individual landowners, occupiers and tenants, whether commercial or residential (Jacobs, 1961). The co-location of types of development with different values within a particular use category (e.g. high- and low-income residential, prime and low-value commercial, community buildings and amenities) is implied by the concept of mixed use as it is employed in this chapter. Underpinning the rationale for such a mixed-use approach to development are the functional relationships that exist between these different types of land use and the flexibility of a city neighbourhood to accommodate changes and diversify over time (in levels of income, production and consumption).

Displacement of small-scale enterprise

Large-scale commercial developments may also displace small-scale business and service enterprises, resulting in the reduction of labour-intensive livelihood opportunities in city centres. Affordable space in older individual and family-owned properties that offer economic adaptability through subletting is lost with the purchase and demolition of existing buildings. Rarely is sufficient provision made in redevelopment plans for central re-accommodation of small-scale enterprises, many of which provide a critical service function to larger-scale businesses and their employees. Without ready access to such markets, it is difficult for such enterprises to survive.

When households are moved to more peripheral locations, they may be forced to travel long distances to their existing workplaces which, even if affordable in time as well as money, is likely to place a significant strain on household resources. Travel times and costs increase for poor households, and the increased travel has an impact on the environment through increasing energy use and air pollution. Alternatively, people relocating in peripheral areas will be forced or choose to find sources of livelihood that are closer at hand – making use of employment opportunities that have less variety and are more spread out than in central areas. Finding these alternatives will inevitably take time and place further strains on the household.

Even when people work from home, they are bound by location, relying on networks of local vendors for raw materials, and on central wholesale markets, street markets or hawking in better off and more densely populated central locations to sell their wares. Most service activities, like domestic service, are based in wealthier areas where the poor cannot afford to live or where they are under constant threat of eviction in order to make way for higher-value development uses, rendering the resident low-income populations very vulnerable to displacement. The dispersal and relocation of existing communities – whether through planned relocation or eviction, or through a slower process of gentrification – leads to the disruption of existing networks that tie communities together within neighbourhoods and link neighbourhoods to nearby city districts through commercial, political and other contacts – in other words, to the haemorrhaging of social capital.

Land tenure and property rights

The nature of the land tenure or property rights of a resident low-income community affects their status and security. Land tenure can be defined as the mode by which land is held or owned, or the set of relationships among people concerning land or its product. Property rights are similarly defined as recognized interests in land or property vested in an individual or group, and can apply separately to land or development on it. Rights may cover access, use, development or transfer, and may exist in parallel with ownership (Payne, 1997, 2001). In the core areas of developing country cities, there may be different tenure systems in place, sometimes in tandem: formal, informal, indigenous and religious. While informal tenure arrangements are generally regarded as illegal, many of those with such arrangements have a sense of security. This implied security has occurred either as a result of the local authority providing infrastructure and services to informal settlements, or because the public sector has neither the capacity nor the political will to offer alternative living solutions to such large numbers of people. In addition, there may be legal provisions that give occupiers – whether legal or not – rights to be rehoused should the site they occupy be subject to redevelopment by the owner. An example of legislation that attempts to enforce (although rarely with success) the on-site provision of low-income dwellings is the 1 : 3 : 6 policy introduced by the Indonesian government, requiring six low-income residential units and three middle-income residential units to be provided for each high-income residential unit built (Max Lock Centre, 2002a).

Regularization of the tenure of unauthorized occupants may be perceived as yielding benefits, for example, improved access to formal credit and an incentive for an individual occupant to 'invest' in his or her property. However, often regularization programmes have been shown to distort property and land markets, increasing values and reinforcing the exclusion of the poorer sections of a community. An alternative approach is to increase the security of occupancy, extending existing customary arrangements where appropriate (Max Lock Centre, 2002a).

The stakeholders

In practice, in any centrally located area there are a range of stakeholders who have a varying degree of interest in taking a sustainable mixed-use approach to core area development. They include:

- planning authorities, public development agencies and other urban management bodies who may own the land, or who can play a role in facilitating partnerships between stakeholders in core area developments
- developers, land agents, landowners and financial institutions, who are most likely to be the initiators of development and the prime beneficiaries (in commercial terms) of redevelopment, but who, for political reasons, may need to negotiate with existing low-income communities and urban authorities in the course of developing core area sites
- NGOs, consultants and technical aid organizations who may be involved in aiding low-income urban communities on the ground
- policy-makers in donor organizations, governments and city institutions who may be responsible for framing policies to enable the implementation of balanced, sustainable and integrated pro-poor development in core areas of cities
- low-income communities themselves, who need to negotiate with landowners, developers, employers and city institutions to ensure that any development acknowledges and addresses the accommodation and livelihood needs of the existing residents and small enterprises.

Each of these actors has interests that may conflict. Some are more powerful than others, and an equitable partnership is easier to achieve in principle than in practice. Part of the process should be to define common areas of interest with a view to achieving a 'win–win' outcome. In the urban context, development negotiations can be complex, lengthy, costly, slow, easily blocked, and frequently fruitless. On the other hand, there are few circumstances in which a stakeholder will not benefit from some type of development or redevelopment. One area of common interest, then, is in ensuring that development takes place at all.

Poor communities may have more to gain than most, but they also have the most to lose. Because they are traditionally the weakest participants and are often ignored by the more powerful actors, they are the most vulnerable. An important aspect of the discussion in this chapter is how to empower poor communities and promote their effective participation in the decision-making process. A major hurdle to empowerment arises out of the internal diversity of communities of the urban poor themselves. The term 'community' is used here in the broad sense of a group of people living and working in a particular neighbourhood and sharing an interest in their common environment. However, such generic neighbourhood-based communities are clearly not homogeneous. Residents' incomes and social status vary. Many different interest groups exist, whether organized or not: people related through economic activity, origin, ethnic background or kinship ties, or sharing common interests of gender or age group. Such diversity undermines political coherence and unity. Problems with neighbours and individual, family and household interests are frequently of greater concern than community issues, with resulting fragmentation of the stakeholder group (Max Lock Centre, 2002a). Mechanisms that address this fragmentation (through promoting community cohesion) are therefore a critical element of a sustainable, equitable, mixed-use approach to core area development.

CORE AREA COMMUNITIES AND THE RESEARCH PROCESS

The research on which this chapter is based sought to address this range of issues. Within the city studies that formed the major part of the research, the chosen sites housed large communities (5000+ inhabitants) of low-income households in informal, long-established neighbourhoods with limited or no security of tenure. The sites selected were of a minimum size (four city blocks or approximately 4 hectares) to allow for consideration of a full range of building and street types, access and layout arrangements. For the most part, they were subject to commercial pressures for redevelopment and/or pressures from public development authorities for redevelopment according to an official master plan. In some instances the latent commercial value of the site was hardly evident because of a perception of it as fixed in its present, low-value use. This was particularly the case where residents had been granted some form of security of tenure, however limited, where some upgrading had occurred, and where planning restrictions limited the future potential for market-based land redevelopment.

Typically, sites were located in areas with the following characteristics:

- within or close to the commercial core or central business district of the city
- close to new or existing commercial subcentres outside the central business district
- close to nodal points such as large transport interchanges.

A detailed examination of the livelihoods pursued by households in the study settlements in Delhi and Jakarta, using data from special household surveys, revealed the critical importance of location for most residents. In the Motia Khan neighbourhood in central Delhi, for example, most people were too poor even to afford public transport, and relied on being within easy walking distance of livelihood opportunities. The community relied on access to the tourist trade, to nearby middle-class neighbourhoods for domestic employment, and to the wholesale markets of Old Delhi for supplies and markets for home-produced goods. Valuable social capital, in the form of networks of business contacts built up over time, was threatened by planned relocation of the community. Even local employers expressed concern at losing people with whom they had built up trust and in whose training they had invested, through relocation to suburban sites. Residents of core area settlements in other city study locations were equally reliant on easy access to the central area economy, to which they were an important source of informal labour and services. In Jakarta, the availability of informal open space where small-scale local economic activities can locate is a crucial component in maintaining livelihoods. Such pockets of activity (frequently overlooked in planned settlements) support life on the street.

The research team undertook feasibility studies for each of the sites identified, comprising a site analysis and proposals. A range of mixed-use development options with different proportions of commercial and residential provision (including low-, medium- and high-income provision) were considered for each. Workshops were undertaken in each city to present and discuss the issues and development options identified. The field studies and follow-up workshops involved local research organizations, NGOs, community representatives, developers and city representatives.

Surveys showed that typically around 50 per cent of residents preferred to be rehoused on site, while the remainder preferred to be relocated elsewhere in the area or at better space standards in more peripheral locations. In each of the major studies it was established that higher-density, mixed-use redevelopment incorporating an element of cross-subsidy from commercial development would allow for this level of rehousing on site at basic space standards, but with a much higher level of local services and with access to commercial work space.

Drawing on these feasibility studies and a review of failed redevelopment projects in the same cities, a more appropriate approach to the renewal of core areas is proposed in the following section.

GOOD PRACTICE IN CORE AREA DEVELOPMENT: AN APPROACH TO RENEWAL

The hypothesis underlying the approach to development in core areas suggested here is that higher-density, mixed-use redevelopment, incorporating an element of cross-subsidy from commercial development, allows for the rehousing of a substantial proportion of the existing low-income population on site at basic space standards. This allows a higher level of local services, amenities and community buildings to be provided, as well as access to commercial workspace. Commercial redevelopment that fails to acknowledge the needs of an existing low-income community has the same effect as gentrification: land values rise and low-income residents are consequently priced out and displaced. The approach to development advocated here is an attempt to arrest the process of gentrification and displacement, enabling the profile of an area to transform through new commercial redevelopment, while at the same time protecting the position and interests of an existing low-income community. Potentially such an approach would enable:

- improvement in the health and quality of life of ultra low-income service workers and their dependents
- a reduction in development impact on the environment, as more sustainable patterns of living and working are developed
- the securing of a balanced and integrated community and a balanced mix of land uses, providing vitality and security in core commercial areas
- maintenance of a viable local service workforce
- facilitation of new employment and small business development opportunities.

Situations in which such a mixed-use approach to core area development may be appropriate are:

- where there is commercial pressure (or commercial potential), but re-development is constrained due to conflicting interests of the developer or landowner and the site occupants, the nature of ownership, or illegal occupation of the site
- where local or central government has the political will to address the issue of sustainable livelihoods for the urban poor in core areas, or to improve or regenerate core areas (including those pockets of land that may have developed incrementally)
- where there is a site sufficiently large for redevelopment, with a number of buildings of different uses and configurations (2–3 hectares minimum), and where the area is either in single ownership or a number of owners are willing to cooperate.

Land development mechanisms

The approach is primarily concerned with capturing (and releasing) the premium on land values from development for the benefit of low-income households and communities. A number of mechanisms may be used to achieve this outcome in different contexts. In general, these mechanisms depend on public intervention, through policy or project facilitation. First, it is necessary for each indigenously acceptable tenure rights system to be established, recognized, and worked with and through for each development. It is important that the intrinsic values of rights as understood by the various stakeholders are understood and evaluated (Max Lock Centre, 2002b). In addition, there are a number of formal mechanisms that may be used, such as planning obligations[3] (used in the UK); Transferable Development Rights[4] (used in India, the USA and Brazil); incentive-based planning codes[5] (used in the USA, Hong Kong, India); or land pooling or readjustment[6] (widely practised in East Asia). Such mechanisms enable individual developers to make an acceptable level of profit while providing social benefit in the form of low-income accommodation or land for infra-structure or social facilities. Alternatively, local authorities can act as inter-mediaries between landowners/developers and resident communities in brokering land-sharing arrangements,[7] providing a guarantee in situations of high risk and allowing 'locked-up' land values to be realized for the bene-fit of both parties. Thus a government can enable mixed-use development through the use of mechanisms that:

- bring the land under central control
- pool and reallocate land, and/or
- ensure developer compliance through conditions or incentives.

Community organization

Where communities are weak and disunited in the face of commercial development pressures, the opportunities for achieving social benefit through redevelopment are easily lost. To realize such opportunities, com-munities need to act collectively (Max Lock Centre, 2002a). Within an exist-ing community, there may already be active community groups or organizations, some of which may be informal and known about only within the community itself. It may be appropriate for a community to engage in the development process through these existing organizations, building on the groups' experience. The public agency needs a clear under-standing of what groups or organizations are in existence, and the relation-ships between them (World Bank, undated). Alternatively, support may be given by government or an NGO to developing community organization.

Typical scenarios

If a core area site (or part of a site) is occupied by unauthorized settlers and is subject to commercial (or political) pressure for redevelopment, the introduction of mixed-use development can allow profits generated from commercial development to cross-subsidize the provision of appropriate housing for existing residents. Under conditions where it is not possible to clear the existing residents from the site, it allows a landowner to regain control of the site and realize its economic potential while rehousing all or part of the population already living on the site. It provides an alternative to either eviction or regularization and upgrading of the existing settle-ment. The latter process can block commercial development potential for an extended period.

In a situation where a site subject to commercial pressure for redevelop-ment is legally occupied by low-income residents, it is often possible to increase the density of development to allow commercial development while rehousing all or part of the existing low-income residential popula-tion on site. The scenario assumes an early awareness on the part of the community that individual acquisitions are in a developer's mind.

If a site is legally occupied by low-income residents, is not under immediate pressure for development, but has potential commercial value, then usually some kind of catalyst is required to kick-start development. Without community action, a process of gentrification and the subsequent loss of low-income accommodation is likely to take place in the longer term as the commercial potential of the area becomes apparent. Individual owners will be able to realize the value of their plots, but the loss of centrally located, low-income accommodation will be permanent, with considerable costs to the city as a whole.

Where it is not possible to rehouse low-income settlers on the site they currently occupy, then it may be appropriate to rehouse them elsewhere in the neighbourhood. Examples might include street dwellers or those squatting on dangerous or unhealthy sites. In such cases, the local government or an NGO could initiate development by actively pursuing a planning policy that would result in the development of low-rent residential and business premises. This can be achieved within an overall development plan by identifying and enabling the comprehensive development of suitable central sites where there are no legal or illegal residents, but where high land values could be exploited for on-site cross-subsidization. While suitable vacant sites may be in short supply in core areas, it is often the case that previously developed land falls derelict as a result of economic change or physical obsolescence, for example, land previously used for goods yards adjacent to central railway stations or for heavy industry and warehousing. Renewal strategies for such areas should consider using a policy of cross-subsidization to provide accommodation for the poor in these key locations.

Principles for a core area development process

Based on the above discussion, it is possible to identify a number of mainly social and economic principles underpinning the approach, which is based on a three-way (public–private–community) partnership, a principle that is becoming a key element of current policy thinking on urban governance and local development. These principles, which build upon those identified for land-sharing arrangements by Angel and Boonyabancha (1988), are listed in Box 12.1.

Box 12.1   Principles of sustainable core area development

Sustainable local development
Ensure that new development respects the local urban context and population and addresses wider environmental concerns.

Acknowledge the rights and contribution that existing core area communities make to the sustainable economic success of redevelopment.

Counter the economic and social argument put forward by commercial developers that mixing uses reduces value and creates social conflict.

Ensure diversity and sustainability through maintaining local, long-term, urban, low-income livelihoods, housing and workspace (affordable, needs-oriented); minimizing work–home travel distances and maximizing local choice and opportunity.

Maintain social capital and promote community economic development (and acknowledge the hidden costs in terms of loss of social capital associated with relocation policies).

Create management frameworks for perpetuating low-income occupation in core areas.

Maintain an economic balance between lower-value and higher-value activities; balancing commercial development with social benefit.

Enable land markets to work, understanding their potential and capabilities.

Capture value (development gain) from commercial development to ensure low-income inclusion as an integrated part of core area redevelopment.

Balance capital investment to ensure stakeholder commitment: commercial, public subsidy and investment by the community.

Establish community investment through access to appropriate/flexible banking and mutual aid.

Community organization

Establish ways of strengthening community organization to enable effective negotiation.

Enable indigenous leadership to drive the process – a community can lead as 'developer' or act as a strong development partner to other interests.

Ensure support to communities from outside organizations and capacity-building programmes.

Establish cooperatives and/or development trusts to ensure long-term community interests and rights.

Participatory and partnership-based approach

Achieve 'political' and stakeholder commitment to the process.

Establish open and cooperative stakeholder dialogue early.

Municipal and/or NGO support to facilitate negotiation and partnership.

Align community aspirations and expected outcomes.

Ensure the process contributes to broader social aims: social integration, institutional development and economic viability.

Governance: appropriate controls and mechanisms

Municipal flexibility and innovation; address existing statutory constraints/conflicts; operate outside 'normal' processes or review existing controls.

Develop appropriate regulatory mechanisms; conditions and incentives or partnership approaches to address constraints and create a level playing field.

Establish a flexible planning framework, to operate at the wider city scale and within core commercial areas, and respond to specific sites with briefs/guidelines based on local community interests as well as commercial success.

Create certainty through binding agreements and legal enforcement by the statutory authority, setting out details of any negotiated and agreed development plans.

Higher densities and reconstruction

Increase residential densities to release land for commercial purposes, which will in turn subsidize the residential development.

Reconstruction (either part or whole) of the residential element is usually a necessity to increase residential density.

Balance residential and commercial densities to create the potential for only partial rehousing of existing communities; displaced residents to be compensated and/or relocated.

THE REDEVELOPMENT PROCESS FOR MIXED-USE CORE AREA COMMUNITIES

The process for achieving sustainable mixed-use development in core areas can be based on a participatory approach (Figure 12.2). The principle of involving all the stakeholders (and giving active support to the participation of the weakest and most vulnerable) is to ensure that the outcome aligns with their aspirations. Who initiates and drives the process will depend on the particular development scenario (as outlined above). The reason for initiating such a process may be to release or 'unlock' prime land for commercial development (developer/landowner); to regenerate a core area, encouraging investment and addressing the poor living conditions of poor residents (local government); or to improve the situation of a core area community under threat (local community). It is likely that technical and professional support will be required to facilitate the process (Figure 12.2).

Involvement of all the stakeholders ensures that the proposals and the suggested reallocation of land are appropriate, commercial and sustainable in the long term, providing mutual benefit to the different parties involved. While the costs of any proposed mixed-use development can only be estimated, approximate values should be drawn wherever possible from the average costing of similar types and sizes of development locally. Financially, the intended outcomes can be achieved through subsidy from the commercial investment, although it is important to ensure that the low-income provision does not rely entirely on a commercial subsidy, as a contribution from the residents will often foster a sense of ownership and stewardship (Max Lock Centre, 2002a). Sources of funding can include commercial capital, private finance, borrowing and other initiatives such as local credit schemes. The availability of other kinds of financial support, including government subsidy, tax incentives or external finance, should also be explored (McLeod, 2001). Alternative proposals should be tested in social and commercial terms through stakeholder workshops.

The role and power of the local community within the process will depend on several factors. Apart from the existing strength and cohesion of the community itself, support from outside organizations (local and central government; NGOs) can contribute significantly, enabling a community to effectively participate or initiate the process. If a community

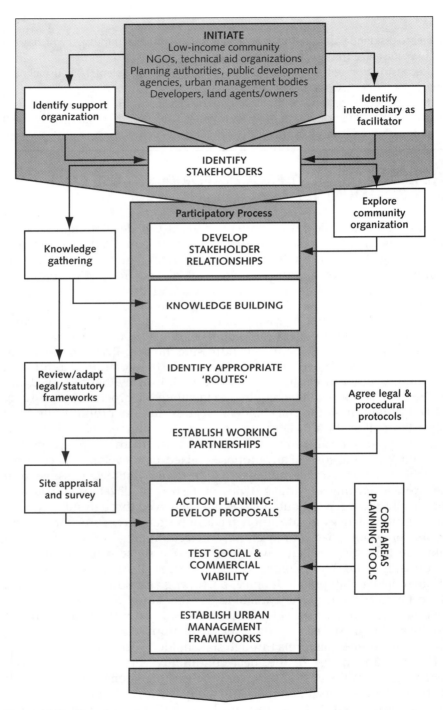

Figure 12.2   Key stages in a core area community redevelopment
Source: authors

can reinforce its position by forming a legal entity, this will further influence its power to initiate, drive or participate effectively in the process. The 'knowledge-building' phase of the participatory process should ensure that all stakeholders have a shared understanding of the situation, the constraints and the available options. This stage may require an intermediary to act as 'honest broker',[8] enabling objective round-the-table negotiation and discussion.

POLICY IMPLICATIONS

The case studies investigated in the research covered a range of political, institutional and development contexts, highlighting different implications of the implementation of a mixed-use approach to core area development. The conditions that need to be considered in determining whether such an approach can be taken include physical criteria, governance factors, socio-economic issues and stakeholder attitudes. The role of local or central government in addressing any conflicting frameworks and attitudes and facilitating the process is of crucial importance. Conflicts within existing policy may necessitate the mixed-use development process taking place outside existing frameworks and policies (as a 'pilot' or demonstration project).

For instance, in Delhi all land and development rights are, in principle, publicly owned and vested in the Delhi Development Authority (DDA), a Government of India body. Cross-subsidization of low-income housing takes place on a city-wide basis, with the DDA using development of the more valuable, central sites to subsidize low-income provision in cheaper, peripheral locations. The Delhi Master Plan, which zones land use for the whole city, prescribes all development. The objective in the Delhi case study was to demonstrate not only that this policy fails to take account of the largely hidden – but significant – social and financial costs of relocating core area communities, but also that cross-subsidization at the local level can be made to work. Given public ownership of land, it is a relatively simple matter to institute an integrated, mixed-use approach. The main hurdle is bureaucracy and institutional inertia. Rigid planning policy works against the interests of the poor and the development of the sort of mixed-income and mixed-use neighbourhoods that occur naturally in the less-regulated areas of the city. The current policy results in the break-up of existing communities and relocation of poor households to peripheral housing estates far from the centres of employment. In the case of the Motia Khan site (Delhi), the Authority built four-storey flats on the outskirts of the city to enable relocation of the poor households. The relocation was planned for March 2001, but since completion the flats have lain vacant, as the low-income families say they cannot afford (and hence refuse to pay) the contribution that the Authority is requesting prior to occupation of the flats. In the case of Delhi, despite initial interest, further work remains to be done in convincing the DDA that a mixed-use approach, implemented through changes to planning guidelines and/or the use of site development briefs, can be economically implemented.

In Jakarta, the development context was particularly crucial. The research took place in the wake of the East Asian financial crisis of 1997 and the subsequent collapse of what had been a booming property market. In this context, the property development company with an interest in the study site was no longer in a position to continue with its gradual plot-by-plot site assembly and large-scale commercial 'clean sweep' redevelopment. In the post-crisis situation, the local authority has a potentially important role to play in facilitating site redevelopment and rehousing of the established low-income community in the medium term by encouraging land pooling and collective action. Thus the developer could be enabled to gain access more quickly and securely to those parcels of land critical for the commercial element of the proposed development. This suggests a need for a long-term planning strategy, allowing for phased redevelopment as market conditions become more favourable, but with strong community involvement in the process. In Jakarta, local government (an arm of central government) had already instituted planning gain rules requiring provision of a fixed proportion of low-income housing in new developments, but in the boom met resistance from the development industry. The tools developed in the research could enable local authorities to take a more flexible approach to planning gain, allowing for changing market conditions and adapted to local circumstances.

In Recife, a strong popular movement by the residents of informal settlements in the late 1970s, combined with democratic decentralization in the 1980s, resulted in the institution of a system for granting security of tenure. As in Delhi, such rights of occupancy have the tendency to 'lock-in' land values and make it difficult for land markets to work effectively. Moreover, even with upgrading, such settlements tend to remain sites of social exclusion and continue to be stigmatized and perceived as outside the 'formal' city. The inclusion of *favelas* within the formal planning system as ZEIS (Zonas Especiais de Interesse Social, special zones of social interest) reinforces this situation. Although the residents of Santa Teresinha had been granted leasehold rights to their plots for up to 50 years, constraints on the sale of properties imposed by ZEIS-specific zoning regulations prevent them from realizing the potential increases in the value of their land through partnership with the neighbouring shopping centre. This suggests that, as in Jakarta, the planning approach to informal settlements needs to be more subtle.[9] Alongside security of tenure, more emphasis needs to be given to allowing land markets to work, and to the long-term development of livelihood opportunities through community development initiatives.

The difficulties encountered during the course of the feasibility studies enables a number of the conditions which are necessary for the advocated approach to be feasible to be identified. These are summarized in Box 12.2.

Box 12.2   Conditions and criteria

Availability of appropriate sites

Sites need to be large enough to accommodate both rehoused residents and a significant level of commercial development.

Potential access and services need to be adequate to support new commercial development.

Potential to increase the density of development to accommodate as many of the existing residents as possible alongside new commercial development,

Positive attitudes of stakeholders

Commitment to the development objectives and a willingness to communicate and cooperate with the other stakeholders, as the process relies on a participatory approach.

Commercial development pressure

Commercial viability will enable cross-subsidization of low-income accommodation and community amenities.

Adequate financial capability of the low-income population

Ability to contribute at least a minimum towards the cost of their housing and community amenities.

Ability to access appropriate finance.

Ability of local government to accommodate and enable the process

Ability to adapt/override inappropriate policy mechanisms (planning, housing, funding, tenure).

Adequate inter-agency coordination.

Ability to deal effectively with the development of private land.

Adequate resources and political will to enforce developer compliance.

CONCLUSIONS

The sites investigated in the research reported here support the basic contention that low-income communities are threatened by commercial development in core areas. In the city studies, the central question addressed was what approach to development would enable low-income communities to resist commercial pressures and continue to live close to the source of their livelihoods within the commercial centres of these cities, without prejudicing commercial redevelopment and improvement. The feasibility studies and subsequent workshops suggested that mixed-use development undertaken at a higher density than existing informal settlements, incorporating a level of cross-subsidy from commercial development, can achieve the commercial returns required and also allow the rehousing of a significant number of existing residents on site. This approach to development in the core areas of cities can also ensure a level of social, economic and environmental sustainability.

Potential constraints related to attitudes and economics. Local government has a key role to play in facilitating such an approach, and could overcome some of the constraints by adopting an 'action planning' approach (with an outside organization as an intermediary), while enabling the community to take an active role in managing the development process and negotiating for their best interests.

The findings indicate that there are a range of land management mechanisms whereby stakeholders can arrive at a 'win–win' solution, in which the interests of low-income communities can be reconciled with those of the planning authorities and private developers (Max Lock Centre, 2002b). However, further work needs to be done on implementing the approach; its application in different contexts; and building interest in and the capacity to adopt it on a wider scale. Issues that still need to be addressed include:

- the extent to which governments and local authorities are capable of adopting the degree of flexibility necessary for the integrated development approach advocated
- whether low-income communities can realistically engage in such a process alongside more powerful stakeholders
- how to address and control any unintended gentrification impacts of the proposed redevelopment approach
- how to address the concerns of developers or landowners that mixed-income and mixed-use development is insufficiently attractive to the market and would therefore prove difficult to fund and might not achieve profitability.

While further investigation of these areas would enhance understanding and practice, the mixed-use participatory approach to core area development advocated in this chapter (and tested through research) represents an important step towards challenging accepted practice, in order to combat urban poverty and achieve sustainable development in both social and economic terms.[10]

CHAPTER THIRTEEN

Ambitious aims, persistent problems: an evaluation of low-income urban housing policy in Iran

M.R. Dallalpour Mohammadi[1]

INTRODUCTION

This chapter analyses the evolution of housing policies in Iran, distinguishing between the pre-revolutionary period, the period from 1979–93, and more recent housing policies. The outcomes are evaluated broadly for the earlier periods and in more detail for recent years. It will be seen that, to some extent, the evolution of housing policy in Iran has reflected broader trends in housing theory and practice, which moved from a focus on the construction by public sector agencies of complete housing units in the 1960s to the provision of serviced plots and upgrading of informal areas in the 1970s, and an emphasis on market enablement through concentrating on ensuring a supply of finance and land since the 1980s (Pugh, 1994). However, the ideological underpinning and content of housing policies in Iran was strongly influenced by the 1979 revolution, at least temporarily. Some aspects of housing policy have received more attention than others, including the organizational framework, the housing finance system, and land policy, and these are discussed in greater detail for each period, while neglected areas are identified.

HOUSING POLICIES BEFORE THE 1979 REVOLUTION

Programmes and projects

The low-income housing programmes that were executed by the pre-revolutionary government between 1945 and 1978 in Tehran and other cities suffering from serious housing shortages can be classified into four stages and types. The first programme provided complete houses, primarily for government employees. This programme targeted particular categories of employees, mostly those in middle- and high-income groups. In addition, it was concentrated in Tehran so could not fulfil the housing needs of many other state employees (Ahary, 1996). The second programme distributed public land to government employees so that they could build their own houses. It appears that, in many cases, the land was allocated to those who had no real housing need. As a result, the cities lost large parcels of land without any real contribution being made to solving their housing problems. The third programme, which started in 1963 and is still operating in a modified form, has been implemented through the Mortgage Bank. The primary function of this Bank was to provide credit amounting to 50 per cent of the total monetary value of a mortgaged property, for a maximum loan term of 15 years and an interest rate of 10 per cent per year (Khavidi, 1978).

None of these government housing programmes benefited the poor. As most poor families were not state employees, did not have steady jobs with fixed monthly incomes, did not have the considerable savings needed to make a down payment, and could not pledge anything to the bank in order to get a loan, they were unable to access the sites, houses or loans provided. The poorest took refuge in unauthorized settlements.

Although the planners who prepared the third and fourth National Economic Development Plans (NEDPs) (1962–67 and 1968–73, respectively) recognized that housing was a widespread problem, the percentage of planned investment devoted to housing was far from sufficient to resolve the problem. In fact only 5.6 per cent of the total investment for the third plan period was allocated to construction and housing, and the number of units constructed during this plan period was nowhere near adequate to overcome the shortages caused by accelerated rural–urban migration. Furthermore, these houses were not necessarily affordable by those in the low-income category.

In the fifth NEDP (1973–78), although the government paid more attention to the housing problem, the outcome remained the same. In this plan, about 64 billion Rials were allocated for the construction of housing for the three military forces and also to meet the housing needs of the Gendarmerie, police headquarters, Savak prisons and army officers, but only 60 billion Rials for other people throughout the country (£1 = 120 Rials in 1973). Although the government, after revising the fifth plan, increased its investment in housing to 230 billion Rials, an increase of about 155 per cent (Kayhan, 1974), the problem persisted because of political instability and increases in military housing expenses (Daneshmand, 1982).

In 1971 the Ministry of Housing and Urban Development (MHUD) introduced a Ten Year Housing Plan and comprehensive national housing policy, which used regional and urbanization criteria to define the overall strategy for housing development. Availability of credit, family income, urbanization needs and trends, agro-industrial development and cost of housing were the major factors taken into account in formulating the policy. The United Nations guideline of spending 5 per cent of GNP for housing was used as the financial goal during the period 1972–81 (Daneshmand, 1982). The objectives of the national urban housing policy were:

- to develop a housing programme for all income groups
- to improve sanitation and the social situation through housing

■ to develop housing units near employment locations for low- and middle-income workers
■ to build housing of a standard above a minimum level
■ to initiate an urban renovation programme
■ to build housing on land allocated in accordance with urban plans
■ to control the price of land which would be used for housing

(Spillane, 1972).

Although intended to be comprehensive, the implementation of the plan and policy failed to improve the well-being of squatter dwellers, low-income groups and industrial workers. The first five years of implementation was an era of active government intervention in housing. It was the first time that specific programmes had been introduced for the provision of low-income housing in Iran. However, data that would allow an assessment are unavailable. According to Khavidi (1978), between 1971 and 1976 only three public housing projects containing 1884 units were completed in Tehran. These projects, apart from being far from adequate to house even newly formed households, had a number of weaknesses. In many respects housing policy was improvised. The government reacted to problems only when they became overwhelming, and anticipatory policies were not adopted. Hence there was no effective institutional machinery to coordinate housing activities and programmes. In the end, housing policy was inadequate and inappropriate at both national and local levels. The enduring housing shortage in Iran was due to the fact that government housing programmes were unable to keep pace with rapid urbanization and fast population growth. The government tended to leave the field almost wholly to private efforts, restricting itself to the provision of a limited number of residential quarters for its officers. As Dehesh (1994) points out, the pre-revolution regime conceptualized housing as a social expense, and not as a sector capable of making a positive contribution to human and social development. In the following sections, some aspects of housing policy that received more attention than others (the organizational framework, the housing finance system and land policy) are discussed in greater detail.

Housing organizations

The first organization established in Iran for the purpose of solving housing problems was the Plan Organization in 1940. Then in 1964 the Ministry of Housing and Development was established, becoming the Ministry of Housing and Urban Development (MHUD) in 1974. In addition, the Worker's Welfare Bank operated a housing finance programme for all government workers, under the general supervision of the Ministry of Labour (Sevald, 1972). Although after the revolution of 1979 there were some changes in the organizations involved in public housing, MHUD is still the main government agency concerned with housing. It is responsible for preparation, implementation and coordination of all plans for building projects by the Ministry and other government institutions, as well as specifying standards for all housing projects. In 1974, it was also assigned responsibility for the supervision of all the housing and urban development activities of the private sector (MHUD, 1976). Thus, MHUD has both policy and operational responsibilities:

- general responsibility for the preparation and implementation of comprehensive urban physical development plans and linkages between sectoral investments and activities, including their location and the requisite infrastructure
- sectoral responsibility for housing for urban and rural development, as well as for supervision and provision of technical assistance to the construction and building materials industry.

The major area of concern before the revolution was the Ministry's failure to complete implementation of any master plans for cities with a population of over 25 000, although plans were prepared for about 95 urban areas (Daneshmand, 1982).

Housing finance policies

Before the 1979 revolution, the lack of a specific and coordinated policy to provide housing loans for low-income people was a major problem. Many of the bank and credit institutions had their own way of financing housing, their activities were not coordinated, and they were not managed effectively. The public banks and savings and loans companies would lend 70 per cent of the total price of a building to the buyer. Interest rates were controlled, giving rise to excess demand. These banks and companies preferred lending to the least risky borrowers, and what little mortgage credit was made available was channelled to rich customers with ample collateral. Low-income households and poor groups, who did not have the 30 per cent down payment, were excluded by such rationing.

Land policy

Before the revolution of 1979, land price increases, which formerly characterized Tehran, spread to other urban areas. The first reason was that, after the oil embargo of Arab countries in 1973, oil-producing countries in general, and Iran in particular, raised the price of oil. As a result both government revenue and incomes rose, the demand for urban land increased, and consequently its price went up. According to published information, land prices increased by 35 to 40 per cent between 1970 and 1972 (Mohammadi, 1990). The second reason for land price increases was corruption among top government officials connected with the previous regime. These officials were also the major landholders in large urban areas and, because of their social and political influence, most of the land regulations were interpreted or changed to their benefit.

A few years before the revolution, public opinion had been that, if repeated land transactions could have been prevented, the urban land problem would also have been solved. As a result of public pressure, the government passed the Act for Forbidding Repetitive Land Transactions and introduced a Land Transfer Tax in May 1975 (Kayhan, 1983). According to this Act, all the undeveloped land located inside the serviced area of cities (five-year service line) could be transferred only once to somebody else, and further transactions were not permitted unless the land had been developed. Transgressions were to be punished, and possession taken of the land by MHUD for future urban development (MHUD, 1976). As a result a major part of profiteers' investments, which were being spent on land transactions, were diverted to building houses and apartments, which were then sold at very high prices. The restriction on land transfers led to the purchase of derelict and old buildings by investors for reconstruction and provision of high-standard and luxury houses for the high- and middle-income groups, because of the large profits to be made. This process of demolishing buildings before they had reached the end of their life span increased pressure on the housing stock available for low income households on the one hand, and increased the price of housing available, due to the construction of high-standard housing, on the other. The imposition of taxes on land transactions did not work, because the taxes were levied by the Finance Ministry according to the current price of the land, which would sometimes show an increase of more than 200 per cent compared with the previous year. Although the tax was linked to the price of land, it was inconsistent with the government's objective of curbing land speculation. Payment of the land transfer tax was transferred from sellers to buyers, so taxes and land prices had a reciprocal impact on each other (Kayhan, 1983).

HOUSING POLICIES AFTER THE 1979 REVOLUTION

Introduction

After the revolution in 1979, a number of regulations and limitations affecting urban housing were lifted. Urban migrants were able to build informal dwellings without having them demolished the next day by government agents. The extensive growth of unauthorized settlement led to the adoption of a policy of control in 1981, which aimed to restrict further development of these areas. However, during the first two years after the revolution, given the availability of open land, new, spontaneous settlements appeared not only on the outskirts of the cities, but also in built-up sections along highways and adjacent to factories (Zandi, 1985). With respect to policy, the post-revolution period can be divided into two: 1979–93 and 1993–97. The policies and achievements of the two periods are analysed, with more detailed consideration given to the second. Lastly, the three key components of housing policy discussed above (organizational framework, finance and land policy) are also analysed.

Housing policies, 1979–93

The first step toward tackling Iran's housing problems was the establishment of the Housing Foundation in 1979, with responsibility for promoting and providing housing for low-income families. This Foundation, during the period from 1979 to 1982, provided 191 665 housing units for the urban poor throughout the country (Muhajeri, 1982). The next important step was the nationalization of urban land and the establishment of the Urban Land Organization (ULO). The ULO, from its establishment up to 1985, created an average of 150 000 plots per year, which were distributed to low-income people. The important housing policies that were adopted after the revolution were as follows:

- land for housing, under which undeveloped land was acquired by the government and allocated to beneficiaries at less than cost, or free
- sites and services, comprising the provision of land, with utilities such as water supply and electricity, and social services such as schools, clinics and markets
- upgrading and improving squatter areas
- constructing low-cost apartment units.

The supply system operated in two basic ways: first by allocating land or complete housing units to low-income households according to family size; and second by allocating land or complete houses to cooperatives to be divided among their eligible members.

A plan prepared for the period 1983–88 was not implemented due to the war with Iraq. In the 1989–93 period, NEDP housing policies were restricted to sites and services (*Amadehsazi*) and upgrading. The quantitative goal of the plan was to construct 1 582 000 housing units in the urban areas (316 000 per year; Dorkoosh, 1990). According to Danil (1997), between 1986 and 1996, 439 000 serviced plots were allocated and, by the end of 1993, 466 sites and services projects had been implemented on a total land area of 42 864 hectares. Housing units made available through sites and services projects between 1986 and 1996 comprised 38 per cent of housing construction. Although during this plan period an average of 200 000 plots were allocated per year (Rafiie, 1997), the number of completed housing units did not exceed 102 000 units per year (Kano, 1996). The implementation of sites and services as a main policy encountered the following problems.

- Lack of an established legal framework and lack of coordination between the responsible agencies.
- Misunderstanding of the ability of low-income groups to participate. While housing policy stated that the low-income groups were the target population, no real preference was given to low-income families.

In providing plots, fixed sizes were used rather than various options being offered.

■ Basic services and utilities were not provided by government agencies in an integrated way. Furthermore, in some projects infrastructure provision occurred after occupation by households, increasing construction costs.

■ Slow construction process: the planning time for these projects was intended to be two to three years; in practice, most took over seven years to complete.

As a result, not only was the target not achieved, but also middle- and high-income groups gained access to serviced plots. Low-income households, due to their inability to provide sufficient resources to build a house within the specified term (one year from the date of allocation) were forced to sell their plots. Although some restrictions were imposed in the early years to avoid such transactions, such as issuing title only after five years of residence, it did not stop informal speculation.

Housing policies 1993–97

In the second NEDP (1993–97), due to the expiry of the urban land nationalization law and the ineffectiveness of the revised law, as well as difficulties connected with the acquisition of publicly owned land, and the high cost of providing serviced plots, the general thrust of the plan focused on adjustments to housing markets and financial policies. The main reasons for the changing policy initiatives included the inefficiency of the housing market and limited effective demand. One of the typical characteristics of housing markets in rapidly growing cities is huge but not effective demand. Most people in need have no reliable financial resources, and therefore there is little incentive for private developers to invest in housing. Moreover, as the demand is ineffective and disorganized, no clearly defined relationships exist between users and suppliers in terms of operational criteria, cost components, and so on. The proportion of housing construction built for sale or rent by private developers during this plan period was very low (15 per cent). The residential consumer sector was characterized by traditional forms of construction, and limited capacity for professionalized and industralized ways of building. Central Bank of Iran statistics show that between 1986 and 1993 over 90 per cent of housing units were built by individuals and untrained labourers, while professional developers were involved in the construction of only 8–10 per cent of houses.

The main intentions of the second NEDP, therefore, were first to organize the housing demand and supply sides so that they could respond to each other; second to increase private developers' share of construction activities, therefore increasing the financial and technical resources available for housing; third to increase the proportion of rental housing; and finally, to reduce the average floor area of dwellings, in order to increase their affordability. The main strategies for achieving these aims were to promote production capacity in the housing sector and to provide houses for low-income families. In order to realize these objectives, the main policies were the provision of land and financial support and further controls on the housing market. These were based on three key concepts (*PAK*): saving (*Psandaz*); mass production (*Anbouhsazie*); and small-size buildings (*Kouchek-sazie*). The provision of three types of housing was recommended: free market housing; protected housing; and social housing. It was intended to build 2 590 000 housing units in the country as a whole. Urban housing was to comprise 60 per cent of the total. The shares of the public and private sectors were expected to be 5 and 95 per cent, respectively (Bagerian, 1994). The government intended also to lend over 150 billion Rials (£1 = 5000 Rials in 1993) to the Housing Bank every year for the construction or purchase of houses for government employees (Mirzadeh, 1995). The characteristics of, and targets for, each of the three types of housing are analysed in turn, followed by an assessment of progress.

Free market housing

This type of housing was built by the private sector for households with sufficient income, and received no governmental support. The public sector played an indirect role by issuing building permissions and taxation. This type of housing was to be 53 per cent of the total (828 000 units).

Protected housing

Protected housing was defined as a dwelling built according to the Consumption Criteria: a housing unit with a floor area not exceeding 100 m². The government contributions were to provide cheap land and low cost loans (interest-free, but to which the operational costs of administering the loans were added) and to subsidize utilities, such as water supply, electricity and gas. In fact, the purpose behind this policy was to encourage middle-income families to save and transform their housing need into effective demand. Individuals or companies building over 20 housing units of a certain size (a floor area of 50–75 m² in Tehran, Tabriz, Esfahan, Sheraz and Mashhad, and 100 m² in other cities) were to benefit from 5–8 per cent interest exemption. For this purpose 2159 billion Rials were to be allocated during the plan period. The target for this type of housing was 30 per cent of the total (476 000 units).

Social housing

Social housing was intended to respond to the housing needs of the poor. The average floor area of this type of housing was 50 to 75 m² in urban areas, and it was supposed to be financed by the government, banks, the Social Security Organization, the savings of households and the sale of bonds. Dwellings were allocated for rent, or for rent with provision for ownership. The proportion of social housing was intended to be 16 per cent of the total (MHUD, 1994). Both public and private sectors were to be involved in the construction of social housing. Housing cooperatives were also encouraged, with the basic structures and core house provided by the cooperative, and the house completed through the self-help of allottees.

Nothing was mentioned in the plan about the way in which the desired contribution by the different types of housing provision was arrived at. However, it seems that it might have been based on income distribution. For instance, about 20 per cent of the population earned between 200 000 and 400 000 Rials per month. The latter was the poverty line, while the minimum income required for participation in social housing projects was 180 000 Rials.

In the second plan, due to the constraints mentioned earlier, land allocation was restricted to new urban settlements and, to some extent, to upgrading areas in the centre of cities. Between 1993 and 1996, 290 000 serviced plots were allocated. Available data show that, by the end of 1996, over 650 000 housing units had been built. In the construction of 25 per cent of these dwellings, subsidized loans and low-cost land were provided by government agencies, while 75 per cent, including free market housing, was sponsored by the private sector. Although these figures represented considerable progress in increasing production capacity in the construction industry, they were still far short of the targets defined in the plan. In addition, they were based on high-technology solutions. It was thought that housing problems could be solved by mass building of mostly high-rise flats. The policy failed to recognize the complexity of pre-fabrication and industrialized housing systems. In addition, the construction of free market housing, mostly for upper-income groups, negatively affected lower-income families, by giving rise to increases in the prices of land, labour and construction materials. The important role allocated to the private sector was intended to redirect investment to construction from other sectors of the economy, and to slow down the rate of inflation, but it led to the construction of many luxury houses.

The government's aim of providing protected and social housing also relied on the participation of the private sector. By the end of 1996, 170 000 subsidized housing units had been constructed, of which 10 500 were social and the rest protected houses. These comprised fewer than 50 per cent of the targeted figures. Concerning the construction of protected housing, the main problem was the inadequate supply of land, and inefficiency of financial and technical aid. The costs of construction and providing services also increased. Therefore, the units produced were not accessible to the initial target population. The proportion of loans made available to buy a house rather than for construction of new housing increased by about 88 per cent annually between 1993 and 1996 (Rafiie,

1997). This increase in the number of loans, as well as in the total sum available for lending, had an inflationary impact on the price of second-hand housing and on other goods. The provision of social housing also faced problems, including the lack of incentives to private developers to invest in this form of housing, incompatibility of social housing standards with current planning regulations, and unclear priority criteria in identifying eligible households. Nevertheless, this type of housing was more affordable to low-income households than other types.

The policies pursued between 1993 and 1997 did not entirely achieve the objective of providing a decent dwelling for low-income families. The success of free market housing benefited people on high incomes. The policies emphasized size and quality and paid little attention to the needs of the beneficiaries and current planning regulations. Although the adoption of these policies was intended to control as well as encourage the housing market, implementation has been weak. In the following sections, changes that have taken place in the institutional framework, housing finance and land policy since the revolution are discussed.

Housing organizations

After the revolution in 1979, the Housing Foundation was established for the purpose of providing low-income housing. This Foundation was very active between 1979 and 1982. Later, following the approval of nationalization of urban land during the first parliament in June 1982, a new organization called the Urban Land Organization (ULO) was established. The Housing Foundation, which had given priority to rural development and coordination between rural and urban areas, focused its activities in rural areas. The main responsibility of the ULO was to take possession of unutilized urban land under the Nationalization of Urban Land Law and distribute it among homeless urban families. The ULO was very active until 1995, but then, due to the change in housing policies from land provision to mass production of small houses, it was merged into the MHUD. Changes in the administrative structure caused a lack of stability and continuity, and the resulting housing management problems affected programme implementation.

Housing finance policies

After the revolution, the Mortgage Bank of Iran and some 16 of the savings and loans companies were consolidated into the Housing Bank. Only the Worker's Welfare Bank and the Sepah Bank remained from the earlier period, with an obligation to provide housing loans only to specific groups. The credit and loan facilities of the Housing Bank increased from 37.6 billion Rials in 1978 to 610.4 billion Rials in 1992 (an average of 22 per cent a year). The average loan also increased 14 per cent a year, from 1.7 million to 10.8 million Rials, during this period. Similarly the Workers'

Bank's credit facilities for housing construction increased from 15.2 billion in 1978 to 56.3 billion Rials (an average of 9.8 per cent a year) (Bagerian, 1994). During the second plan period, the amount available for loans also increased, to 1.5 million and later to 2.5 million Rials. These Banks provided loans to owner-occupiers, either for building or buying houses, repayable in monthly instalments over 20 years with interest rates of 16 per cent. The Banks granted loans to government employees or to businessmen who were considered able to repay the loans. Although the housing policy gave strong support to achieving increased housing construction through the extension of loans to individuals with savings, many people were unable to save sufficient money and had to wait several years for loans to be granted.

Land policy

For all the reasons mentioned above, before the revolution low-income people were excluded from the formal land market. The arguments advanced after the revolution for the nationalization of land ranged from those based on broad ideological considerations to those urging the use of nationalization as an efficient tool to benefit the majority and achieve an immediate solution to the problem of urban land supply.

Between 1979 and 1987, three laws regarding urban land were enacted. According to the first law, the Urban Waste Landownership Abolition Law, passed in 1979, private ownership of all waste lands was abolished and this land was nationalized. The second law was the Urban Land Law, enacted in 1982 for five years. According to this law, the ULO could acquire land that was currently unused, but with a previous history of use. The third attempt was the revision and enactment of a new Urban Land Law in 1986 (Aziz, 1995). The government also gave landholders the right to keep in perpetuity 1000 m^2 of undeveloped land in large urban areas and 1500 m^2 in small urban areas, to be developed within a designated time. In addition, as mentioned previously, the allocation of urban land was carried out by the ULO, and urban land transactions not subject to regulations were prohibited. Land plots were allocated by the ULO for a payment sufficient only to cover the cost of utilities. Title was issued after five years, providing development had taken place. After 1986, when the Urban Land Law was revised and prohibitions on land transactions removed, land prices increased considerably. Although the law kept the right of priority in acquisition for public purposes, including housing projects, due to difficulties in the acquisition of land because of ever-increasing prices, land availability again became a critical factor in major urban areas.

The limited validity of the Urban Land Law, together with the exclusion of smaller tracts of land from nationalization and lack of an adequate management system to control the urban land market, are the main reasons for the unresolved problem of delivering land for the construction of housing, particularly to persons with low incomes.

Neglected areas

An appropriate national housing plan, apart from estimating the number, type and standard of dwellings to be constructed by the public and private sectors, should specify the sources and volume of funds. In addition, the amount of land, materials, equipment and manpower necessary for attaining these targets should be calculated, constraints on supply identified, and the manner in which they are to be made available explained. The ancillary infrastructure, services and community facilities required, including their estimated cost and timing, should be assessed. Finally, the agencies responsible for executing and/or financing certain components of the proposed programmes should be identified. National housing plans before and after the revolution have fallen short with respect to issues such as identifying key building materials and instituting support measures to promote the supply of materials, and making an inventory of skills available and required, with policies to address the shortfalls. The results, once rapid private construction was encouraged, were bottlenecks and rising prices. There were also major shortcomings in the arrangements for coordination of the institutions and firms most active in the housing sector. Municipal electricity, water, gas departments and so on operated under the supervision of different ministries. No specific policy statement or organization existed to ensure coordination of these institutions or, perhaps more importantly, to prepare national housing sector plans.

CONCLUSIONS

Urban housing, particularly for low-income families, has always been, and still is, an acute problem in Iran. The continuing housing deficit results partly from high rates of population growth and urbanization, but especially from the absence of comprehensive and appropriate housing policies. Before the 1979 revolution, no effective policies were adopted to tackle the housing problems of low-income households. Housing policies were generally designed in favour of government officials and did not benefit poor families. After the revolution, the government attempted to intervene on a large scale in the provision of housing for low-income people. The initial policies, basically involving sites and services and upgrading, were effective due to the availability of cheap land, resulting from the nationalization of unused urban land. However, other policies to increase supply and decrease the cost of housing had limited results.

Changes in policy in the 1990s were intended to bring about further participation of private developers in housing production and to create equilibrium in the housing market. Increased construction of free market housing resulted, mainly for high-income groups, and demonstrated private sector capacity for large-scale involvement in housing construction. Constraints on further increases in private sector construction included scarce managerial and entrepreneurial skills, inadequate land supply and delayed provision of public services. The realization of this goal had some adverse effects on achievement of the other aim, which was to increase the availability of affordable housing for low-income households. Construction of better housing for high-income groups negatively affected low-income people due to the rising costs of construction which ensued, because most trained labour as well as limited supplies of building materials were channelled to this type of building. There were no major changes in land and housing markets, and the new policies did not, in practice, succeed in increasing the affordable housing available to low-income families. The proportion of completed social housing units (in comparison to other types) was very low, due to the weakness of public sector construction capacity and bureaucratic relationships. Difficulties of land acquisition, provision of urban utilities and access to financial assistance also led to the protected housing strategy not achieving satisfactory results.

Although, in some respects, the policies pursued in the mid–1990s had major strengths, such as encouraging private sector participation in housing construction, their shortcomings – particularly limited success in the provision of low-income housing – should not be neglected. Bearing in mind the relatively important contribution of earlier policies, such as sites and services, in increasing the availability of low-income housing, it might be argued that it would have been better to address the shortcomings of these schemes than to replace them with other approaches. It has also been revealed in this chapter that, in accordance with successive housing policies, major changes took place in the institutional framework, financial arrangements and land policy. These changes, however necessary, were not permanent. The nationalization of undeveloped urban land expired after five years of implementation. Soon after, land prices and availability again became critical problems. The ULO, which had responsibility for providing land for housing, was abolished. Housing finance policy, apart from a relative increase in the amount available for loans and credit facilities, did not solve the problem of access for people who lacked a permanent occupation and reliable monthly income. Therefore it was clear that some aspects of the policies in force in 1997, particularly issues concerning the availability of affordable land and finance, needed to be rethought.

CHAPTER FOURTEEN

Developing appropriate housing standards and procedures

Theo Schilderman and Lucky Lowe

WHAT IS WRONG WITH CURRENT HOUSING STANDARDS AND PROCEDURES?

Current housing standards and procedures in many developing countries are inappropriate in a context of rapid urban development and decreasing resources. Many argue that a certain minimum standard of housing is desirable, for example to guarantee the health and safety of residents, but there is often disagreement about what that minimum level should be. In many countries, regulations were put in place by colonial powers, copied almost verbatim from those in force in the North. In many countries, this legal legacy has not been amended. Current housing standards and procedures in many countries are inappropriate because (Schilderman, 1992):

- they are not affordable, by individual households, local industries or countries as a whole; entire populations cannot be housed at the level of current standards
- being so often imported or imposed, they are not in line with local conditions, culture or building traditions, for example they fail to recognize that housing construction is more often an incremental process than a one-off exercise
- contrary to the International Organization for Standardization's definition, they are not based on consensus but are set by a small elite, and fail to take into account the opinions and priorities of major stakeholders such as consumers or local authorities, who may then be inclined to ignore them
- being specification-oriented, they restrict the materials and technologies that can be used, often favouring imported materials and skills; they do not encourage innovative or alternative materials or technologies that might be more appropriate and affordable, and do little to stimulate the local economy
- they are not user-friendly, as they are written in language accessible only to professionals
- building a house according to the procedures tends to be complicated, lengthy and expensive, which facilitates corrupt practices

■ standards and regulations are useless unless they can be enforced, usually the responsibility of engineers at local authority level; thus inspection becomes a constraint for authorities and residents alike.

It is clear, then, that a substantially different approach is needed to housing standards and procedures in poor countries. This has been recognized in many international and national policy documents, which have advocated public sector enablement of the private sector, such as the Habitat Agenda (UNCHS, 1997). Yet housing development in most countries is still framed by standards and procedures that disable a major proportion of the urban populace, the revision of which often remains very exclusive. It is for these reasons that the Intermediate Technology Development Group's (ITDG) international shelter programme is focusing on reforming legislative frameworks, in order to improve poor people's access to legal shelter and livelihoods. Work in this area started with an international research project funded by the UK Department for International Development, the outcomes of which are described in this chapter. Local researchers analysed recent housing standard revision processes in two countries, Kenya and Zimbabwe. They also checked urban residents' and other stakeholders' awareness and opinions of those standards. From this it emerged that it is not enough merely to revise standards to the benefit of the urban poor; in addition, a substantial effort is required to stimulate their uptake, and this is where NGOs such as ITDG can play a major role. Ultimately, the impact of the revisions was positive in both countries, although it was recognized that further revisions would be useful. These two experiences were compared with 12 case studies of revisions in other countries and with the global literature on the issue (Lowe, 1999). As a result, the team was able to identify a limited number of innovative approaches to the revision of housing standards, and to make recommendations related to revision processes, partnerships and alliances, and information and dissemination.

THE REVISION OF HOUSING STANDARDS IN KENYA AND ZIMBABWE

The process of revision

In Kenya, it had long been recognized that the existing by-laws governing human settlements were outdated. As a result of a review just after independence, in 1963, two grades of by-law were introduced by 1968, with the lowest applying essentially to the urban fringe. However, even this level was still out of reach to many of the urban poor. In Kenyan towns and cities, between 50 and 70 per cent of the population now live in informal settlements. A further review was commissioned by the government in 1979; this took place in the early 1980s, using a rather top-down approach, but its recommendations were never implemented. Faced with the unaffordability of existing standards, and under pressure from major donors, some local authorities did adopt lower planning and building standards for specific projects. Agencies involved in the development and promotion of innovative materials and technologies were also becoming frustrated by the restrictive standards, and began campaigning for change. A number of NGOs and academics became interested in the debate. In 1990, ITDG organized a national seminar to highlight and discuss constraints on revising the by-laws. This process led to the establishment of a task force charged with their review, whose members were drawn from the public sector, the private sector and NGOs. There was initial disagreement in the task force as to the extent of change required. Visits to informal settlements in Nairobi, exposing its members to prevailing popular housing standards, finally convinced the task force that a radical change towards performance standards was essential. A report was produced recommending standards that were flexible and allowed the use of inexpensive materials and technologies. Code '92, a set of amendments to the building code applying to low-cost housing, and a manual of 'deemed to satisfy solutions' were published in 1993 and disseminated, particularly to local authorities. They were gazetted by the government in 1995, after which they became known as Code '95 (Yahya et al., 2001, pp. 75–77).

Similar concerns about the decreasing affordability of the prevailing standards were a major factor in revising the standards in Zimbabwe. Although other agencies, such as major donors and NGOs, influenced the process, two key ministries mainly undertook the review in a top-down manner during 1992. The process was not lengthy, and failed to create ownership among other key stakeholders, even at lower levels of government. The standards remained prescriptive but did allow for a wider range of materials and reduced plot sizes. ITDG concentrated on creating acceptance of affordable building materials such as stabilized soil blocks and artisanal (farm) bricks (Yahya et al., 2001, pp. 100–102, 168–169).

Awareness and opinions among key stakeholders

Among the first research activities undertaken by ITDG, in 1996, were surveys that aimed to assess the perceptions of key stakeholder groups in Kenya and Zimbabwe. Researchers focused on consumers, producers and a range of professionals involved in housing in a total of 15 towns, using questionnaires, focus group discussions and in-depth interviews with over 700 individuals (Agevi and Yahya, 1997; Mugova and Musandu-Nyamayaro, 1997).

In Zimbabwe nearly 90 per cent of residents thought standards are necessary and useful for reasons of beauty, safety, durability and protection from poor workmanship. The small number opposing standards questioned their affordability and enforcement. In Kenya, the majority felt standards were desirable, though not relevant as they were living in illegal settlements.

While the key concern of professionals was quality, the majority of residents in Zimbabwe were of the opinion that plot size is a key issue, as is the need for a wider range of allowable designs and materials. In Kenya, residents' concerns focused on water supply, sanitation, space and accessibility.

Levels of awareness varied considerably between the two countries. In Zimbabwe, the lack of initiatives to disseminate the revised standards is evident from an awareness rate of only 9 per cent among households. In Kenya, 77 per cent of the households were aware of the existence of standards, and 56 per cent of the revised standards. More attention is paid to these issues in Kenya through bodies such as the Shelter Forum, which disseminates information through its network of 800 members using a variety of media. In Kenya, in particular, residents were disillusioned with public institutions. In both countries corruption and political issues undermine the credibility of the building control system.

Professionals were generally aware of standards and procedures, although few had been involved in their revision. They expressed concern that their opinions were not heard, yet were sceptical about wider involvement due to the additional cost and time this would involve. In addition, they perceived the revision of standards as a specialist task. Local authority staff were often informed directly about changes through centrally issued government circulars, and often felt revised standards had been imposed from above, despite the fact that they are adoptive at the local level. The resultant lack of local ownership means that revisions may be ignored by those responsible for ensuring implementation.

Towards wider uptake

It is not sufficient just to review standards. The experience from Kenya and Zimbabwe shows that their implementation has been rather ad hoc. This has been partly attributed to four factors: poor information flow; lack of institutional support at both local and national levels; inadequate resources; and administrative rigidities. The challenge of reforming legislative frameworks does not end with official recognition. An aggressive dissemination strategy is required to sensitize local authorities and the general public to the potential benefits that can be derived from applying revised standards. ITDG's strategy has included workshops for civic leaders and technocrats, trainers and community-based leaders; aggressive publicity through publications and the national media; and demonstrations. What follows is a more detailed description of some of these activities:

Participatory house type design and construction

Construction of demonstration houses was found to be essential in testing and demonstrating the viability of options permitted under the revised standards. While these enable cost-effective and efficient use of materials and building methods, they do not guide the builder on spatial arrangements, efficient use of the site, or appearance. This implies a need for architectural services that are accessible and affordable. The dissemination efforts in Nakuru, Kenya therefore sought first to involve consumers in the house design process, and second to intellectually equip artisans, technicians and draughtsmen to prepare designs for simple, single-storey buildings. While this may appear an obvious step to take, it was in fact rather innovative and risky as the architectural profession enjoys statutory protection in Kenya and professional architects therefore might resist such a move. In the event, the Municipal Council of Nakuru (MCN) was sympathetic, and it was possible to hold several training sessions with the help of the Architectural Association of Kenya (AAK) to develop a dossier of community-inspired designs, based on an extensive analysis of consumer needs.

In facilitating the participatory design of 22 demonstration houses, the project was keen to illustrate that, given the right conditions, community-based housing agents are best placed to articulate their preferences in the design of house development schemes. A demonstration project aimed at convincing professionals and consumers of the viability of alternative technologies enabled under the revised by-laws is shown in Figure 14.1. Such a shift from expert-driven to community-based organization (CBO)-facilitated housing designs is likely to contribute to more community-responsive models for affordable housing programmes. As part of the MCN's commitment to

Figure 14.1   Existing housing next to demonstration housing built in accordance with Kenya's revised by-laws in Nakuru Municipality
Photo: ITDG

the revised by-laws, it has also accelerated procedures and now approves housing designs within 30 days. Using simplified approval processes and appropriate building technologies, low-income urban communities are now better placed to gain access to decent, affordable and legal housing.

A handbook

While researchers in Zimbabwe also demonstrated the application of the revised standards by way of a few houses designed with residents in three locations, a local workshop of stakeholders also expressed the need to disseminate these in the form of a manual. The publication of a simple information booklet (Mugova and Musandu-Nyamayaro, 1998) and the dissemination of 3000 copies enabled individuals and local authorities to deploy existing resources by freeing up public sector staff time. The handbook in question answers a range of questions often asked by people on first approaching their local authority, creating greater awareness of the procedures to be followed. Provision of information directly to local people can reduce procedural costs by eliminating the need for intermediaries and enabling people to deal directly with local authority staff. It also reduces the cost to local authorities of answering enquiries.

Partnerships and alliances

The process of revising housing standards and procedures involves many individuals and institutions who can pool resources, learn from one another, and offer mutual support and encouragement. Although partnerships are a means to an end, they have now come to be regarded as a desirable goal in their own right because of their enormous potential for empowerment. Traditionally, partners in the shelter sector were government, consumers and delivery agents (such as local authorities, national housing agencies or contractors). The circle may be broadened to include NGOs, donors, private developers and researchers. However, such new institutional relationships are not without challenges, for example how to accommodate partners' various agendas, or variance in resource endowments and working cultures.

Projects and collaborative efforts usually start with inflated expectations on all sides. As time goes on, attitudes can change and roles become more clearly defined. Table 14.1 shows the collaborative activities and partnership web stretching across the shelter delivery scene in Nakuru. The range of stakeholders involved and their desire to create synergistic relationships are paramount in achieving change in the regulatory environment, and also in implementing revisions and making an enabling environment a reality. Consumers, investors, regulators and promoters are all key players in understanding the need for change, formulating new legislation, supporting it with the necessary resources, and ensuring that the political will exists to achieve sustained and sustainable change. The wide range of

Table 14.1 Collaborative activities

Stage	Activities	Partners
Changing the law	Identifying shortcomings Learning from others Reviewing codes Drafting legislation Passing legislation	Government, researchers, consultants, legal advisers, legislators, activists, donors
Sharing knowledge	Disseminating the rules Training Assessing technology	CBOs, local authority, media, training establishments, artisans, professionals
Enforcing the law	Simplifying procedures Streamlining control Tightening enforcement	Local authority, security forces, builders, CBOs, NGOs, landlords
Distributing inputs	Developing new designs Developing new materials and technologies Making land available Supplying services Providing mortgages	CBOs, NGOs, local authority, private sector, utilities, finance houses, savings associations, private merchants
Building	Supplying materials Constructing Renovating and expanding	Manufacturers, merchants, artisans, builders, local authority, NGOs, CBOs, individuals

stakeholders and interests in the built environment means there is plenty that can be done if partnerships can create understanding of each others' strengths, and clearly define roles for action by each. An example was the involvement of the AAK in participatory house design, showing its new-found eagerness to appear relevant in the fight against poverty.

One stakeholder group that can constrain the uptake of revised standards and associated materials and technologies is the financiers. In Zimbabwe, for example, building societies have refused to provide credit to prospective house-builders intending to build timber and terra block houses in Mutare. They have also spoken against the use of artisanal bricks. In Nakuru, financiers were specifically targeted, for example by inviting them to workshops and promotional events, in order to influence their perceptions of new housing options. New linkages between community savings groups and financiers like the National Cooperative Housing Union and the Kenya Rural Enterprise Programme have been brokered, resulting in financial agreements between these groups and CBO members. Workshops have been a key element in engaging academics, politicians, donors and NGOs in the debate, generating recommendations on approaches to the future revision of standards and engendering a sense of ownership among these influential stakeholders. Donors and international development agents can bring their influence to bear on national governments and encourage the uptake of pro-poor policy instruments.

Project experience in Zimbabwe and Kenya has shown that local councillors can significantly influence local uptake of revised standards and practices; yet reaching and influencing them remains difficult. In Kenya, newly elected councillors are given two days' training, of which maybe two hours will be spent considering the whole gamut of regulatory issues governing every aspect of life. It is not surprising, then, to learn that the subject of housing standards is not given much meaningful consideration. The limited term for which councillors are elected, as well as the absence of accessible local language dissemination materials, add to the difficulties of reaching this target audience effectively.

Collaboration with research establishments and standards organizations to increase access to scientific information has also proven significant in influencing professionals who might otherwise act as an effective barrier to change. For example, the MCN engineer was pleased to report the materials testing he had undertaken with local partners in order to prove the strength of stabilized soil blocks produced by local artisans.

Information sharing and training

Information sharing and training are important inputs into partnership-building. Artisans and technicians are key players in building local capacity to produce alternative building materials and construction services. Shortages of building materials have been found to be real barriers in accessing housing. Both formal training sessions and exchange visits increased awareness of available housing options, and built knowledge and skills to employ preferred technologies. An ongoing challenge is one of quality assurance, which is critical in the promotion, or can be instrumental in the demise, of alternative technological options. There are high levels of dissatisfaction with much low-income housing in Harare, for example, steel-framed houses in Kuwadzana or timber houses in Dangamvura. A combination of several factors has led to poor performance and/or overwhelmingly negative popular perceptions of the technologies concerned, which tend to affect views of all potential technological alternatives in the housing sector. In Nakuru, artisans are seen as key agents in supervising production and construction technology, to ensure that performance standards are adequate and longer-term viability assured.

Having an impact

In 1998, the Ministry of Local Authorities in Kenya was persuaded to relaunch Code '95 three years after it was gazetted, to create greater publicity and recognition. The Ministry informed all 167 local authorities about Code '95, and a year later 30 authorities had adopted the revised by-laws. In some locations, the project managed to motivate active involvement of low-income housing agents in the standards development and review process. As a result, the MCN introduced flexibility and speed into their building plans approval process, for example approving 50 plans en bloc. Project activities in Kwa Rhonda and other neighbourhoods of Nakuru have resulted in an increase in the housing stock, improved living conditions, increased incomes for landlords and artisans, and the uptake of new housing technologies. Additional impacts are summarized in the following section.

Poverty impact

Cost comparisons of the newly developed units as opposed to conventional buildings indicate that a 30 per cent reduction in building costs has been achieved in demonstration houses in both Zimbabwe and Kenya. Low-income households are now finding it practicable to mobilize resources for decent and officially sanctioned housing. Replicating the demonstration house nearby, a new home was built by a family in Chitungwiza, Zimbabwe for 30 per cent less than the cost of conventional technologies. There has been substantial replication in several locations in both countries; for example, in Nakuru 25 per cent of CBO members who had attended workshops, exchange visits or meetings organized by the project had started on improved house construction within a year. The increased demand for locally produced building materials and construction has created income-generating opportunities. Several groups or individuals are now involved in producing materials such as stabilized soil blocks, concrete blocks, concrete tiles, doors and windows, or in construction.

Empowerment

Participation by CBO representatives in group meetings, exchange visits and training workshops organized by ITDG locally and nationally have increased knowledge and confidence in the design and construction of affordable housing technologies. Above all, exposure to information on housing technologies and regulations has increased people's capacity to understand institutional requirements and procedures. In Nakuru, 42 per cent of CBO members who had participated in events organized by the project had shared the knowledge gained with others within a year. In addition, meaningful dialogue with partner agencies has enabled CBOs and artisans to present propositions for closer interaction with key partners, such as credit providers.

Gender impact

The national workshop held in 1998 in Kenya on housing standards highlighted the roles played by men and women in housing development and management (Agevi, 1998). Specifically, the event underscored the value of conducting gender analysis of housing needs in order to build on the skills of women, men and youth. Project teams have proactively involved both women and men in the planning and implementation of project support initiatives. For instance, during the participatory design of demonstration houses, the designers ensured that the preferences of both women and men were taken on board. Women's groups in three neighbourhoods of Nakuru have established savings and credit schemes for housing, and several women are making plans to build. One of the shortcomings recognized at a national workshop in Kenya in 1998 still appears to be the inability to select and train young female designers and artisans. In Zimbabwe, however, several women's groups are deriving benefits from building materials production for the informal sector.

Sustainability

Housing agents interviewed in both countries agreed that lasting and innovative technologies using local materials, as well as effective partnerships, were key factors in sustaining project results. An additional factor in Kenya was cost-sharing by CBOs, and in Zimbabwe a reduction in plot sizes. Trained artisans will be key actors in ensuring technical sustainability via peer training. In terms of organizational sustainability, the project's activities have had the effect of enhancing CBOs' capacity to design, plan and organize house improvement programmes. One CBO in Nakuru has mobilized members' savings to buy several block presses; the group is currently producing stabilized soil blocks for its members and has developed an income-generating strategy. In addition, an umbrella CBO, the Nakuru Affordable Housing and Environmental Committee, has emerged and developed into a key partner of both the local authority and external development agencies. There also has been a remarkable transformation in the MCN's Engineering Department, which increasingly interacts with and responds to the needs of housing agents in low-income settlements. Furthermore, the Council's commitment to keeping up the momentum of the implementation of revised by-laws is evident in its ongoing policy of approving house designs within 30 days. In Zimbabwe, momentum has been generated through the dissemination of the handbook and via partnerships between ITDG and the Housing People of Zimbabwe, the Civic Forum on Housing, the municipalities of Marondera and Chitungwiza, and the Ministry of Local Government and National Housing (MLGNH). These organizations have the capacity to sustain the activities initiated by the project. The MLGNH is embarking on a participatory review of plot sizes and infrastructure standards for housing development, thereby addressing the long-term need to review standards continuously.

Environmental impacts

Environmental sanitation issues have, in designated areas of Nakuru, been the mandate of Localizing Agenda 21, a key partner with whom ITDG has maintained close working relations. Area committees often mobilize residents to conduct clean-up campaigns. Partner agencies have also trained CBO members in solid waste management and sanitation. In its agreements with housing agents, ITDG is paying as much attention to the design and costing of latrines and soak-pits as to the construction of demonstration houses. Stabilized soil block production still poses a challenge in that holes may be left behind; it has been suggested that these could be used for soak-pits or latrines. The negative aspects of previously used materials, such as asbestos cement sheets, are substantially reduced by the use of less energy-intensive and environmentally degrading materials such as stabilized soil blocks or micro-concrete tiles.

THE REVISION OF HOUSING STANDARDS ELSEWHERE

As part of this research, ITDG analysed more than 350 documents (Lowe, 1999) and commissioned case studies of the revision of housing standards in Egypt, Uganda, Botswana, Malawi, Zambia, South Africa, Senegal, Jamaica, China, Sri Lanka and India, as well as a study of the development of regional standards for earth construction in Africa. The global trend in human settlements policies suggests increasing awareness of the importance of an enabling regulatory framework in addressing the growing need for adequate and affordable shelter. Despite good intentions, however, there is plenty of evidence to show that the actual impact of standards has been at odds with their intended impact. They have marginalized people, resulting in millions of houses being declared 'substandard' and thereby illegal. Revisions have occurred only sporadically in poor countries, perhaps due to a lack of resources and political will. While there are numerous examples of revision on a project-by-project basis, few have been scaled-up to the national level. Where political backing exists at the highest level, and resources are focused on the needs of the poor, standards can enable people to take control of the building process, resulting in affordable and adequate shelter and infrastructure. Some promising examples follow.

User-led standards

Sri Lanka's Million Houses Programme is perhaps the most extensive example of a people-led housing process, in terms of both its geographical reach and its duration. Standards were established by way of a people-centred approach, facilitated by professional and technical support staff. The Urban Development Authority made provision in its laws for reduced standards in settlements designated as special project areas. A reduction in minimum plot size, from 150 to 50 m², fitted the limited land availability. Other basic minimum rules include: 'no-one should build beyond his or her plot boundaries and all plots must have a minimum open space of two feet at the front and back'. Building codes specific to a settlement were formed by some 20–25 participants in a two-day workshop; in which three to five resource people and 15–20 community members (with at least seven women) addressed a range of questions about the building regulations and how they should be enforced. Subsequent to the initial community action planning workshop, half-day issue-based workshops were organized to consider any subject a community wanted to raise, such as planning principles and technical guidelines, or community building guidelines and rules. This process put the urban poor in the driving seat, with the state acting as supporter and partner (Sirivardana, 1999).

Incremental development

Where the urban poor cannot meet standards at the outset, an incremental approach can help. In Jamaica, the Association for Settlement and Commercial Enterprise for National Development (ASCEND) is a national coalition of private, public and non-governmental organizations which was formed in 1993 to examine and address the issue of providing shelter for people living below the poverty line. In 1996, ASCEND's working committees produced a series of manuals aimed at assisting in the planning and development of low-income settlements: a Starter Standards Manual; a Community Development Manual; an Affordable House Types Manual; a Beneficiaries' Policy Manual; and a Beneficiary Selection Policies Manual. The Starter Standards aim to ensure rational use of community (and external) resources in incremental settlement development. The Manual was prepared on the basis of detailed discussions with government agencies, professional associations, and local and overseas consultants. A separate guide has been developed to enable self-help builders by providing 60 small house designs which can be personalized (McHardy, 1998).

The concept of incremental development can be applied in various ways. It can be used to allow a house to grow in size from a small core; this concept has been applied in various countries, including Zimbabwe in the 1992 revision. Incremental development can also apply to improving quality over time, as for poor people size often matters more than quality initially; this concept was applied to the Traditional Housing Areas of Malawi, where it did not entirely match expectations (Okonkwo, 1999). Moreover, it can work to improve the existing housing stock, as in the upgradable plots approach in India.

Incorporating innovation

The reduction of housing costs is often hampered by the fact that more affordable materials or technologies are either not standardized, or not listed among those that are allowed within prescriptive standards. A regional approach may help to overcome the time-consuming and costly development of new standards. This was what CRATerre-EAG did to introduce Compressed Earth Block standards in Africa (Lowe, 1998), driven by a desire to ensure that affordable building with earth was not discredited through poor performance, and to support national initiatives by eliminating research and development costs, avoiding duplication and thereby increasing acceptability and market access. The participatory approach evolved in order to overcome strong opposition at the national level, and to create consensus and ultimate ownership of the outcomes. South Africa, on the other hand, has adopted agrément certification, much used in France, for example, which aims to demonstrate that innovative materials and technologies are fit for a certain purpose. Its Mantag certification is particularly geared to low-income housing, and is based on four simple principles: the evaluation of fitness for purpose is based on essential health and safety considerations only; it provides technical information to help builders, owners, authorities and others to assess suitability; the assessment includes the feasibility of incremental upgrading; and it is meant to include self-help building methods (Kraayenbrink et al., 1998).

Simplified procedures

De Soto (1989) wrote that it took 43 months to obtain a piece of state land in Peru, in a process involving 207 bureaucratic steps. To obtain the necessary building permits and develop the plot took another 40 months. Needless to say, this was also a costly process. Based on the recommendations of De Soto and his Institute for Freedom and Democracy, the Peruvian government adopted a much simpler property regularization policy at the national level. In 1996, they established COFOPRI (La Comisión de formalización de la Propriedad Informal), a commission to regularize informal property. With support from the World Bank, a massive land-titling effort began, and today COFOPRI claims to have issued 1 million new titles to previously informal properties (Turkstra and Kagawa, 2001). According to Turkstra and Kagawa, COFOPRI had such a huge impact largely because it focused initially on government land on the outskirts of coastal towns in Peru, which was basically unoccupied desert. But Camaiora (in Durand-Lasserve, 1996) also attaches importance to the decentralized organization of the new body, and the simplicity of the procedures it adopted. By taking services into the settlements and engaging with residents, the system developed in response to feedback from trials involving all stakeholders, remaining simple, efficient and accessible. Improvements to housing have followed regularization.

CONCLUSIONS AND FUTURE DIRECTIONS

This final section highlights the conclusions that have emerged from the international research. It also offers recommendations for the next phase of interventions perceived as critical in meeting the universal goal of adequate shelter for all. These reflections have been grouped into those concerning the processes of revision; partnerships and alliances; and information and dissemination.

Processes of revision

- The revision of housing standards reflects political and policy rhetoric focused on improving people's living conditions and reducing poverty.
- Revision is not a one-off event, but should be an ongoing process.
- The process requires champions: a core of committed and knowledgeable reformers. It creates its own momentum; once it is under way, it is possible to push for progress.
- Genuine concerns about health, safety and potential hazards must be addressed in a professional manner, as they are likely to evoke emotional reactions and move the debate to the political arena.
- Appropriate standards are required not only for housing, but also for services and facilities at neighbourhood level. While planning regulations exist and are extensively used, their synchronization with emerging dwelling standards is far from satisfactory. For example, they often forbid the incorporation of economic activities in houses and even in residential neighbourhoods, or fail to provide suitable guidelines for the regularization of informal settlements. Land titling procedures also need to be simplified.
- Whereas most stakeholders would agree that standards and procedures are useful and important, they do have different priorities. For example, where authorities and professionals seek quality and effective control, residents tend to favour space, a wider range of options and speedy procedures. Review processes need to deal with such varied interests, but also to redress the balance between the opinions of dominant professionals and residents, as demonstrated in Sri Lanka.
- Enabling standards should limit the elements decided centrally to a minimum, and devolve more decisions to the local level; a move towards performance standards would be part of this.
- Particular attention should be paid to increasing the options available to low-income residents and builders. This will require work on the standardization or inclusion of hitherto unstandardized or innovative technologies, such as building with earth; regional collaboration and the agrément system are two ways of taking this forward.

Partnerships and alliances

- Review processes to date have benefited from considerable external support. Thus the question arises whether, and how, future efforts can be localized. It is essential to build national capacity to resource and sustain continuous revision of housing standards, but given that government resources are declining, that will not be easy: all the more reason to develop partnerships.

■ Although much has been said and written about participation, the concepts and techniques are still developing. It remains a challenge to engage all stakeholders in meaningful reviews. To allow a greater voice for the concerns of low-income dwellers, builders or materials producers, pressure is needed on the stakeholders who now control them; coalitions of like-minded individuals or organizations have achieved a degree of success.

■ At the national level, investments in terms of funds or international expertise must be accompanied by political commitment and relentless prodding by concerned activists and reformers.

■ Donors must contribute more than money. They can guide policy orientation, supplement technical expertise and internationalize revision efforts.

■ NGOs such as ITDG can play a role as catalyst in moving revision processes forward and strengthening dissemination efforts.

■ Major revisions to legislation governing the built environment are undertaken at the national level, but effective operationalization is very much a local affair. Writing a technically competent code is only half the battle; it is necessary to win the minds and imaginations of those who build.

■ Recognition is an important issue for public officials who often feel ignored and underrated. While consultants and NGOs may receive monetary benefits, officials may have little to show for their efforts, although they may have been the ones who initiated and directed the whole process. Committees can grind to a halt because of inadequate compensation for members.

■ A key group, which is insufficiently heard in most review processes, is local authority staff. They are pivotal, because they are often sceptical about centrally imposed rules and decide whether to adopt or change centrally developed standards or procedures at the local level; they are the link between authorities and dwellers, where participation should begin; and they control the implementation of standards and procedures. However, the resources of local authorities are often stretched, and this needs to be taken into account when developing standards and procedures.

■ Participating communities and institutions need clear definitions of goals, objectives and roles. An approximate time frame is also useful as delays cost money and sap commitment.

Information and dissemination

■ While the revision of legal instruments is a major step forward, it marks the beginning of a new struggle to get them adopted and implemented throughout a country. This task can be more challenging than the revision process itself, and requires a great deal of effort in marketing changes in the standards.

- The research surveys highlighted the need for proactive and imaginative interventions by concerned individuals and groups to help municipalities to popularize the new codes.
- Residents need to be convinced of the quality of alternative technological options, via appropriate information and demonstration, backed by detailed financial analysis possibly using the life cycle approach. However, existing financial information is usually rudimentary and grossly inadequate.
- Information and training packages for various community groups and stakeholders are important, while a clear communications strategy is essential. An important activity is the packaging of new provisions into user-friendly and comprehensible formats.
- Demonstration projects designed and implemented by ITDG in collaboration with municipalities and CBOs yielded enormous benefits, in terms of enabling poor people to access affordable technologies; simplifying plan approval procedures; introducing improved sanitation; promoting house-building and ownership among women; increasing design capacity in local communities; and strengthening the organizational and management capacities of CBOs.
- Reviewing standards and procedures takes a great deal of time and resources, which developing countries can hardly afford. Access to information on developments elsewhere, as well as regional collaboration on specific standards, can reduce costs.
- There appears to be a lack of information across the board. Residents are often ill-informed on current standards or available technological options enabling compliance with them. Local authority staff have little exposure to innovative solutions, and play safe by going for known technologies. Professionals rarely hear about examples of best practice elsewhere. It is important for relevant information to be exchanged internationally and for local information providers to reach the whole range of stakeholders concerned.

In conclusion, the process of reforming the regulatory frameworks affecting shelter development is complex and lengthy. It requires the establishment of partnerships and alliances pushing for change that will benefit the poor. It is ineffective to stop when revisions have been gazetted, as a major effort of dissemination, which may include working closely with low-income communities, is required to raise awareness and demonstrate what the revisions mean on the ground. Above all, it is important to monitor the impact of revisions and feed information back into a continuous process of change.

CHAPTER FIFTEEN

Public–private partnerships in urban land development

Geoffrey Payne

BACKGROUND AND CONTEXT[1]

The starting point for any discussion of partnership approaches to urban land development has to be the increasing disenchantment with the ability of either direct state provision or unrestrained market systems to satisfy ever-increasing social needs. The collapse of communism in eastern Europe and the recent economic downturn in south-east Asia have served to reinforce awareness that alternative approaches are needed in countries at all levels of economic development, but particularly in developing countries, where the gap between needs and resources is greatest. While this issue affects all key development sectors, none is more affected than land and housing.

Within the rapidly expanding cities of developing countries, the demand for land is without historical precedent. Many metropolitan centres accommodate more than 10 million and are increasing by up to 1000 people a day, while many smaller cities are doubling in population every decade or less. It has been estimated that, in India alone, approximately 600 000 hectares, or enough land to accommodate 20 more cities the size of Mumbai, will be needed within the next 20 years to accommodate the projected increase (von Einsiedel, 1995). It is hardly surprising that this level of demand has placed conventional methods of supply under intense pressure. Public sector land acquisition, land nationalization and development controls have all been tried in order to stimulate the supply of land for approved uses, yet hardly any city can claim to have met demand on a long-term basis.

The ever-increasing attraction of land as a source of secure and profitable investment has intensified a commercial market system to the point where urban land in some cities is well beyond the affordability of even middle-income households. In Mumbai, prices rose so fast that in early 1996 the city could boast (if that is an appropriate term) land prices that were among the highest in the world. Although prices fell to a more sustainable level during the late 1990s, they are still far higher than most local people can afford, and many other cities are now finding that access to land is the greatest single obstacle to the improvement of urban living conditions (UNCHS, 1993, p. 61).

As land has become increasingly commercialized, even areas that were previously considered marginal (along railway lines or drains, or on the sides of steep hillsides) have acquired a market value, reducing future options for access by low-income households. The potential value of public landholdings has increased, so that the opportunity cost makes their allocation for low-income groups difficult to sustain when the need to raise revenues and put land to economically productive use is almost irresistible. Such pressures have led to several recent instances in Mexico City, Dhaka, Manila, Rio de Janeiro and Santiago where the government has evicted well-established communities on the grounds that the land they occupy can be put to better use, for example as conference centres or for highways.

Estimates of the proportion of people excluded from formal land and housing markets vary widely. Durand-Lasserve (1996, p. ix), for example, suggests that an average of over 40 per cent internationally, and between 15 and 70 per cent of the urban population in developing countries, are unable to access land and home ownership through formal channels. Improving access to land markets is therefore a prerequisite for improving the housing situation and economic prospects for low-income populations.

The ethos of public sector agencies is often based partly on the assumption that they should compensate for the failure of private housing markets by providing directly for those in need. Whilst this is well intentioned, it fails to take into account the large numbers of those in need and their low incomes, thereby putting public supply systems under intolerable pressure. By acting as developers, government agencies have invariably failed to meet their goals of providing land or housing for more than a token proportion of those in need. In some countries (especially in sub-Saharan Africa), land nationalization was adopted to control land markets, while in others, such as India, Sri Lanka, Egypt, Mexico and Tunisia, attempts were made to regulate markets more tightly (Durand-Lasserve, 1996, p. 51). Both approaches have failed because of a lack of support from key urban actors, inadequate human and financial resources, or simply because of bureaucratic inflexibility and corruption. At the same time, the formal private sector has shown little, if any, inclination to address the needs of low-income households, leaving informal developers, mafia gangs and low-income groups themselves to fill the gap.

In many countries, the gap between the public and private sectors is wide and deep, and reflects cultural as well as practical differences. Despite the limitations of public sector projects, many officials still regard themselves as the protectors of the poor against what they consider a regressive market system. Viewed from the other side of this chasm, private sector developers often view the public sector as incompetent, inflexible and corrupt. In most countries, landowners dread the threat of compulsory purchase by local authorities who offer compensation levels well below the potential market value of their land. Official standards and procedures are often so inappropriate to levels of affordability that it is impossible for private developers to both meet social needs and conform to official requirements. Delays in processing proposals and the cost of obtaining permissions erode profit margins, forcing many developers to increase prices to stay in business.

Against this background of mutual distrust, an awareness is gaining ground that new approaches are required, based on ideas that work in practice and enable all parties to satisfy their legitimate interests. The current impasse has made it clear that neither the public nor the private sector on its own is able to address, let alone resolve, the problem of housing an increasing urban population. This recognition is the first step in paving the way for innovative approaches through which the roles and relationships of the two sectors, together with third sector groups such as NGOs and community-based organizations (CBOs), can be radically transformed.

Public–private partnerships are, therefore, being widely promoted, for several reasons.

- It is now generally recognized throughout the world that direct government supply of urban land and housing has proved ineffective and unsustainable in meeting varied needs at the scale required.
- Increasing globalization of the world economy reduces public sector options and makes some form of partnership an effective option for influencing urban land markets. (This may be considered both positively, as a more effective approach; or negatively, as an option of last resort).
- Their incorporation as a central element of the Habitat Agenda agreed at the City Summit in Istanbul in 1996.
- The private sector is considered to be more efficient than the public sector in meeting diverse housing needs, based partly on the assumption that competition will filter out inefficient or unresponsive suppliers. It is also regarded as more efficient than public sector agencies in achieving high levels of cost recovery. Many people see government as having a responsibility to help the less affluent, to the point where many in receipt of government assistance do not consider they have an obligation to repay costs, especially when they see others fail to do so with impunity.

TYPES OF PARTNERSHIP

There are currently a wide range of partnership arrangements in the fields of finance and credit (e.g. UN, 1978; Lloren, 1991; Munjee, 1992; Mitlin, 1993; UNCHS, 1993, pp. 61–71) and infrastructure provision (e.g. Gidman et al., 1995; Batley, 1996). Surprisingly, less attention has been paid to initiatives in the field of land development (UNCHS, 1993, p. 60), even though land is a precondition for any housing development.

The first comprehensive review of public–private partnerships was published by UNCHS. This stated that partnerships can be taken 'to mean more than a simple link or interaction between two or more actors in the shelter process'. Partnership implies (UNCHS, 1993, pp. 9–10):

- an active and deliberate process, even if the activity of the partners consists of *not* doing something, for example not imposing controls on land or rents
- a process of working together in a mutually interdependent fashion, often with shared responsibilities . . . The most successful partnerships are those in which each partner derives something beneficial, and gains access to something that it does not have from the other partner or partners in the relationship.
- a common agenda and goal, even if the interests, benefits and powers of the partners differ
- a relationship in which accountability and transparency are crucial.

The report goes on to say that responsibilities may vary, and there is certainly no need for successful partnerships to be equal in terms of investment or effort, although they do imply a deliberate commitment on the part of the actors involved to contribute something distinctive towards a common goal – adequate shelter for all. The examples reviewed include land sharing, land pooling and readjustment, allocation of public land for development by third sector groups, development corporations made up of public and private sector interests, and concessions to planning regulations to attract private investment.

Concern over the need to stimulate a partnership approach was also reflected at the Delhi Conference on Security of Tenure, held in January, 1996 (UNCHS, 1996a). During this conference a working group on formal private sector participation, including public–private partnerships, was organized, which produced a set of guiding principles, including the following.

- Partnerships based on principles of equity, economy, efficiency, flexibility and participation can lead to better land management and greater access to land and security of tenure.
- Effective partnerships between government and private business and landowning sectors need to be fostered through facilitating access to land, and land development opportunities for these sectors.
- In current forms of such partnerships, redistribution of value added benefits is inequitable and to the advantage of speculators/brokers
- The role of governments should be to inspire, enable and facilitate formal private sector initiatives through an appropriate policy framework, rather than to involve themselves in project implementation.
- NGOs are well placed to mediate between communities, governments and private sector actors.
- Capacity-building for communities, local governments and CBOs is needed to ensure their effectiveness in land management.

■ Mechanisms for formal private sector participation should be designed to ensure that they include access to land for the urban poor and other disadvantaged sections, and partnerships should take cognisance of any impediments affecting women or particular groups.

Partnership initiatives have a long tradition in many industrialized countries. They were part of the New Deal in the USA in 1932, and were established in Canada and the Netherlands by the late 1960s (UNCHS, 1993, pp. 27–50). They were adopted increasingly in the United Kingdom during the 1980s, examples including the formation of joint enabling agencies, with variations in objectives, membership, organization and resources. Some were the result of initiatives by private development companies, which took advantage of new public policies to increase the role of the private sector; others were initiated by local authorities, which sought to protect their interests against central government policies. These initiatives have not all been exhaustively assessed, and there is considerable scope for reviewing their relevance to contemporary urban problems in the cities of the South.

The UN review provides a good working basis for further analysis, especially in its emphasis on relationships rather than formal contracts. However, the examples cited are relatively formal, public and, sometimes, contractual relationships between the partners. This issue of definition is of more than academic relevance. Several observers (e.g. Baker and Sims, 1991, p. 32; UNCHS, 1993, pp. 60–61; Edwards, 1995) suggest that formal partnerships have been limited in scale to date, and have had only a modest impact on low-income access to land. This may well be because the definitions used have excluded less formal associations, arrangements, partnerships or relationships between the public, private and community sectors. A more useful definition would be a recognized working arrangement that addresses the interests of both public and private sectors in developing land for housing. This more inclusive definition can include arrangements that, while not within the conventional definition of formal, transparent relationships, directly address the needs of low-income groups.

It is clear that there are a number of ways in which informal relationships or arrangements have evolved between the public and private sectors, in which both sides are fully aware of the impact of their actions and act for a perceived mutual benefit. For example, officials in local government may find it easier (and more profitable) to relax regulations and official standards than to change them, so that private developers can develop land at standards that people can afford, and still make an acceptable profit (Box 15.1). In other cases, public agencies may turn a blind eye to the unauthorized subdivision and development of land, and eventually provide such settlements with services, knowing that such action is more effective than direct state provision in helping low-income groups.

Box 15.1   Examples of partnerships in India

Many examples of innovation in relationships between the public and private sectors currently exist in India, and some have been operating for many years. These include Town Planning Schemes, based on British planning practice; Participatory Development Schemes, by which the private sector is permitted to undertake large-scale land development in return for the provision of a social housing component; land compensation schemes to benefit Project-Affected Persons; and Transferable Development Rights, by which private landowners in areas where development is restricted are compensated by disassociating development rights from their existing plots and issuing transferable development right certificates for use in other approved areas. Another example is the Slum Redevelopment Scheme recently introduced in Mumbai, whereby the commercial private sector, together with slum cooperatives and NGOs, is offered land-based incentives to upgrade existing slums.

Inevitably, these approaches cannot address, let alone resolve, all the problems facing India's expanding cities, and some depend on a buoyant land market. However, they are proving a realistic, generally progressive weapon in the armoury of those responsible for regulating urban land and housing markets and seeking ways of enabling low-income groups to gain access to land for housing, as well as a range of other benefits for the wider urban community.

In Navi Mumbai, or New Bombay, the City and Industrial Development Corporation (CIDCO) found an effective way of encouraging the participation of local villagers in developing the new city. Instead of offering compensation for their agricultural land under terms that have traditionally evoked strong opposition, they offered a combination of cash payments at existing use rates, and a number of developed plots in the subdivided urban development, according to the size and value of land acquired. So attractive were the terms offered that some farmers have become rich. The positive aspect is that the principle of this approach has now become very popular – the downside is that expectations have been raised and demands have increased as a result. Managing these expectations is, therefore, increasingly the critical element in managing the programme.

CIDCO has also exploited the popularity of trains as the major means of travel into and out of Mumbai to develop commercial projects above and adjacent to railway stations and, until recently, was recovering sufficient funds from selling these to pay for the capital costs of the infrastructure. Unfortunately, the recent collapse of land prices in central Mumbai has dramatically reduced the demand from commercial enterprises to move to new, lower-cost locations such as Navi Mumbai, so that many new properties are lying empty and returns are falling.

Finally, an example of what can be achieved by the Slum Redevelopment Scheme can be seen in central Mumbai, where a cooperative has implemented a project with support from a local architect. Squatters were living in basic huts near a main road. Although the land had a potentially astronomical value, it could not be developed with the squatters in residence. An agreement was therefore reached between the landowner and the squatters, by which the local authority granted planning permission for a large commercial housing scheme to be developed along the main frontage (Figure 15.1), on the understanding that sufficient area would be left to construct blocks of small apartments for the squatters, who would become legal occupants. This land-sharing project cemented good relations between the parties to the point where residents in newly valuable apartments decided not to encash their new-found wealth by selling out, and instead opted to create a community fund to finance the education of children in the settlement. While this example is probably the exception, rather than the rule, it clearly demonstrates some of the potential benefits of a partnership approach.

Figure 15.1   The planning authorities allowed the landowner to develop the maximum commercial units on the main road frontage as part of a land-sharing project in Mumbai
Photo: G. Payne

A further example of such an informal partnership is the guided squatting approach, or incremental development concept, which has been adopted in Hyderabad, Pakistan and Conakry, Guinea (Durand-Lasserve, 1996, p. 63). Guided land development has been particularly effective in sub-Saharan Africa (e.g. Guinea, Cameroon and Rwanda before 1994), where it has helped to overcome obstacles to developing land held under customary tenure. This was achieved by associating customary owners with all phases of the operation, from the choice of site to the development and sale of plots (Durand-Lasserve, 1996, p. 65). The approach has also been applied in Lima, Peru. In Mexico, joint ventures between *ejidos* and the private sector have been implemented for many years (Varley, 1985; Jones and Ward, 1998, p. 15). One common practice involved private developers acquiring *ejido* land in return for making private land of equal value elsewhere available to the occupiers. In practice, the valuation of the *ejido* as 'agricultural', even when it was adjacent to an urban area, allowed the developer to acquire a large quantity of prime land for less than the market value. Many partnerships have also involved the provision or sale of public land, as a means of attracting private sector investment in land development and housing construction.

Such tacit partnerships maintain the fiction of official norms, while permitting more realistic responses and, if maintained on a long-term basis, might evolve into a form of sustainable, de facto partnership. In practice, many of the actions undertaken by the public sector are within the spirit of the Habitat Agenda, in that they involve inclusive, participatory forms of land development and management to the benefit of all sections of society, particularly the poor. While including such informal arrangements may be stretching the concept of partnership to its limits, it remains true that possible forms of collaboration between the public and private sectors represent a continuum that needs to be more fully understood.

All this is not to imply that informal partnerships are preferable to formal, transparent ones. The informal sector provides as many examples of exploitation, manipulation and inefficiency as other forms of development. However, it exists largely because the regulatory framework which determines official standards, regulations and administrative procedures is all too often inappropriate to the social, cultural, economic and environmental realities of developing countries. Under such conditions, the inability or refusal to reform such standards, regulations and procedures forces lower-income households into the informal sector, and leaves a range of informal arrangements or partnerships as the only viable means of assisting them. In cities where the authorities are interested in adopting a partnership approach, attention should be given to assessing the need for reform of the existing regulatory framework, so that partnerships can be developed at a large and sustainable scale.

The essential quality partnerships embody is that of complementarity, in which the relative strengths and weaknesses of each partner are offset against each other to produce developments that combine the best attributes of each, namely developments that are economically efficient, socially responsive and environmentally sustainable. However, it is likely that the concept of partnerships means different things to different people. To some, it may be a series of discrete projects; to others, a way of doing business. While acceptance of such variations may be necessary in winning support for the concept, it does present problems in defining and assessing examples. These issues can be resolved only by assessing the objectives and outputs of different approaches.

ISSUES INVOLVED IN PUBLIC–PRIVATE PARTNERSHIPS

An approach that involves redefinition of the role of the state and its rela-tionships with the private and third sectors raises several major issues. A central one concerns the reason why partnerships are adopted. If it is seen by the public sector as representing the only effective means of maintain-ing an influence over land and housing markets, or by the private sector simply as a means of extending its share of total supply, any partnership is likely to be of limited impact and duration. Such an arrangement would be a marriage of convenience between partners speaking different languages. While self-interest is an essential element, partnerships should be seen as offering each party benefits that cannot be achieved when operating inde-pendently. Partnerships will not be sustainable unless they are founded on such recognition.

A first step in this process is for actors from each sector to understand and acknowledge the legitimate interests of the others. For the public sec-tor, this involves protecting the wider public interest, and particularly the needs of vulnerable groups such as those unable to gain access to the legal land and housing market (Box 15.1). The state is also ultimately responsible for maintaining an effective and appropriate legal, policy and administra-tive framework within which other actors can operate on equal terms – the famous 'level playing field'. In theory, this means drawing up and monitor-ing contracts, regulating contractors, preventing monopolies, coordinating suppliers, and informing consumers and other groups of their rights and responsibilities. In practice, the state is never a disinterested onlooker and invariably favours some groups over others, so that many groups find themselves kicking uphill over bumpy ground. For the private sector, the primary interest is to maximize returns on investment, while minimizing costs and risk. For commercial developers, investment will be defined pri-marily in terms of finance, while for NGOs, it may be seen in more social or political terms.

However, improved understanding is an insufficient basis for partner-ships, and may even be seen as reinforcing opportunities for control over the other sector, rather than cooperation. The common antipathy between public and private sectors will require a major shift on both sides – for public sector agencies to become more market sensitive, and for the private sector to become more socially responsive. Formal private sector developers will have to accept a social responsibility for working in areas that involve lower profit margins and undertaking mixed developments that benefit lower-income groups. At the same time, public sector staff will need to relate proposals to prevailing market conditions and the resources of their target populations. As Durand-Lasserve (1996, p. 52) notes, this requires a better knowledge of how land markets operate, and the changing relationship between demand and supply. Training mater-ials, based on the findings of sound research, can help officials to under-stand the implications of such factors, while examples of successful partnerships can help build confidence in establishing more productive relationships.

The mechanisms essential for making such adjustments may not yet exist in some countries (Asobur et al., 1991, p. 318). As Batley (1996, p. 749) notes, the adoption of a market-enabling role may also bring transaction costs associated with the control and coordinating roles which government has to assume, and a full assessment of privatization should take into account the cost to government of undertaking these new roles, and its capacity to do so. Research on such transaction costs would help prepare the ground for new partnership approaches.

New roles will also require new rules. These will vary from one level of government to another, with central government creating the policy, legal and administrative framework within which local authorities can create a range of partnerships to suit local conditions. Striking the right balance, and adapting it to changing market conditions, will not be easy. Failure to adapt the administrative system would render partnerships more a public relations exercise than a transformation of government roles in land development. Action at both levels will therefore be vital if past experience with the sites and services approach is to be avoided. Instead of signalling a greater role for developers and residents in housing provision, these remained as a series of discrete projects, often undertaken by a separate unit in a land development agency and with minimal impact on the wider operations of urban development authorities. According to Gore (1991, p. 209), the site-specific nature of early partnership projects in Britain limited the contribution they were able to make to the overall regeneration of an area. For partnerships to escape this cul-de-sac and permeate institutional corridors will require a greater effort of will at both national and local levels.

Responsible officials and the wider public will also need to be reassured that procedures are formulated to ensure a modicum of transparency and accountability. This is difficult enough for elements such as infrastructure provision, where variations in unit costs are relatively small within a given city. However, land is unique in that its value or market price varies dramatically from one parcel to another, depending upon location, tenure status and site conditions. The propensity of land to attract substantial investment from the informal economy also provides ample scope for abuse. The task of formulating administrative procedures that are able to provide both consistency and flexibility will therefore challenge the most capable administrators.

Another issue concerns the tendency for local authorities to offer a relaxation of official regulations or standards as a contribution in kind towards a partnership approach. This has the attraction of being a cost-free means of attracting private investment and increasing public sector leverage over developers, and several examples are presented in this chapter (see, for example, Box 15.1). However, the scope for such relaxation is proportional to the extent to which such standards and regulations impose requirements (and costs) that conflict with market trends. In this sense, the more unrealistic, complex and expensive the regulatory framework, the greater the scope for selective relaxation. Under such conditions, relaxation may increase the leverage exercised by a local authority and enable it to maintain the fiction of official regulations, although such practices may virtually remove the incentive to reform an inappropriate regulatory framework. Any system that depends on the perpetuation of outmoded and unrealistic regulations as a front for a series of deals with private sector groups runs the risk of institutionalizing inefficiency and corruption.

In partnerships between the public and formal private sectors, some form of contract will generally be required in order to clarify the roles of each partner and the distribution of investment, risk and benefit. This presents several issues. First, how can contracts adopt an administratively manageable form and yet still allow for the uniqueness of different sites and partnership arrangements? Second, how can the opposing needs of transparency and commercial confidentiality be met? Third, how can contracts be enforced when the state itself is one of the interested parties? Contracts may not be feasible when a partnership is between public agencies and informal sector developers, which are the largest single channel for urban land development in many countries. As most of the latter will be operating outside the officially sanctioned norms, it is understandably difficult for agencies to support what are seen as illegal activities or groups. This makes the issues of transparency and accountability even more difficult to resolve, although it does not mean that benefits may not accrue to all parties, including those in need of housing. Research covering the outcomes of different contractual arrangements would help to identify parameters for satisfying the priority interests of key partners.

Whether contracts are applied or not, the ability of partnerships to succeed in areas occupied by, or designated for, low-income groups presents a major practical problem. The potential for commercially attractive returns will be lower in such areas, and development will therefore require a greater public sector contribution to ensure viability (Durand-Lasserve, 1996, p. 60). Yet these are the main areas in which partnerships are required, as commercially attractive areas can be developed by the private sector without external intervention. To date, the ability of the state to provide the necessary level and types of support at the scale required is, at best, unproven. Even if such investment is available, the value of the final development may increase to a level that either puts it out of reach of poorer households, or requires subsidies to ensure their access. The latter, in turn, add to market distortion. This issue is likely to be of particular relevance in cities where public authorities hold areas of land in, or adjacent to, prime central locations. In such cases, should a local authority sell land at the full market price for private sector development and use the revenue generated for other projects targeted at low-income groups, or should it forgo such revenue in order to enable poorer households to live in central locations near employment areas? Assessment of the options should include the costs of any direct and/or indirect subsidies to arrive at a 'true' cost.

Speculation, and the desire to prevent it, is another common objective of public policy dealing with land markets. Just as subsidies are intended to enable households to obtain land and housing they would not be able to afford at a market-determined price, so attempts to control speculation have sought to reduce market prices to facilitate market access by the poor. Public–private sector partnerships offer a means of avoiding this problem, by encouraging developments that maximize 'added value', but incorporate elements that enable a proportion of the (speculative) increase to accrue to the wider community, or to specific groups defined as deserving by the wider community. Realizing the potential benefits of this approach will, however, require public sector agencies to reassess planning policies, particularly those relating to development control, and to revise them in ways that can facilitate a partnership approach. Case study research on examples that have succeeded in balancing the need for commercial viability and accessibility by low-income households possibly represents the area of greatest potential value for lesson learning by policy makers and partnership project designers.

Finally, partnerships will contribute to more sustainable forms of urban development only if they can demonstrate an ability to satisfy the primary needs and interests of all key stakeholders, especially the intended beneficiaries. Procedures will, therefore, need to be developed to identify and address these needs and interests, and to formulate criteria that can be used in assessing the costs and benefits of each development. This is not a process that should be restricted to either the public agencies or private developers, but would need to include representatives of NGOs and community groups.

CRITERIA AND CONDITIONS FOR SUCCESSFUL PARTNERSHIPS

Recent research on partnerships in land assessed examples according to the extent they had:

- increased the supply of urban land for housing
- improved the efficiency of urban land markets in effecting both transfers and development
- improved access to land for low-income groups
- provided the basis for a more productive relationship between the public, private and third sectors.

The research revealed that successful partnerships are likely to embody:

- an efficient way of identifying different and changing needs
- adequate trust between partners

- clarity concerning the purpose of the partnership and individual roles within it
- adequate leadership
- the ability of each partner to fulfil their roles
- adequate access by all partners to essential information
- the availability of necessary financial and other resources
- compatibility with the prevailing political and legal climate
- the potential for wider application.

Inevitably, any partnership development will achieve more success in meeting some objectives than others. The list above should therefore be regarded only as a framework. For example, some partnerships have succeeded in improving land market efficiency, but have resulted in increasing land costs which, in turn, reduced low-income access to land (Durand-Lasserve, 1996, p. 57). Despite its reputation for overbearing bureaucracy, India has generated a range of partnership initiatives (Box 15.1) which have opened up new possibilities for managing the process of urban growth and meeting the needs of low-income groups within market-led urban land development. While not all these initiatives are completely successful in meeting the criteria outline above, they provide a valuable basis for future progress.

This suggests that the issue of whether any sectoral activity is best undertaken by the public, private, or other sector, or some partnership between them, should be determined not on the basis of political dogma, so much as on the nature of the activity concerned and the local considerations which apply at the time (Batley, 1996). This, in turn, suggests that regular reviews should be undertaken by all agencies in the field of urban development, to stimulate a wide range of supply options and assess the costs and benefits of each. The first question that needs to be continually asked is: What is best value? The second question should be: How do we define best value? Each stakeholder will probably have a different definition of what constitutes good value, and it is difficult to identify a single set of parameters by which performance, and therefore success or failure, can be measured. Any assessment should therefore attempt to include political, social, cultural and environmental factors, as well as financial and economic ones.

The roles of central, regional and local government will need to be identified and revised within this framework. As argued throughout this chapter, it is also important that the concept of partnerships should be widened to include a wide range of stakeholders, including developers, landowners, NGOs, CBOs and local residents. On this basis, attention should be directed to creating multi-stakeholder partnerships, rather than the conventional and narrower public–private partnerships. Successful partnerships will be those that recognize the primary interests of each partner and balance the strengths of one against the limitations of others. Although partnerships will never solve all problems, they can improve urban governance by giving the poor and vulnerable a voice, and making decision-making more transparent and flexible. The essential value of a partnership approach should not be measured in terms of whether or not a particular example is successful. The need to change institutional cultures and working practices is not a short-term task, but a long-term challenge – cities cannot realize their economic and social potential unless they meet the needs of *all* their citizens, not just the wealthy and powerful. That is why it is important to make an early start.

CHAPTER SIXTEEN

Conclusions: some building blocks for sustainable urban settlements

Carole Rakodi

In the first section of this conclusion, the main findings that emerge out of the diverse contributions are summarized. The overall contribution of the collection is then reviewed, and some further research questions identified. Finally, a number of key principles or criteria that might constitute some of the building blocks of a more environmentally and socially sustainable approach to urban development are identified.

COMMON THEMES AND FINDINGS

The first part of the collection is concerned with the potential contradictions between economic growth and environmental sustainability at different levels, and the form and effectiveness of regulatory frameworks which are intended to ensure that the environmental impact of urban development processes is mitigated. In all the cases, the difficulty of achieving a balance between diverse economic, environmental and social interests is stressed, although the weight and importance attached to each varies between situations and actors.

In both China and Thailand, although there is a formal commitment to sustainable development, in practice the priority at both national and local levels is economic growth, and the institutional framework for environmental management is weak and uncoordinated. In Shanghai, Shaw and his colleagues observe that, although the new industries being attracted to locate in the city in large numbers do not generate high levels of pollution, many existing industries are highly polluting. Environmental management objectives are set for the city as a whole by the Shanghai Municipal Environment Protection Board, which is part of the municipal government, but many of the tasks are devolved to lower levels of local government which compete with each other for economic development. As a result, the effectiveness of regulation is reduced by the difficulty of ensuring vertical and horizontal coordination. In Thailand, likewise, despite the presence of legal requirements (in this case for environmental impact assessment, EIA), the process of regulation is uncoordinated, with development and pollution control systems running in parallel to EIA requirements. As a result, Pimcharoen and Shaw conclude, although quality assurance mechanisms ensure that good EIA statements are produced, these often have no impact on the decision to construct a particular project. Because the development control process operates separately, permission is often given and construction started before the EIA is conducted. Only mitigation measures can be included, and even for these, enforcement is weak. Because EIA is not integrated into the decision-making process at an early stage, it does not function as an anticipatory tool able to prevent or mitigate adverse environmental effects, and moreover is seen by project proponents as an unnecessary bureaucratic hurdle, containing conditions to be ignored when inconvenient. Until there is both political and administrative support for stricter environmental regulation and better integration of various regulatory systems, they conclude, it is unlikely that the achievement of environmental management objectives will improve.

Hameed and Raemaekers also stress the lack of consistency between land-use planning, development control and pollution control. They conclude that a regulatory framework for housing and industry is gradually being put into place in Pakistan. They suggest that in future there is potential for achieving greater compliance than at present, because government and foreign direct investment are susceptible to pressure to meet higher environmental standards. However, any such improvement is likely to affect only large-scale industry, leaving small-scale industry located in close proximity to housing, 40 per cent of which is itself unregulated and built in locations close to industry so that its occupants can gain access to jobs. Such residents have little influence on industry's waste management practices and, in any case, the scope for pressurizing such industry to comply with regulations is constrained by the limited space and finance available to the small manufacturing plants.

Tipple, Coulson and Kellett are also concerned with the potential contradictions between poor households' ability to access income-generating activities and the quality of the environment in which they live. They note that home-based enterprises, comprising a great variety of manufacturing and service activities, are regarded with disfavour by the regulatory authorities because they are seen to generate poor working conditions, impinge on scarce domestic space and harm the residential environment. Drawing on studies from Cochabamba, New Delhi, Surabaya and Pretoria, they show that the benefits that low-income residents, especially women, derive from being able to make a living from or use the services provided by home-based enterprises outweigh any environmental concerns they raise. They conclude, therefore, that regulations which prohibit the use of domestic space for business enterprises are inappropriate, because home-based enterprises are congruent with the needs, priorities, practices and attitudes of most residents. Instead, income-generating activity in the home should be taken into account in regulations relating to permissible/desirable plot and dwelling size, affordability calculations and infrastructure provision, in order to provide residents with a wider range of choices.

The contributions in the second part of the book are concerned with the need and prospects for producing lasting change in a quest for more environmentally sound, equitable, socially empowering and culturally acceptable patterns of urban development.

As in the earlier chapters, Brand's starting point is the contradictions between a free market economic growth model based on taking advantage of globalization and environmental aims. The social conflicts and contradictions that arise out of such a model of economic growth include greater inequality, privatized social welfare, and increased crime and violence. In this situation, the ability of local government to ensure social welfare and safety has been whittled away, in turn reducing its legitimacy. Because city government no longer has sufficient leverage over work and services, in the case of Medellin it has focused instead on 'space', or the local environment. By concentrating on developing a shared vision, values, policies and actions for the environment, Brand suggests, the city government has used the discursive, institutional and financial resources of sustainable development policy to help contain social conflicts and restore social harmony. Social relations have been redefined environmentally through the affirmation of a biological collective identity, stressing the vulnerability of all residents to environmental risks and calling on common environmental values. Although the effectiveness of the environmental action that ensues is not his main concern, it does depend, he suggests, on obtaining wide support for the common values and actions identified through such a discourse.

Rakodi is also concerned with organizational capacity, but in her case for poverty reduction rather than city-level environmental management. She argues that the process of developing sustainable capacity at municipal and community levels is as important as the content of policy. For municipal services, regulatory functions and targeted interventions to be appropriate, they need to be based on a sound understanding of the characteristics and causes of poverty and deprivation. To ensure this, residents need to be able to articulate their needs and assert claims on resources through the political and administrative systems. Despite the difficulties, therefore, systematic local administrative structures are needed, in 'communities' or at a sub-city level of government, as well as state and non-state organizations with the capacity both to respond and to weigh the claims of various local groups and competing policy objectives to ensure viability and equity. Imposition of standard models of representative democracy and traditional project-based innovation are rarely sufficient to achieve such outcomes, so need to be complemented by opportunities for direct democracy and a process approach to project design, implementation and learning. Given existing organizational weakness and the complexity of urban situations, incremental change building on existing capacity is more likely than dramatic transformation to produce structures, processes and actions that can achieve lasting poverty reduction.

Jenkins also considers means for achieving appropriate and lasting pro-poor policy, in his case for housing. What are needed, he suggests, are political and institutional mechanisms that connect poor households with the state. In particular, he analyses the potential role of civil society organizations in mediating and interpreting the needs and demands of households to policy makers. The outcome depends both on the characteristics of civil society in the country concerned, and on the type of regime. Where both the state and civil society are weak, he concludes, there will be serious obstacles to developing appropriate and effective policy. In South Africa and Mozambique, attempts to reconcile the demands of organized political groups and wider society seem to be leading to the development of authoritarian regimes supported by technocratic elites, in which civil society is either subordinated through consociational structures or incorporated only in specific institutional areas. The way forward, Jenkins suggests, is to strengthen civil society to ensure that the needs and demands of the wider population, not just organized interests and elites, are reflected in policy.

The next two chapters are both assessments of attempts to do just this. Lopes and Rakodi assess whether the aim of strengthening community-level organization is realistic, or merely romantic. Taking the example of community-based organizations (CBOs) in Florianópolis, Brazil, which had had support from an NGO for a period some five years previously, a systematic set of dimensions or indicators of empowerment was developed and used to assess whether lasting community capacity had been developed. The study concluded that, because of the approach taken by the NGO concerned, the ability of communities to obtain access to new resources had improved. These resources were material (land, water, electricity, etc.); social (defensible life space, social organization and social networks); and personal (an individual sense of potency). Residents were enabled, with NGO support, first to challenge practices regarding the allocation of land to low-income populations, and subsequently to negotiate in the political sphere, initially for access to secure tenure, services and infrastructure, and later in the wider political process through participatory budgeting.

Smith is much less positive in his review of an attempt by the state, with external assistance, to strengthen 'community self-management' in a large, low-income settlement on the edge of the capital city of Costa Rica. Community self-management was, in this instance, he asserts, used as a means of stabilizing an increasingly explosive and unmanageable situation, and reducing the public resources required to meet low-income housing needs. Portrayed as opening up 'space for negotiation', community self-management was in fact largely a process of co-optation, to overcome social unrest and increase state legitimacy with relatively limited resources. It did not develop either lasting capacity for community self-management (because the support depended on external resources which were, in any case, available for only three years), or the ability of low-income residents to make claims on the government. One of the key differentiating factors between the outcomes described appears to be the wider political context, which was more favourable to community organization and demand-making in democratizing 1990s Brazil than in Costa Rica.

In the final chapter in this section, Al-Naim emphasizes that, for the urban living environment to be appropriate (culturally acceptable and socially suitable), it is important to reflect social structures and relations in the organization of the physical/home environment. He demonstrates how, although cultural values and family structures change in response to economic change and are threatened by changes in the physical environment, they are deeply embedded, even when they are not recognized by contemporary housing policy. As a result, even an unsuitable built environment may be adapted to increase its acceptability.

The third part of the book continues this theme of change and adaptation. It focuses on the process of development and transformation of the urban built environment, paying particular attention to the public and private actors involved in managing the development process, with the objectives of ensuring that the built environment is environmentally sustainable and more suited to the needs of poor people.

Romaya argues for as much attention to be paid to managing change in the built environment as to accommodating new growth, identifying a range of issues that need to be given more attention in the quest to achieve more environmentally sustainable development. He suggests a planning process and a specific tool, the sustainability matrix, that could be used to mainstream sustainability objectives in all levels of urban planning, and to assess the impact on sustainability objectives of development proposals. Lloyd-Jones and Carmona are also concerned with the transformation of the built environment, advocating an approach to core area development or redevelopment that can utilize the potentially high land values of undeveloped or illegally occupied inner-city land to provide low-cost housing for poor residents whose livelihoods depend on their inner-city location. Such an approach depends, they suggest, on government being willing and able to mediate between private landowners and poor residents to achieve win–win outcomes, as well as the availability of appropriate support for the residents concerned from public or NGO sources. As in Tipple et al.'s earlier contribution, both Romaya and Lloyd-Jones and Carmona advocate mixed uses, primarily in the interest of poor residents' livelihoods, but also because of their contribution to the vitality and interest of the urban environment.

Dallalpour Mohammadi's review of evolving housing policy in Iran finds that shifts in housing policy (particularly the radical reforms after the 1979 revolution and a further set of changes in the mid–1990s) were accompanied by major changes in the institutional framework, financial arrangements and land policy. However, rather than learning from experience and introducing incremental changes to consolidate gains and overcome problems, policies and organizational arrangements were often overturned or reversed. The new arrangements and policies made only limited contributions to solving the problems, and sometimes exacerbated them.

While this review is comprehensive and wide-ranging, the remaining contributions are concerned with particular aspects of housing policy. Schilderman and Lowe's starting point is the frequently inappropriate regulatory environment for producing low-cost housing, which reduces the chances of low-income households being able to access legal housing.

They advocate a process of producing and institutionalizing change that will win support from professionals, residents and builders, build capacity to sustain an ongoing process of revision at the national level, and be implementable. Such change processes need to involve all stakeholders, be backed by key actors (such as local government professionals and politicians), and potentially be supported by donors and NGOs playing the role of catalyst. Schilderman and Lowe reinforce the messages of earlier contributions by devoting considerable attention to the need to develop understanding and acceptance of the new regulatory processes and standards, in order to institutionalize new practices.

Finally, Payne identifies innovative approaches that bring together public and private sector actors, together with NGOs, CBOs and local residents, to overcome the problems typically faced by low-income residents trying to access urban land – bureaucratic public systems and increasing prices. Arrangements for collaboration, he suggests, need to be based on an understanding and acknowledgement of the legitimate interests of other parties; the generation of benefits for all concerned that cannot be achieved by working independently; transparency leading to trust; and ongoing commitment even if a particular partnership experiences problems. The aim of such partnerships should be to make available the resources of the private sector (finance, land) in areas attractive to low-income residents, with public backing and support to provide incentives where the commercial returns are uncertain. One of his examples is land-sharing, on which Lloyd-Jones and Carmona's model is also based. However, he also notes first that, given the variety and complexity of local situations, models cannot simply be transferred from one city to another; and second that the changes to institutional cultures and working practices implied by new alliances between public and private actors constitute a long-term challenge.

CONTRIBUTION, LIMITATIONS AND RESEARCH QUESTIONS

This volume is a major addition to the debate about how to increase the contribution of human settlements to sustainable development. However, it is neither a definitive nor a complete guide. The principles outlined below are soundly based in the experience and evidence reviewed by the contributors, although many are not new. Most attention has been given to meeting economic, social, cultural and political needs. In the introduction, the environmental impacts of urban settlements were noted as the use of resources and generation of waste. Relevant objectives should focus on first, minimizing the use of non-renewable and sustainable use of renewable resources; and second, minimizing or managing waste in appropriate ways, especially not overtaxing natural sinks for waste disposal. Many of these issues have been touched on this volume. For example, Romaya and Schilderman and Lowe pay some attention to resource use for construction, and the early chapters consider pollution and waste-management issues arising from industrial development. However, these issues are not analysed systematically, and none of the chapters is centrally concerned with programmes to clean up or reduce air or water pollution.

The difficulty of achieving a balance between economic growth and environmental goals is not a new debate. The contribution of this volume is to review some of the issues from the point of view not just of government policy-makers and industrial operators, but also of low-income residents who live in close proximity to industrial and other enterprises, in their neighbourhoods or homes, and for whom the livelihood benefits of this proximity generally outweigh the adverse effects on their living environments. This is not to say that regulation is not needed, but that it needs to be sensitive to the importance of location in livelihoods. However, transportation in all its guises (user of resources, generator of waste, determinant and result of land use and travel patterns) is not discussed systematically in this collection.

The volume also contributes to ongoing discussions about the appropriate level for exercising regulatory functions. Shaw et al. argue for a stronger municipal framework to prevent local autonomy contradicting higher-level objectives which have environmental as well as economic concerns, and to ensure consistency. Tipple et al., on the other hand, argue for greater local autonomy for land-use and development control with, in low-income neighbourhoods, permission being based on agreement by residents rather than a formal plan prepared at a higher level. The advantages of such local decision-making in relation to the dangers, including possibly a lack of transparency, objectivity and even-handedness, needs further discussion.

The contributors emphasize the importance of developing sustained capacity to deal with environmental matters, urban management, poverty reduction and appropriate policy formulation and implementation, at local and municipal levels, and in public and civil society organizations. Most stress that this is a far from straightforward process, because capacity can be destroyed by political change or economic crisis, while it is relatively slow to develop in many cases because of the need for new ways of working and attitudinal changes. At each level, not all the relevant issues have been addressed in this volume. For example, none of the contributions deals systematically with issues of water and sanitation, and although the importance of the political system to building sustainable settlements is mentioned by many, the precise political arrangements and their outcomes are discussed by only a few.

Inevitably, many of the contributors identify outstanding questions to which they are unable, on the basis of existing knowledge, to produce answers. In addition, questions arise about how far one can generalize from findings in one city, and the wider applicability of an approach tried in one situation. For example, it would be interesting to know whether the mobilization of environmental values and meanings has had a similar role in cities other than Medellin, and whether it has resulted in more effective environmental management in Medellin and elsewhere by gaining political and public backing for the environmental policy agenda of environmental improvements and increased regulation.

Arising from Jenkins' discussion is the issue of the actual and potential roles of what he terms 'primordial' civil society in strengthening contemporary civil society and its ability to interact with the state, in comparison with so-called 'modern' civil society. While problems of definition abound, questions around the roles of old-established social organizational arrangements, compared to those of relatively new organizations, have wider relevance than southern Africa. Much published research focuses on externally driven attempts to support the poor in the production of housing, and their interactions with the state and 'formal' market. Many of these attempts have limited success, and research into the mechanisms by which the urban poor provide themselves with housing and interact with the state and large-scale enterprises might help improve future interventions. One example is the informal land development partnership arrangements that have evolved in many towns and cities. The strengths and weaknesses of these informal arrangements need to be analysed, to identify the circumstances in which alternative arrangements might both be effective and have pro-poor outcomes.

Finally, there is a need to evaluate the outcomes of attempts to address sustainability objectives in processes of planning and regulation, and to assess their compatibility with poverty reduction objectives. Although sustainability is one aim among others for some contributors, on the whole it is treated as a constraint on other goals such as economic growth or achieving secure livelihoods for the poor, rather than an end in itself. This ambivalence reflects the conceptual problems discussed in the introduction, and general international experience of trying to operationalize the broad umbrella concept of sustainability. Much conceptual, analytical and practical work remains to be done to identify the characteristics of 'sustainable urban settlements' and how these might be assured. From the contributions in this volume it is possible to identify a number of pointers, which are outlined in the final section.

SOME PRINCIPLES FOR BUILDING SUSTAINABLE URBAN SETTLEMENTS

The contributions in this volume concentrate on the scope and prospects for achieving physical patterns of urban development that can assist in achieving the overall goal of sustainable development, but also focus on the economic, social and political dimensions of urban development. Attention has been paid to organizational arrangements, actors and their capabilities, and processes of achieving change. With respect to these 'city-building' aims, it is possible to identify a number of key principles.

Building human settlements that provide satisfactory environments for economic activity and everyday life

- A planning and regulatory framework is needed that permits mixed land uses and home-based enterprises, with relatively few exceptions, both to enable poor households to develop secure livelihoods, and to help achieve sustainability objectives by reducing the need for travel.

- Attention needs to be paid to managing the transformation of the existing – as well as the production of new – urban built environments, with a view to reducing poverty as well as achieving sustainability objectives.

- A combination is needed of a political system in which residents, particularly poor people, can make their voices heard and claim their rights, appropriate policies and organizational capacity. Although in some situations this will require dramatic transformations, in most circumstances, following radical changes, a process of incremental change and consolidation is needed. Increasing capacity and institutionalizing new working relationships at community and municipal level takes time and is unlikely to be achieved in unfavourable political circumstances, by frequent organizational or policy shifts, or by short-term donor contributions.

- Changes should more often be based on learning from experience. While sometimes radical changes are needed, the cost of establishing new organizations and instituting new administrative systems, and the long period needed to institutionalize new working relationships and practices, should be recognized. More attention should be given to the need for, and management of, incremental change based on existing arrangements and capacities.

- Managing a process of change to produce new and sustainable attitudes, practices and working relationships needs care. It should include paying attention to the discourse through which shared knowledge and values are developed, building alliances for change, involving all relevant stakeholders, providing support to the various parties involved, and increasing awareness of and compliance with new approaches.

- The role of public sector organizations in producing satisfactory urban environments needs to be carefully defined. Public sector agencies clearly have a key role in initiating change, leveraging private action or investment, mediating between residents and private actors, and ensuring that the needs of the poor are addressed. However, all these are potentially problematic and contradictory, as the public sector is not neutral, nor does it generally have adequate financial or administrative capacity to play the lead, or even a major role.

- A strong civil society is needed to interact vertically with the state, and also to define and implement society-led development where large sections of the population are increasingly isolated from both the state and formal market mechanisms. There is potential for this to occur at the community level, given a favourable political climate and appropriate support. However, in view of the ease with which communities can be co-opted or bought off in clientelistic political systems, alliances between poor groups or an organized political movement may be needed to achieve more than token improvements.

- An appropriate policy is one that is adapted to local realities, while recognizing the importance of social and cultural values that underpin family life and social organization. Thus any process of change needs to be nuanced in order to achieve a balance between respecting existing values and social organization, and the need for reform to reduce poverty and inequality.

Managing the impacts of urban development on the natural environment

- Integration, both vertical and horizontal, of planning and regulatory systems is vital, but the trade-offs between centralized control, city-level autonomy and decentralization to the local or sub-city level are difficult to resolve.
- Adequate enforcement powers are essential, but depend on recognition and acceptance of the need for regulation as much as on legal powers. Brand's discussion of the mobilization of shared environmental values to reconstitute social relations and legitimate local government is relevant here. The experience of Medellin shows how – in a society where economic growth is outside public control, inequality has grown and crime and violence have increased, reducing the scope for effective action – political and public commitment to environmental improvement can first be mobilized and, in turn, can increase the legitimacy of local government.

In the Introduction it was suggested that 'sustainable urban settlements' might be understood as settlements in which democratic and accountable city and municipal authorities ensure that the needs of people within their boundaries are met, while minimizing the transfer of environmental costs to other people or ecosystems, or into the future. The principles derived from the evidence and discussions collected here demonstrate that it is possible, given sound analysis, an appreciation of the needs and views of poor residents as well as other urban actors, and political commitment, to produce and maintain physical patterns of urban development that contribute to more environmentally sustainable consumption and waste management; provide a conducive environment for economic, social and cultural activities; and result in safe and healthy living and work environments for all residents.

Notes on authors

Mashary A. Al-Naim is an architect with degrees from King Faisal University, Saudi Arabia and a PhD from the University of Newcastle-upon-Tyne, UK. He is Chairman of the Department of Architecture, College of Architecture and Planning, King Faisal University, Dammam. His research interests are in the symbolic and cultural aspects of architecture, traditional and contemporary Arab architecture, and the relationships between housing architecture and social change.

Peter Brand completed his doctoral thesis on urban environmentalism at the Joint Centre for Urban Design, Oxford Brookes University, in 1998. He is currently head of the Postgraduate School of Urban and Regional Planning at the Universidad Nacional de Colombia (Medellín campus) where he has worked since the 1980s. Recent publications include 'The sustainable city as metaphor' [in: Jenks, M. and Burgess, R. (eds), *Compact Cities – Sustainable Urban Forms for Developing Countries*, E & FN Spon, London, 2000] and *Trayectorias Urbanas en la Modernización del Estado en Colombia* (Tercer Mundo, Bogotá, 2001).

Peter J.B. Brown is a senior lecturer and the Director of Undergraduate Studies in the Department of Civic Design, University of Liverpool. He is a Chartered Town Planner and Fellow of the Chartered Institute of Transport. His research interests lie in the fields of urban and regional analysis (including geodemographics and GIS applications) and transport planning. From 1996 to 2000 he was an Honorary Professor of East China Normal University in Shanghai in connection with the Waigaoqiao Free Trade Zone Environmental Baseline Study.

Sarah Carmona is a researcher and part-time lecturer in urban design at the Bartlett School of Architecture and Planning, University College London. Her research interests are primarily housing- and development-related: recent work includes an examination of the working relationships between housing providers and planners in the UK, and an investigation into urban development in the context of developing countries, undertaken at the University of Westminster. She is a chartered architect and urban designer, and has worked on community-based and commercial development projects in the UK and overseas.

Justine Coulson is a Research Associate in the School of Architecture, Planning and Landscape, University of Newcastle-upon-Tyne, UK, and a staff member of the Centre for Architectural Research and Development Overseas (CARDO). She has a BA in Latin American Studies from the University of Liverpool and a doctorate from the University of Newcastle-upon-Tyne. She was the Research Associate on the DFID-funded research project on 'The Environmental Effects of Home-Based Enterprises', and is currently researching the issue of disability in low-income areas.

Rizwan Hameed lectures in town planning in the Department of City and Regional Planning, University of Engineering and Technology, Lahore. His Master's degree in planning from there involved research into housing provision. His PhD from Heriot-Watt University, Edinburgh, concerned town planning and pollution control.

Paul Jenkins is Director of the Centre for Environment and Human Settlements in the School of Planning and Housing, Edinburgh. An architect/planner by training, he has worked with a wide range of central and local government, NGO, private sector, international aid and community-based organizations. He has worked in urban development, housing, architecture and construction, in policy, practice, training and research, with some 20 years in Southern Africa. His main practice and research interests are widening participation, community empowerment and the changing relationship between the state and civil society in the urbanizing world.

Peter Kellett is Senior Lecturer in the School of Architecture, Planning and Landscape. After qualifying as an architect he worked in Latin America for several years before joining the Centre for Architectural Research and Development Overseas (CARDO) in 1985. His PhD was based on an ethnographic study of informal housing processes in northern Colombia, and his main research interests continue to focus on housing, particularly on understanding how disadvantaged households create, use and value dwelling environments. Much of his recent work focuses on how meanings of home are socially constructed and the application of ethnographic methodologies to housing research.

Tony Lloyd-Jones is a senior lecturer and researcher in urban design and development at the University of Westminster, London. He is part-time urban and physical planning adviser to the Department for International Development, with a special responsibility for urban livelihoods and United Nations human settlement issues. With a background as a practising community architect and planner, he has conducted urban development-related research in Asia, Africa and Latin America. His research interests focus on the link between urban poverty reduction, urban livelihoods, spatial planning and urban governance.

Denise Martins Lopes graduated in Architecture and Urbanism from the Federal University of Santa Catarina in 1994. In 1998, she obtained her MPhil at the University of Wales, Cardiff. Back in Brazil, she worked for 18 months in the NGO CECCA – Centre for Studies, Culture and Citizenship – developing quality-of-life indicators for the city of Florianópolis, resulting in a book which she co-authored, entitled *Quality of Life and Citizenship*. In 1999 she joined the University of Southern Santa Catarina (UNISUL).

Lucky Lowe trained as a site manager in the UK construction sector, and then worked as a low-cost housing adviser with the Agricultural Development Bank of Nepal. On returning to the UK, she took up a marketing position with the Chartered Institute of Building before gaining an MSc degree in infrastructure engineering for developing countries at Cranfield University. She has worked for the Intermediate Technology Development Group since 1995, as Shelter Specialist and now Information Services Unit Manager.

David W. Massey is a senior lecturer in the Department of Civic Design, University of Liverpool, where he has been associated with the editing of *Town Planning Review* since 1971. His current research interests focus on coastal zone planning and management, and he has contributed to the preparation of strategic guidance for the management of the estuary of the River Mersey and the planning of the coast of the north-west of England. From 1996 to 2000 he was an Honorary Professor of East China Normal University in Shanghai in connection with the Waigaoqiao Free Trade Zone Environmental Baseline Study.

M.R. Dallalpour Mohammadi is an associate professor in the Department of Geography and Urban Planning, University of Tabriz, Iran. An urban geographer with a particular research interest in housing, he has a PhD from Cardiff University and has published two books and fifteen papers in the areas of housing policy and land use planning. He also served as Dean of the Faculty of Humanities and Social Sciences in the University of Tabriz for five years, Vice Chancellor for four years, and has recently been elected Chancellor of the University.

Geoffrey Payne is an independent consultant who specializes in urban housing, local land development, land tenure and project design issues in developing countries. He has taught in several universities; undertaken consultancy, research and training in most parts of the world; and published on land and housing. Recent and current assignments focus on public–private partnerships in land for housing, and innovative approaches to the provision of secure tenure for the poor, together with the development of multi-stakeholder urban projects in Lesotho, Cuba and elsewhere.

Orapim Pimcharoen is a senior urban planner with the Bangkok Metropolitan Administration, working on the revision of various strategic planning documents including the Bangkok Master Plan, liaising with Districts as they prepare their local plans, and developing the Green Area Strategy for Bangkok. She gained an MA in Metropolitan Planning from the Department of Civic Design at Liverpool University. Subsequently she stayed on to complete a PhD evaluating the effectiveness of EIA programmes in Thailand.

Jeremy Raemaekers lectures in the School of Planning and Housing, Edinburgh College of Art/Heriot-Watt University, Scotland. He has served as a planner in regional government in Scotland. Prior to that, he researched and taught primate ecology and behaviour in Southeast Asia for 10 years.

Carole Rakodi is a Professor of International Urban Development in the International Development Department, School of Public Policy, the University of Birmingham. Until recently she was a professor in the Department of City and Regional Planning, Cardiff University. She is a geographer and town planner, with professional experience in Zambia and Kenya. Her main research interests are in urban planning and management, land and housing markets and policy, and urban poverty. She has carried out research in Zambia, Zimbabwe, Kenya, Ghana and India.

Sam Romaya is an architect/planner specializing in urban planning, urban design and urban conservation. He practised as an architect in Iraq, and taught urban design for many years in the universities of Nottingham and Cardiff, as well as lecturing on short courses in a number of universities including Zimbabwe, Nigeria, Malaysia and Lesotho. His research interests include lighting in offices, urban regeneration and urban conservation. He is currently engaged in research, consultancy and voluntary work related to urban design and conservation in Wales.

Theo Schilderman is an architect and currently ITDG's senior shelter specialist. Before joining ITDG, he lectured at the Institute for Housing and Urban Development Studies and worked as a researcher for COOPIBO. He spent 10 years in Africa for these two organizations, and in his current post travels widely to support projects in six developing countries. He has published a range of papers, most recently on how the urban poor access information, urban income generation, housing standards and building materials production.

David Shaw is currently Head of the Department of Civic Design, Liverpool University. Before joining Civic Design in 1994, he held academic positions at the College of St Mark and St John, Plymouth, and the universities of Malawi and of Central England in Birmingham. His research interests focus on environmental planning and management and the process of European integration and its impact on spatial planning in the UK. He has a particular interest in comparative planning, having worked in Malawi and with colleagues in several Far Eastern countries.

Harry Smith is a Postdoctoral Research Fellow at the Centre for Environment and Human Settlements (CEHS), Edinburgh. He trained in architecture in Spain and in planning in the UK, where he has engaged in professional practice: recent activities include research on housing in Costa Rica; teaching planning and housing at CEHS; and the management of community self-build projects in Scotland. His current research interests include planning for sustainable urban development, housing policy, participation in planning and housing, and bottom-up processes in urban development, with a focus on low-income groups, particularly in developing countries.

Graham Tipple is Reader in Housing Policy and Development and Director of the Centre for Architectural Research and Development Overseas (CARDO) in the School of Architecture, Planning and Landscape, University of Newcastle-upon-Tyne, UK. He qualified as a Town Planner at the University of Sheffield and holds a doctorate from the University of Newcastle-upon-Tyne. He spent seven years in Africa (Zambia and Ghana) as a planner and lecturer in planning. His main research interest is in housing, with current work on issues of homelessness in developing countries.

Xiangrong Wang is a professor in the Department of Environmental Sciences and Engineering and Director of the Institute for Urban Ecological Planning and Design in Fudan University, Shanghai. He has also held academic appointments in Hubei University (Wuhan), East China Normal University and Tongji University (Shanghai). He is interested in ecology, the environment and urbanization. He has played a significant role in developing methods and applications of eco-environmental planning in China's urban modernization processes, including special studies on the Shenzen Special Economic Zone.

Notes

CHAPTER 1

1. We are grateful to the many officials, industrialists and residents who gave their time in interviews, and to Irfan and Kashif, who assisted with the interviews.
2. Environmental impact assessment (EIA) has great potential as a tool for applying the principle that prevention is better than cure in securing more sustainable development. However, EIA is only as good as the regulatory regimes within which it operates. Even within a strong regime like UK town planning, the influence of EIA on development decisions is by no means always clear (Glasson et al., 1999, pp. 180–184). In weaker regimes there are numerous cases of token use of EIA. The Pakistani government issued revised procedures for EIA in August 2000 (Pakistan Environmental Protection Agency, 2000), and the nation's leader, chairing its highest environmental body in February 2001, directed all sectors to implement them. The EIA procedures, however, do not make clear what mechanisms will guarantee that proposed projects are notified to the environmental protection agencies in the first place.
3. World Bank (2000b) reports literacy in Pakistan as 58 per cent among men and 29 per cent among women, while the government puts it at about 30 per cent overall (MELGRD, 2001, p. 8).

CHAPTER 2

1. The authors wish to acknowledge the support of the British Council for the project entitled 'Environmental Planning and Management of the Waigaoqiao Free Trade Zone, Shanghai', on which this paper draws. The project was funded under the Academic Links with China Scheme (ALCS) award number SHA/992/290, and has also received support from the Waigaoqiao Free Trade Zone Administration. We are particularly grateful for the assistance and collaboration of Ms Xu Xinli and Mr Zhu Bin of the Waigaoqiao Free Trade Zone Administration.

CHAPTER 4

1. This research on 'The Environmental Effects of Home-Based Enterprises' was sponsored by the UK Department for International Development (DFID) under its Engineering Knowledge and Research Programme (DFID Research Contract No. R7138). The views expressed are the authors' and do not necessarily represent those of DFID.

CHAPTER 6

1. The participatory urban appraisals were carried out as part of the project preparation process for a proposed Kenya Urban Poverty Programme to be funded by the UK Department for International Development.

CHAPTER 7

1. The core content of this chapter was initially presented as a paper at the 15th Inter-Schools Conference on Development, held at the Department of City and Regional Planning, Cardiff University in March 1998. It was subsequently expanded and published as an article in *Third World Planning Review*, 1999, 21(2).
2. This theme is more fully drawn out by Carley et al. (2001), who present two chapters dealing with the role of civil society in urban development in more detail; see also Jenkins (2001a, 2001b).
3. A distinction is made between civil society (e.g. neighbourhood associations, women's groups, religious groupings) and political society (e.g. political parties).
4. Young also argues that '. . . the new social construction of identity bore the heavy imprint of colonial practice and policy – ethnic classification, records of "ethnicity" and language unification strategies' (Young, 1991, p. 39). Or as Lonsdale put it, 'In Africa today invented tribes intertwine with still more imaginary nations'.
5. According to Hyden (1992), in Africa the partial abdication of sovereign authority for policy-making to the World Bank and IMF has undercut the political legitimacy of state elites. See also Simon et al. (1995).
6. National NGOs are, more often than not, created with support from international NGOs, which themselves were increasingly used to direct emergency relief (and to a lesser extent development) activities outside the state from the mid-1980s, as various international donors either did not want to support the state, or considered it corrupt and/or ineffective. This has been extensively documented; see Hanlon (1991).
7. Grest defines 'international community' in Mozambique as follows: 'The notion of "the international community" is imprecise, and shorthand for a set of interests and organisations which are certainly not homogeneous and which only on occasion speak with a single voice, but which represent the dominance of a loose coalition of Western European and North American interests' (Grest, 1998).
8. The Forum initially included the then government, but this pulled out, leaving the Forum non-statutory in status. However, the Forum carried sufficient force for its recommendations to be adopted almost immediately by the previous government, and so it acted as the de facto policy-making institution; see Rust and Rubenstein (1996).
9. The National Housing Department created a policy section in 2000, but this is still relatively new and understaffed.
10. The 1 million housing target was formally abandoned by the government, as indicated specifically in President Mandela's speech opening Parliament on 6 February 1998.

CHAPTER 8

1. Since 1992, CAPROM has stopped working with low-income communities and promoting organized land occupations in Florianópolis. Another NGO, Centro de Evangelização e Educação Popular (Centre for Popular Education and Evangelism, CEDEP) took on the responsibility of keeping grassroots work with the communities going. The two institutions tried to work at the same time, with different emphases in their work. CAPROM was to be responsible for working with the communities that had problems of land irregularity, trying to put pressure on the public institutions to enable them to gain access to secure tenure and housing-related infrastructure; CEDEP was to be responsible for working with the communities that had already solved (at least in part) their land problems, but lacked other kinds of infrastructure and services, such as access to proper education and healthcare, had low incomes, and so on. However, conflicts between the two institutions started to appear when the work of one began to affect the other. According to one source, community leaders began to feel overwhelmed with too much activity, leading CAPROM to decide to completely cease its work in 1992. Although the institution CAPROM still exists legally, it was inactive in the late 1990s.
2. For more information about the reasoning behind the choice of research subjects, see Lopes (1998).

CHAPTER 9

1. Population of the San José Metropolitan Area in 1989: 711 473. Source: Mora and Solano, 1994, p. 42.
2. The 'enabling' approach as promoted by the United Nations and the World Bank with reference to housing and urban development is set out in UNCHS (1987) and World Bank (1991, 1993). For a critique of the implementation of this approach, drawing on a comparison between the cases of Mozambique and Costa Rica, see Jenkins and Smith (2002).
3. This figure is the sum of housing units in bad condition (43 804) and the difference between the estimated number of houses and the estimated number of households (27 947). Source: Gutiérrez and Vargas (1997, Table F.2).
4. These were: Frente Democrático de Vivienda (FDV) and Frente Costarricense de Vivienda (FCV), both linked to the Partido de Liberación Nacional; Coordinadora de Lucha por Vivienda Digna, linked to the Comité Patriótico Nacional, a left-wing organization; and the Frente Nacional de Vivienda, with a Communist outlook. The latter front lasted only from 1982 to 1984.
5. This pledge, as well as how it was subsequently accounted for by the government, was misleading. The Arias government's accounts of housing production were usually a grand total that included all types of housing (from low income to high income), and did not distinguish between actual house completion and the granting of housing loans (Molina, 1990, p. 44).
6. In November 1992 the Supreme Court declared the use of a permanent state of emergency for the purpose of house-building unconstitutional; this meant the effective end of CEV (Grynspan, 1997).
7. The agreement was that FDV would invade San Pedro de Pavas and FCV would invade another large area called Los Guido, with the endorsement of the Guido Monge government. Eventually, the FDV invaded Los Guido before FCV, thus strengthening its position in the political struggle between the three major fronts.

8. The concept of 'community self-management' was explained in the project document as the participation of communities in the '. . . management, at each stage, of interventions that may contribute to improve the quality of life of their inhabitants. This means that the definition of priorities, the formulation of action plans, the implementation of initiatives and the administration and management of the improvements that result from these efforts, should be the responsibility of their managers – the community' (DANIDA et al., 1991, p. 9). This role of the community was to be supported by an 'enabling state'.

9. PROFAC's activities were later extended for a further three years.

10. These institutions include central government agencies (Ministries and Institutes – MIVAH, Instituto Mixto de Ayuda Social – Social Aid Institute, INVU, etc.), local government, local facilities (schools, mental hospitals, etc.), NGOs, religious associations and international agencies (UN Volunteers Programme).

11. This is the 'social contract' component in PROFAC's approach, the other basic component being 'empowerment'.

12. See Figure 8.4 of Smith and Valverde (2001) for a summarized graphic overview of the process.

13. Cuevas (1997) points out centralization as a favourable factor because it means concentrated and focused decision-making, but does not explain how this relates to community participation and self-management.

14. RGP received the highest investment ever in a Costa Rican 'marginal settlement', amounting to US$9 million in the first two years (Cuevas, 1997).

15. These views were expressed by community leaders during one of the fortnightly meetings of the Community Representation, in September 1997, which the author attended. This reaction came at a time when the participatory planning process was coming to an end and PROFAC was trying to pave the way for its eventual 'pulling out' of what was meant to become sustained community implementation and management of the plan. At the end of this stormy meeting, the participants agreed to hold their first independent meeting – without PROFAC – the following 9 October 1997. This meeting did not take place because people did not turn up. The mood at the presentation of the finalized Local Development Plan to the community and institution representatives, on 12 October 1997, was much more positive, and the community leaders came up with a proposal for organization of the Local Development Plan Steering Group and Sectoral Committees.

16. The author took part in this workshop as a participant observer, invited by PROFAC.

CHAPTER 10

1. The author interviewed many people in the area in 1996 and found that a plot in the surrounding blocks cost almost US$50 000, while in this block it cost more than US$100 000 because of the high demand for land in this area.

CHAPTER 11

1. The author wishes to acknowledge the help of the many people who responded to requests and questions during his visit to Cairo, in particular Professor Mohammed El-Barmalgy, Dr. Khaled Samy and Dr. Hesham El-Barmelgy. Acknowledgement is also due to the Aga Khan Award for Architecture foundation for giving permission to use illustrations: Figures 11.1, 11.2

and 11.4. Thanks also to Professor Terry Marsden, Department of City and Regional Planning Cardiff University for his help and encouragement.

CHAPTER 12

1. The core areas research was carried out between June 1997 and March 2001 by teams in London (at the Max Lock Centre, University of Westminster, and GHK Research and Development); Delhi (Max Lock Centre, India, in association with the Delhi Development Authority, Romi Khosla Associates and Moving Images); Jakarta and Bandung (Centre for Urban and Regional Planning Studies, Institute of Technology, Bandung); Recife (Department of Architecture and Urbanism, Federal University of Pernambuco); and Aswan (Department of Geography, University of Glasgow). The authors acknowledge the work of all the team members and the financial support of DFID's Engineering Knowledge and Research programme. However, the views expressed are those of the authors alone and are not necessarily shared by their fellow researchers or DFID.
2. These techniques included the development of a prototype computer-modelling tool (a further output of the research) to help communities and other stakeholders envisage and evaluate different development options. A workshop to pilot the tool was held in London in September 2000 (Anon., 2001). The computer-modelling tool is intended (once complete) to be available for use in core area development projects.
3. Planning obligations are imposed by local authorities on developers, who may be required to provide additional buildings, services or facilities (either on site or within the locality) as part of the development for which planning permission is being sought (Healey et al., 1995).
4. Transferable Development Rights involve landowners surrendering their rights to develop particular pieces of land to the local government, in return for monetary compensation or the development rights to another piece of land in another area of the city (Adusumilli, 1999, p. 36).
5. Incentive-based planning codes offer developers additional buildable space as an incentive to cross-subsidize the costs of slum redevelopment (Adusumilli, 1999).
6. Land-pooling systems involve the land being legally consolidated through the land-pooling agent before it is returned to the owners. Land readjustment involves the consolidation of land by the land readjustment agency before it is redesigned and returned to the landowners, who effectively exchange old title documents for newly developed plots of land (Archer, 1999).
7. Land sharing is an agreement between the illegal occupants of a piece of land and their landlord. It essentially involves illegal occupants moving off high-value land in return for being allowed to either rent or buy a part of the site below its market value (Angel and Boonyabancha, 1988).
8. An honest broker is a neutral intermediary (third party) who acts during the negotiation process to ensure that all information presented is understood by both parties, unbiased and acknowledged as such. This role can be undertaken by an NGO or other voluntary organization.
9. The *Favela do Bairro* programme in Rio de Janeiro is instructive in this respect, with more emphasis given to the strategic provision of infrastructure, in order to link *favelas* to the main public realm of the city.
10. A local capacity-building package comprising a toolkit of partnership-based neighbourhood development methodologies and associated user guides, including web and interactive CD-ROM-based guidelines and neighbourhood

development modelling tools, will be developed to encourage wider adoption of the approach. It is hoped that these will be used in training workshops, building on the methodology developed and tested during the course of the research in Recife (1999) and London (2000), and in the work of Geoff Payne Associates. This would involve training local research partners and municipal agencies in the capacity-building techniques, so that the approach may be disseminated locally.

CHAPTER 13

1. This paper was prepared during a period of sabbatical leave in Cardiff. The author sincerely thanks Professor Carole Rakodi for her constructive and helpful comments. He also expresses his appreciation to Professor Jeremy Alden, then Head of Department of City and Regional Planning, for his kind cooperation and support. Special thanks and appreciation to Dr Pourfaizi, the president, and members of the Research Council of University of Tabriz for granting the author leave and financial support.

CHAPTER 15

1. This chapter is based on a research project funded by the UK Department for International Development (DFID) between 1996 and 1998. It involved fieldwork to assess examples of innovative partnerships in Egypt, India, Pakistan and South Africa, together with commissioned papers reviewing examples from many other countries, including Bulgaria, Russia, Mexico, sub-Saharan Africa, south-east Asia and the UK. The full research was published as Payne (1999).

References

Abbott, J. (1996) *Shaping the City: Community Participation in Urban Management,* Earthscan, London.

Abrahamsson, H. and Nilsson, A. (1995) *Mozambique: The Troubled Transition,* Zed Press, London.

Adusumilli, U. (1999) Partnership approaches in India, in: Payne, G.K. (ed.), *Making Common Ground: Public–private Partnerships in Land for Housing,* Intermediate Technology Publications, London.

Agevi, E. (1998) *Emerging Partnerships for Implementing Sustainable Building Standards – Report on the National Workshop on Housing Standards,* Intermediate Technology Development Group (ITDG) Kenya, Nairobi.

Agevi, E. and Yahya, S. (1997) *Seeking the Standard Bearer – A Study of Popular Knowledge of Shelter Standards in Kenya,* Enabling Housing Standards and Procedures (EHSP) Working Paper 2, ITDG, Rugby.

Aguilar, M. and Gutiérrez, A. (1988) *Análisis de un programa de vivienda de interés social: lotes con servicios,* Dissertation, Universidad Nacional, Heredia, Costa Rica.

Ahary, Z. (1996) Upgrading in Koy-e-Seizdah Aban, (nohom-e-Aban), in: *Proceedings of the Third Seminar on Housing and Urban Development in Iran,* Ministry of Housing and Urban Development, Tehran, pp. 144–159.

Ahmad, M. (2000) Participatory decision-making for sustainable industrial development: the case of the stranded communities in the tannery clusters in Sialkot, Pakistan, *Environmental News,* August: 16–20.

AIT (1972) *Ecological Reconnaissance of the Quae Yai Hydroelectric Scheme,* Prepared for Electricity Generating Authority of Thailand, Asian Institute of Technology, Bangkok.

Al-Hathloul, S. (1981) *Tradition, Continuity, and Change in the Physical Environment: The Arab-Muslim City,* PhD thesis, Massachusetts Institute of Technology, Cambridge, MA, USA.

Al-Hathloul, S. and Anis-ur-Rahman (1985) The evolution of urban and regional planning in Saudi Arabia, *Ekistics,* 52(312): 206–212.

Al-Hussayen, A. (1996) *Women and Built Environment: Case Studies – Ar-Riyadh and Ushaigir,* PhD thesis, University of Edinburgh, UK.

Al-Musallam, A. (1995) *Al-Hassa Traditional House; a case study of Al-Kur District,* Special Workshop in Architectural Design, King Faisal University, Dammam (unpublished).

Al-Naim, M. (1993) *Potentiality of the Traditional House: A Case Study of Hofuf, AlHasa,* MA thesis, King Faisal University, Dammam, Saudi Arabia.

Al-Nowaiser M.A. (1983) *The Role of Traditional and Modern Residential Urban Settlements on the Quality of Environmental Experience in Saudi Arabia: Unyzeh and New Alkabra in Alkasseem Region,* PhD thesis, University of Southern California, USA.

Al-Olet, A.A. (1991) *Cultural Issues as an Approach to Forming and Managing the Future Neighbourhoods: Case Study: The Central Region of Saudi Arabia,* PhD thesis, University of Strathclyde, Glasgow, UK.

Al-Said, F. (1992) *Territorial Behaviour and the Built Environment. The Case of Arab-Muslim Towns, Saudi Arabia*, PhD thesis, University of Glasgow, UK.

Al-Shuaibi, A.M. (1976) *The Development of the Eastern Province with Particular Reference to Urban Settlements and Evolution in Eastern Saudi Arabia*, PhD thesis, University of Durham, UK.

Al-Soliman, T.M. (1991) Societal values and their effect on the built environment in Saudi Arabia: a recent account, *Journal of Architectural and Planning Research*, 8(3): 235–255.

Ali, Kamal Hassan (1985) Inaugural statement: the expanding metropolis – coping with the urban growth of Cairo, in: Evin, A. (ed.), *Proceedings of Seminar 9 in the series Architectural transformations in the Islamic World, Cairo, 11–15 November 1984*, The Aga Khan Award for Architecture, Geneva.

Allauddin, J. (1994) *Environmental Impact of Industries: A Case Study of Lahore*, BSc dissertation, Department of City and Regional Planning, University of Engineering and Technology, Lahore.

Altman, I. (1975) *The Environment and Social Behavior: Privacy, Personal Space, Territory, Crowding*, Brooks/Cole Publishing Company, California.

Amis, P. (2001) Rethinking UK aid in urban India: reflections on an impact assessment study of slum improvement projects, *Environment and Urbanization*, 13(1): 101–114.

Angel, S. and Boonyabancha, S. (1988) Land sharing as an alternative to eviction: the Bangkok experience, *Third World Planning Review*, 10(2): 107–127.

Anon. (1997a) *China Daily*, 2 May 1997.

Anon. (1997b) *China Daily*, 14 July 1997.

Anon. (1997c) *Diario Extra*, 27 October 1997.

Anon. (1997d) *El Espectador*, 23 March 1997, p. 5A.

Anon. (1997e) *La Nación*, 22 September 1997.

Anon. (2001) Focus: guide to good practice in core area development report, *Urbanisation*, No. 12 (May): 4–5.

Anon. (2002a) *Al-Ahram Weekly*, www.caip.com.eg; online Issue No. 575, 28 Feb–6 March.

Anon. (2002b) *Fustat Community Times*, February.

Archer, R.W. (1999) The potential of land pooling/readjustment to provide land for low-cost housing in developing countries, in: Payne, G.K. (ed.), *Making Common Ground: Public–private Partnerships in Land for Housing*, Intermediate Technology Publications, London, pp. 113–131.

Argüello, M.A. (1992) *Housing policy, democracy and the revolution: Costa Rica and Nicaragua during the 1980s*, PhD thesis, London University, UK.

Asobur (Asociación Urbanos), Fonvi (Fondo Nacional de la Vivienda) and Proa (Programa Piloto de Desarrollo Urbano de Alta) (1991) Reorienting housing policy: will the private sector respond? *Cities*, November, 8(4): 315–324.

Ayers, R.L. (1998) *Crime and Violence as Development Issues in Latin America*, World Bank Report No. 17408, Latin America and Caribbean Studies Series, World Bank, Washington, DC.

Azarya, V. (1994) Civil society and disengagement in Africa, in: Harbeson, J.W., Rothchild, D. and Chazan, N. (eds), *Civil Society and the State in Africa*, Lynne Rienner, Boulder, CO, USA/London, UK, pp. 83–100.

Aziz, M.M (1995) Provision of urban public facilities through the development of public commercial land in Iran, *Habitat International*, 19(3): pp. 269–278.

Bacharach, J.L. (1995) *The Restoration and Conservation of Islamic Monuments in Egypt*, The American University, Cairo, Egypt.

Bagerian, M. (1994) Credits and investment in housing sector, in: *Proceedings of the Seminar on Housing and Development Policies in Iran*, Vol 2., Ministry of Housing and Urban Development, Tehran, Iran, pp. 41–67.

Bairoch, P. (1988) *Cities and Economic Development*, Mansell Publishing, Oxford, UK.

Baker, L. and Sims, D. (1991) India: public–private partnerships in land development, final report, PADCO (Planning and Development Collaborative International, Inc.) for USAID, Bureau for Asia and Private Enterprise, Regional Housing and Urban Development Office, Washington, DC, mimeo. (USAID order no. PN-ABH-124)

Barnes, C., Green, C., Miles, N. and Qui, W. (1997) Approaches to regional economic development: the experience of Shanghai in the Chinese transition model, Paper presented at the Regional Studies Association Conference, 20–23 September 1997, Frankfurt.

Barrow C.J. (1997) *Environmental and Social Impact Assessments: An Introduction*, Arnold, London.

Barton, H. (2000) Conflicting perceptions of neighbourhood, in: Barton, H. (ed.), *Sustainable Communities: The Potential for Eco-neighbourhoods*, Earthscan, London, pp. 3–18.

Basiago, A.D. (1999) Economic, social, and environmental sustainability in development theory and urban planning practice, *The Environmentalist*, 19(2): 145–161.

Batley, R. (1996) Public–private relationships and performance in service provision, *Urban Studies*, 33(4–5): 723–751.

Batley, R. (1997) *A Research Framework for Analysing Capacity to Undertake the 'New Roles' of Government*, The Role of Government in Adjusting Economies Paper 23, Development Administration Group, School of Public Policy, The University of Birmingham, Birmingham, UK.

Batliwala, S. (1994) The meaning of women's empowerment: new concepts from action, in: Sen, G. et al. (eds), *Population Policies Reconsidered: Health, Empowerment and Rights*, Harvard University Press, Boston, MA, USA.

Beall, J. (1999) Valuing social resources or capitalising on them? Limits to pro-poor urban governance in nine cities of the South, *International Planning Studies*, 6(4): 357–376.

Benjamin, S. (2000) Governance, economic settings and poverty in Bangalore, *Environment and Urbanization*, 11(2): 35–56.

Bhatt, E. (1989) Towards empowerment, *World Development*, 17(7): 1059–1065.

Blackburn, J. and de Toma, C. (1997) Scaling-down as the key to scaling-up? The role of participatory municipal planning in Bolivia's Law of Popular Participation, in: Blackburn, J. with Holland, J. (eds), *Who Changes? Institutionalising Participation in Development*, Intermediate Technology Publications, London, pp. 30–39.

Blair, H. (2000) Participation and accountability at the periphery: democratic local governance in six countries, *World Development*, 28(1): 21–39.

Bond, P. and Tait, A. (1997) The failure of housing policy in post-Apartheid South Africa, *Urban Forum*, 8(1): 19–41.

Bond, R. and Hulme, D. (1999) Process approaches to development: theory and Sri Lankan practice, *World Development*, 27(8): 1339–1358.

Bradbury, I. and Kirkby, R. (1996) China's Agenda 21, *Applied Geography*, 16(2):97–107.

Brand, P. (1998) *Urban Environmentalism and the Configuration of Urban Space: Contemporary City Development in Medellin, Colombia*, PhD thesis, Oxford Brookes University (Joint Centre for Urban Design), Oxford, UK.

Brand, P. (1999) The environment and postmodern spatial consciousness: a sociology of urban environmental agendas, *Journal of Environmental Planning and Management*, 42(5): 631–648.

Brandt Commission (1983) *Common Crisis: North–South Co-operation for World Recovery*, Pan, London.

Bratton, M. and Rothchild, D. (1992) The institutional bases of governance in Africa, in: Hyden, G. and Bratton, M. (eds), *Governance and Politics in Africa*, Lynne Rienner, Boulder, CO, USA/London, UK, pp. 263–285.

Brown, P.J.B., Massey, D.W. and Shaw, D. P. (1995) *Leading China into the Global Economy? Free Trade Zone Developments and Opportunities in the Pudong New*

Area, Shanghai, Department of Civic Design Working Paper No. 54, University of Liverpool, Liverpool, UK.

Burgess, R., Carmona M. and Kolstee, T. (eds) (1997) *The Challenge of Sustainable Cities: Neoliberalism and Urban Strategies in Developing Countries*, Zed Books, London.

Callaghy, T.M. (1991) Civil society, democracy and economic change in Africa: a dissenting opinion about resurgent societies, in: Harbeson, J.W., Rothchild, D. and Chazan, N. (eds), *Civil Society and the State in Africa*, Lynne Rienner, Boulder, CO, USA/London, UK, pp. 231–254.

Carley, M., Jenkins, P. and Smith, H. (eds) (2001) *Urban Development and Civil Society: The Role of Communities in Sustainable Cities*, Earthscan, London.

Carney, D. (ed.) (1998) *Sustainable Rural Livelihoods: What Contribution Can We Make?* Department for International Development, London.

Céspedes, V.H. and Jimenez, R. (1995) *La pobreza en Costa Rica: concepto, medición y evolución*, Academia de Centroamérica, San José, Costa Rica.

Chaves, E. and Alfaro, L.A. (1990) *La Comisión Especial de Vivienda en el marco de la política de vivienda de interés social en la Administración Arias-Sánchez (1986–1990)*, Dissertation, Universidad de Costa Rica, San José, Costa Rica.

Chavez, E.M., Fallas, S.P., Sancho, M.A., Sancho, C.M., Ruiz, M.V. and Vargas, Y. (1989) *La autoconstrucción como alternativa de solución para el problema de vivienda*, Universidad de Costa Rica, San José, Costa Rica.

Clark, R. (1993) The National Environmental Policy Act and the role of the President's Council on Environmental Quality, *The Environmental Professional*, 15(1): 4–6.

Colenutt, B. and Cutten, A. (1994) *Community Empowerment in Urban Regeneration*, The Barrow Cadbury Fund Ltd and The Docklands Consultative Committee, London.

Concejo de Medellin (1989) *Problemática Ambiental del Valle de Aburrá*, Concejo de Medellin, Colombia.

Concejo de Medellin (1994) *Plan General de Desarrollo para Medellin*, Concejo de Medellin, Colombia.

Cordero, A. (1996) Sistematización de diagnósticos de Rincón Grande de Pavas, Equipo Interagencial de Naciones Unidas, San José, Costa Rica.

Correa, C. (1989) *The New Landscape: Urbanisation in the Third World*, Butterworth Architecture, Sevenoaks, UK.

Cuevas, F. (1997) Proyecto de fortalecimiento a la autogestión comunitaria MIVAH-HABITAT-PNUD (cos 91/003). Estudio de caso. Rincón Grande de Pavas: una experiencia de gobierno facilitador en la autogestión comunitaria, San José, Costa Rica.

Culhane, P. (1993) Post-EIS environmental auditing: a first step to making rational environmental assessment a reality, *The Environmental Professional*, 15: 66–75.

Dale, R. (2000) *Organisations and Development: Strategies, Structures and Processes*, Sage, Delhi.

Daneshmand, H. (1982) *Housing Policy Formulation for Low Income Urban Families With Respect to Socio-Economic and Environmental Aspects of Urbanisation. A Case of Mashhad, Iran*, PhD thesis, Rensselar Polytechnic Institute, New York.

DANIDA (1994) *Evaluation of DANIDA/UNCHS Training Programme in Community Participation*, Volume I, www.ingenioeren.dk/danida/1993–7s.txt

DANIDA, CNUAH–Habitat, PNUD and MIVAH (1991) *Fortalecimiento de la autogestión comunitaria en el desarrollo y operación de los asentamientos humanos en Costa Rica (Proyecto COS/91/003)*, Project Document. San José, Costa Rica.

Danil, V. (1997) Amadehsazieh Zamin Dar Iran land preparation in Iran, in: *Egtesad-e-Maskan*, National Land and Housing Organisation, Tehran, Iran, No. 23: 21–29.

de Soto, H. (1989) (1989) *The Other Path: The Invisible Revolution in the Third World*, Harper Row, New York.

Dehesh, A. (1994) Developmental instability in Iran: its impact on housing since 1962, *Cities*, 11(6): 409–424.

Departamento Administrativo de Planeación Metropolitana (1985) *Plan de Desarrollo Metropolitano del Valle de Aburrá: Para la Consolidacion de la Metrópoli*, Consejo de Medellin, Colombia.

Departamento Administrativo de Planeación Metropolitana (1986) *Plan de Desarrollo de Medellin 1986*, Municipio de Medellin, Colombia.

Departamento Administrativo de Planeación Metropolitana (1990) *Plan de Desarrollo de Medellin 1990*, Municipio de Medellin, Colombia.

Dickens, P. (1996) *Restructuring Nature*, Routledge, London.

Dodds, S.H. (2001) Pathways and paradigms for sustainable human communities, in: Lawrence, R.J. (ed.), *Sustaining Human Settlement: A Challenge for the New Millennium*, Urban International Press, North Shields, UK, pp. 28–54.

DoE (1996a) *Five Years on from Rio: The UK Position Paper*, Department of the Environment/HMSO, London.

DoE (1996b) *Indicators of Sustainable Development for the United Kingdom*, Department of the Environment/HMSO, London.

Dorkoosh, S.A. (1990) Land pricing in new urban settlements, in: *A Report of Studies in the Establishment of New Cities in Iran*, MHUD, Tehran, pp. 15–18.

Dovey, K. (1985) Home and homelessness, in: Altman, I. and Werner, C.M. (eds), *Home Environment*, Plenum Press, New York, pp. 33–64.

Downey, C. (2001) Small government. . .big society: visit to China, *Campaigner*, October: pp. 4–5

Doxiadis, C. (1968) *Ekistics: An Introduction to the Science of Human Settlements*, Hutchinson, London.

Durand-Lasserve, A. assisted by Clerc, V. (1996) *Regularization and Integration of Irregular Settlements: Lessons from Experience*, World Bank, Urban Management Programme, Working Paper No. 6, Washington, DC.

Eder, K. (1996) *The Social Construction of Nature*, Sage, London.

Edwards, B. and Hyett, P. (2001) *Rough Guide to Sustainability*, RIBA Publications, London.

Edwards, M. (1995) Public–private sector partnerships in housing provision: what are the possibilities? *Habitat Debate*, 1(4).

von Einsiedel, N. (1995) Improving urban land management in Asia's developing countries: an overview paper, presented at the Asian Regional Consultation on Access to Land and Security of Tenure, Jakarta, 28–30 August 1995.

Ekeh, P. (1975) Colonialism and the two publics in Africa: a theoretical statement, *Comparative Studies in Society and History*, 17(1): 91–111.

Eldredge, H.W. (ed.) (1967) *Taming the Megalopolis – Volume II: How to Manage an Urbanised World*, Anchor, New York.

Elkin, T., McLaren, D. and Hillman, M. (1991) *Reviving the City: Towards Sustainable Urban Development*, Friends of the Earth, London.

EPA Punjab (1993) *Annual Progress Report of Environmental Protection Agency Punjab Research Laboratories (1993–94)*, Housing, Physical and Environmental Planning Department, Environment Protection Agency Punjab, Government of Punjab, Lahore.

Escobar, A. (1996) Constructing nature: elements for a postmodern political ecology, in: Peet, R. and Watts, M. (eds) *Liberation Ecologies: Environment, Development and Social Movements*, Routledge, London.

Etemadi, F. (2000) Civil society participation in governance in Cebu City, *Environment and Urbanization*, 12(1): 57–72.

Evans, P. (1996) Government action, social capital and development: reviewing the evidence on synergy, *World Development*, 24(6): 1119–1132.

Evin, A. (ed.) (1985) *The Expanding Metropolis – Coping with the Urban Growth of Cairo*, The Aga Khan Award for Architecture, Geneva.

Fathy, H. (1973) *Architecture for the Poor: An Experiment in Rural Egypt*, University of Chicago Press, Chicago.

Fiori, J. and Ramirez, R. (1992) Notes on the self-help housing critique: towards a conceptual framework for the analysis of self-help housing policies in developing countries, in: Mathéy, K. (ed.), *Beyond Self-Help Housing*, Mansell Publishing, London/New York, pp. 23–31.

Fischer, F. and Hajer, M. (1999) *Living with Nature: Environmental Politics as Cultural Discourse*, Oxford University Press, Oxford, UK.

Foucault, M. (1970) *La Arqueologia del Saber*, Siglo XXI, Madrid.

Franzoni, T. (1993) As 'Perigosas' relações entre movimento popular/comunitário e administração pública municipal na Ilha de Santa Catarina', Master's Dissertation in Social Anthropology, Federal University of Santa Catarina, Florianópolis, Brazil.

Friedmann, J. (1992) *Empowerment: The Politics of Alternative Development*, Blackwell, Oxford, UK.

Gajanayake, S. and Gajanayake, J. (1993) *Community Empowerment: A Participatory Training Manual on Community Project Development*, Northern Illinois University, Illinois, USA.

Garaycochea, I. (1990) The methodology of social development evaluation: thematic paper, in: Marsden, D. and Oakley, P. (eds), *Evaluating Social Development Projects*, Development Guidelines No. 5, Oxfam, Oxford, UK.

Germen, A. (1983) *Islamic Architecture and Urbanism*, King Faisal University, Dammam, Saudi Arabia.

Gidman, P., Blore, I., Lorentzen, J. and Shuttenbelt, P. (1995) *Public–private Partnerships in Urban Infrastructure Services*, Urban Management Program Working Paper Series 4, Urban Management Program, UNCHS, Nairobi.

Gilpin A. (1995) *EIA: Cutting Edge for the Twenty-first Century*, Cambridge University Press, Cambridge, UK.

Glasson J., Therivel R. and Chadwick A. (1994) *Introduction to EIA*, UCL Press, UK.

Glasson, J., Therivel, R. and Chadwick, A. (1999) *Introduction to Environmental Impact Assessment*, 2nd edn, UCL Press, London.

Gleeson, B. and Low, N. (2000) Cities as consumers of the world's environment, in: Low, N., Gleeson, B., Elander, I. and Lidskog, R. (eds), *Consuming Cities: The Urban Environment in the Global Economy after the Rio Declaration*, Routledge, London, pp. 1–29.

Goodlad, R. (1996) The housing challenge in South Africa, *Urban Studies*, 33(9): 1629–1645.

Gore, T. (1991) Public–private partnership schemes in UK urban regeneration: the role of joint enabling agencies, *Cities*, 8(3): 209–215.

Government of Pakistan/IUCN (1992) *The Pakistan National Conservation Strategy*, Government of Pakistan/Joint Research Committee–International Union for the Conservation of Nature and Natural Resources, Karachi, Pakistan.

Government of the Punjab (1973) *Master Plan for Greater Lahore*, Housing and Physical Planning Department, Government of Punjab, Lahore.

Government of the Punjab (1998) *Directory of Registered Factories*. Bureau of Statistics, Government of Punjab, Lahore.

Gow, D.D. and Morss, E.R. (1988) The notorious nine: critical problems in project implementation, *World Development*, 16(12): 1399–1418.

Grest, J. (1998) 'A cidade de Maputo, Mozambique: Pressôes globais, reformas locaise a invençâo de uma sociedad civil.' Paper presented to the V Congresso. Al-Luso-Brasileiro das Sciencias Sociais, Maputo, Mozambique, 1–5 September, 1998. (Copies are available from Paul Jenkins, Centre for Environment and Human Settlements, School of Planning and Housing, Heriot-Watt University, Edinburgh).

Groeneweger, P., Fischer, K., Jenkins, E. and Schot, J. (eds) (1996) *The Greening of Industry: Resource Guide and Bibliography*, Island Press, Washington, DC.

Grynspan, R. (1997) El Sistema Financiero Nacional para la Vivienda de Costa Rica: Acceso a la vivienda para las familias de bajos ingresos, paper delivered at the Symposium *La Ciudad Latinoamericana y del Caribe en el Nuevo Siglo*, organized by the Inter-American Development Bank, Barcelona, 13–15 March.

Gutiérrez, M. and Vargas, A.J. (1997) *Costa Rica: Una revisión de las políticas de vivienda aplicadas a partir de 1986*, CEPAL (Consejo Económico para América Latina, Economic Council for Latin America)/UNDP (United Nations Development Programme), Santiago de Chile.

Haddad, L., Ruel, M.T. and Garrett, J.L. (1999) Are urban poverty and undernutrition growing? Some newly assembled evidence, *World Development*, 27(11) 1891–1904.

Hajer, M. (1995) *The Politics of Environmental Discourse: Ecological Modernisation and the Policy Process*, Clarendon, Oxford, UK.

Hamdan, S. (1990) *Social Change in the Saudi Family*, PhD thesis, Iowa State University, Ames, IA, USA.

Hameed, R. and Raemaekers, J. (1999) The environmental regulation of industry in Lahore, Pakistan, *Third World Planning Review*, 21(4): 429–453.

Hameed, R. and Raemaekers, J. (2001) The state, business and the community: abating industrial nuisance in Lahore, Pakistan, in: Carley, M., Jenkins, P. and Smith, H. (eds), *Urban Development and Civil Society: Cities, Communities and Self-Development*, Earthscan, London, pp. 51–67.

Hameed, R. and Raemaekers, J. (2002) Putting over the message: a programme in Pakistan to build capacity among industrialists for pollution abatement, in: Gandelsonas, C. (ed.), *Communicating for Development: Experience from the Urban Environment*, ITDG Publishing, London.

Hanlon, J. (1991) *Mozambique: Who Calls the Shots?* Indiana University Press, Bloomington, IN, USA.

Harbeson, J.H. (1994) Civil society and political renaissance, in: Harbeson, J.W., Rothchild, D. and Chazan, N. (eds), *Civil Society and the State in Africa*, Lynne Rienner, Boulder, CO, USA, pp. 1–29.

Harbeson, J.W., Rothchild, D. and Chazan, N. (eds) (1994) *Civil Society and the State in Africa*, Lynne Rienner, Boulder, CO, USA.

Harms, H. (1982) Historical perspectives on the practice and purpose of self-help housing, in: Ward, P.M. (ed.), *Self-Help Housing: A Critique*, Mansell, London, pp. 17–53.

Harré, R., Brockmeier, J. and Muhlhausler, P. (1999) *Greenspeak: A Study of Environmental Discourse*, Sage, London.

Harvey, D. (1996) *Justice, Nature and the Geography of Difference*, Blackwell, Oxford, UK.

Haughton, G. (1999) Environmental justice and the city, *Journal of Planning Education and Research*, 18(3): 233–243.

Healey, P., Purdue, M. and Ennis, F. (1995) *Negotiating Development: Rationales and Practice for Development Obligations and Planning Gain*, E & FN Spon, London.

Hentschel, J. and Seshagiri, R. (2000) *The City Poverty Assessment: A Primer*, World Bank Technical Paper 490, Washington, DC.

Hilderbrand, M.E. and Grindle, M.S. (1995) Building sustainable capacity in the public sector: what can be done? *Public Administration and Development*, 15(5): 441–463.

Hillier, R. and Hanson, J. (1984) *The Social Logic of Space*, Cambridge University Press, New York.

Hinrichsen, D. (1987) *Our Common Future: A Reader's Guide*, Earthscan, London.

Hodder, R. (1996) Industrial Locations, in: Yeung, Y.-M. and Sung, Y.-W. (eds), *Shanghai: Transformation and Modernisation under China's Open Policy*, The Chinese University Press, Hong Kong, pp. 225–248.

Holmes, A. (1992) *Limbering Up: Community Empowerment on Peripheral Estates*, Delta Press, Brighton, UK.

Hyden, G. (1992) Governance and the study of politics, in: Hyden, G. and Bratton, M. (eds), *Governance and Politics in Africa*, Lynne Rienner, Boulder, CO, pp. 1–26.

IDS Workshop (1997) Reflections and recommendations on scaling-up and organizational change, in: Blackburn, J. with Holland, J. (eds), *Who Changes? Institutionalizing Participation in Development*, IT Publications, London, pp. 135–144.

Instituto Mi Río (1995) *Guía Ecológica y Ambiental*, Instituto Mi Rio, Medellin, Colombia.

International Red Cross (1999) *1999 World Disasters Report*, International Red Cross, Geneva.

IOSCOPRC (1996) *Environmental Protection in China*, Information Office of the State Council of the People's Republic of China, Beijing.

Jacobs, J. (1961) *The Death and Life of Great American Cities*, Penguin, Harmondsworth, UK.

Jenkins, P. (1990) Housing policy development in post-independent Mozambique, in: Mathey, K. (ed.), *Housing Policies in the Socialist Third World*, Mansell, Oxford, UK, 147–180.

Jenkins, P. (1997a) 'Policies and praxis for housing the urban poor in the New South Africa – a case of old wine in new bottles or new wine in old bottles?, in Leonard, J. (ed). Proceedings of the 14th Inter-Schools Conference on Development: Global and Local Development – Nas Agendas, 24–25 March, Edinburgh College of Art and Design/Heriot-Watt University, Centre for Environment and Human Settlements.

Jenkins, P. (1997b) Reports from the 'front-line': difficulties experienced in implementing the new South African housing policy. Is this promoting continuing segregation by race and class?, paper presented at Scotland–Africa Seminar, *Housing in the New South Africa*. Available from the author, Centre for Environment and Human Settlements, Heriot-Watt University, Edinburgh.

Jenkins, P. (1998) *National and International Shelter Policy Initiatives in Mozambique: Housing the Urban Poor at the Periphery*, PhD thesis, Edinburgh College of Art/Heriot-Watt University, School of Planning and Housing, Edinburgh, UK.

Jenkins, P. (1999a) The role of civil society in housing policy development: some lessons from Southern Africa, *Third World Planning Review*, 21(2): 177–199.

Jenkins, P. (1999b) Difficulties encountered in community involvement in delivery under the new South Africa Housing Policy, *Habitat International*, 23(4): 431–446.

Jenkins, P. (1999c) *Mozambique: Housing and Land Markets in Maputo*, Research Paper No. 72, Edinburgh College of Art/Heriot-Watt University, School of Planning and Housing, Edinburgh, UK.

Jenkins, P. (2001a) The role of civil society in shelter at the periphery: the experience of peri-urban communities in Maputo, Mozambique, in: Carley, M., Jenkins, P. and Smith, H. (eds), *Urban Development and Civil Society: The Role of Communities in Sustainable Cities*, Earthscan, London, pp. 33–50.

Jenkins, P. (2001b) Community-based organisations and the struggle for land in South Africa: urban social movements in transition, in: Carley, M., Jenkins, P. and Smith, H. (eds), *Urban Development and Civil Society: The Role of Communities in Sustainable Cities*, Earthscan, London, pp. 139–153.

Jenkins, P. (2001c) Relationships between the state and civil society and their importance for sustainable urban development, in: Carley, M., Jenkins, P. and Smith, H. (eds), *Urban Development and Civil Society: The Role of Communities in Sustainable Cities*, Earthscan, London, pp. 175–191.

Jenkins, P. and Smith, H. (2001) An institutional approach to analysis of state capacity in housing systems in the developing world: case studies in South Africa and Costa Rica, *Housing Studies*, 16(4): 485–508.

Jenkins, P. and Smith, H. (2002) International agency shelter policy in the 1990s: experiences from Mozambique and Costa Rica, in: Zetter, R. (ed.), *Planning in Cities: Sustainability and Growth in the Developing World*, ITDG Publishing, London.

Jenkins, P. and Wilkinson, P. (2002) Assessing the growing impact of the global economy on urban development in South African cities: case studies of Maputo and Cape Town, *Cities*, 19(1): 33–47.

Jenks, M. and Burgess, R. (eds) (2000) *Compact Cities: Sustainable Urban Forms for Developing Countries*, E & FN Spon, London/New York.

Jones, G.A. and Ward, P.M. (1998) Privatizing the commons: reforming the Ejido and urban development in Mexico, *International Journal of Urban and Regional Research*, 22(1): 76–93.

Kano, H. (1996) Urbanisation in post-revolution Iran, *The Developing Economies*, XXXIV(4): 424–446.

Kayhan (1974) Housing finance: an evaluation, *Daily*, Tehran, 8 March 1974, p. 3.

Kayhan (1983) Review on housing projects, *Daily*, Tehran, 12 March 1983, p. 5.

Kellett, P.W. and Tipple, A.G. (2000) The home as workplace: a study of income-generating activities within the domestic setting, *Environment and Urbanization*, 12(1): 203–213.

Khan, A.S. (2001a) *Air Pollution – Government Response and Need for Public Co-operation*, www.environment.gov.pk/Article2.asif.html (accessed October 2001).

Khan, A.S. (2001b) *Industrial Pollution*, www.environment.gov.pk/Article3.asif.html (accessed October 2001).

Khan, A.S. (undated) *Industrial Operations and Interaction with Ecology: The Case of Pakistan*. www.etpi.org.pk (accessed June 2001).

Khavidi, R. (1978) *Low-Income Public Housing and Neighbourhood Planning and Development in the City of Tehran*, PhD thesis, University of Wisconsin, Milwaukee, USA.

Killick, T. (1995) Structural adjustment and poverty alleviation: an interpretative survey, *Development and Change*, 26(2): 305–331.

Kraayenbrink, E.A., Van Wamelen, J. and Schlotfeldt, C.J. (1998) A South African solution to the approval of non-standardised construction methods, *BASIN News*, SKAT, St Gallen, 15: 13–15.

Lahore Development Authority/World Bank/International Development Agency (1980) *Lahore Urban Development and Traffic Study: Urban Planning, Final Report, 1-A*, Lahore Development Authority, Lahore, Pakistan.

Lahore Development Authority/National Engineering Services Pakistan (1998) *Integrated Master Plan for Lahore, Draft Report, July 1998*, Lahore Development Authority, Lahore, Pakistan.

Lall, V.D. (1994) *Informal Sector in Alwar: Status, Development and Action Plan*, Society for Development Studies, New Delhi.

Laloo, K. (1998) Areas of contested citizenship: housing policy in South Africa, *Habitat International*, 23(1): 35–46.

Lam, K.-C. and Tao, S. (1996) Environmental quality and pollution control, in: Yeung, Y.-M. and Sung, Y.-W. (eds), *Shanghai: Transformation and Modernisation Under China's Open Policy*, The Chinese University Press, Hong Kong, pp. 469–491.

Lapidus, I.M. (ed.) (1969) *The Middle Eastern City*, University of California Press, Berkeley, CA, USA.

Li, N. (1995) Pudong – full of hope: an interview with Shanghai's Vice-Mayor, Zhao Quizheng, *Beijing Review*, 8–14 May 1995, pp. 10–14.

Lijphart, A. (1985) Non-majoritarian democracy: a comparison of Federal and Consociational theories, *Publius*, 15: 3–15.

Lipton, M. (1980) Family, fungibility, and formality: rural advantages of informal non-farm enterprise versus the urban-formal state, in: Amin, S. (ed.), *Human*

Resources, Employment, and Development, Vol. 5, Developing Countries, Macmillan, London.

Lloren, J.D. (1991) *The Community Mortgage Programme in the Philippines: A Preliminary Evaluation,* MSc dissertation, University of Wales Cardiff, UK.

Lloyd-Jones, A. (2000) Compact city policies for megacities: core areas and metropolitan regions, in: Jenks, M. and Burgess, R. (eds) *Compact Cities: Sustainable Urban Forms for Developing Countries,* E & FN Spon, London, pp. 37–52.

Lo, C.W.-H. and Yip, P.K.-T. (1999) Environmental impact assessment regulation in Hong Kong and Shanghai: a cross-city analysis, *Journal of Environmental Planning and Management,* 42(3): 355–374.

Lopes, D.M. (1998) Community empowerment: an evaluation of the impact of the work of a non-governmental organization in Florianópolis, Brazil, MPhil thesis, Department of City and Regional Planning, University of Wales Cardiff, UK.

Loughhead, S. and Rakodi, C. (2002) Reducing urban poverty in India: lessons from projects supported by DFID, in: Rakodi, C. with Lloyd-Jones, T. (eds), *Urban Livelihoods: A People-Centred Approach to Reducing Poverty,* Earthscan, London.

Low, N., Gleeson, B., Elander, I. and Lidskog R. (2000) *Consuming Cities: The Urban Environment in the Global Economy after the Rio Declaration,* Routledge, London.

Lowe, L. (1998) *The Current Review Process of the Earth Building Standards in Africa,* EHSP Case Study 1, ITDG, Rugby (based on a case study prepared by CRATerre-EAG).

Lowe, L. (1999) *Literature Review,* EHSP Case Study 10, ITDG, Rugby.

Mackay, C.J. (1995) The development of housing policy in South Africa in the post Apartheid period, *Housing Studies,* 11(1): 133–146.

Mackay, C.J. (1999) Housing policy in South Africa: the challenge of delivery, *Housing Studies,* 14(3): 387–399.

Macnaghten, P. and Urry, J. (1998) *Contested Natures,* Sage, London.

MacPherson, K. (1994) The head of the dragon: the Pudong New Area and Shanghai's urban development, *Planning Perspectives,* 9(1): 61–85.

Mahmud, A. (2001) Hell from leather: are Bangladeshi tanneries to blame for health problems?, *The Guardian,* 7 February 2001, p. 11.

Mani, M. and Wheeler, D. (1998) 'In search of pollution havens? Dirty industry in the world economy, 1960–95,' *Journal of Environment and Development.* 7(3): 215–47.

Marcuse, P. (1998) Sustainability is not enough, *Environment and Urbanization,* 10(2): 103–111.

Marsh, C. (1997) Mixed use development and the property market, in: Coupland, A. (ed.), *Reclaiming the City,* E & FN Spon, London, pp. 117–148.

Martinez-Allier, J. (1997) Environmental justice (local and global), *Culture, Nature, Socialism,* 8(1): 91–107.

Massey, D., Shaw, D. and Brown, P.J.B. (1997) Economic Imperatives v. environmental quality in the Dragon's Head: the Waigaoqiao Free Trade Zone, Shanghai, *Journal of Environmental Management and Planning,* 40(5): 661–679.

Max Lock Centre (2002a) *Good Practice in Core Area Development: Final Report,* DFID research project R6860, unpublished report available from the Max Lock Centre, University of Westminster, London.

Max Lock Centre (2002b) *Guide to Good Practice in Core Area Development,* Max Lock Centre, University of Westminster, London, www.wmin.ac.uk/builtenv/maxlock/

McHardy, P. (1998) *Revising Development Standards in Jamaica,* EHSP Case Study 7, ITDG, Rugby.

McLemore, R. (1995) Shanghai's Pudong: a case study in strategic planning, *Plan Canada*, 35(1): 28–32.

McLeod, R. (2001) Experiences of linking community-based housing finance to formal finance mechanisms, Homeless International, Coventry, UK, www.theinclusivecity.org/bridging.htm

MELGRD (1997) *Pollution and Monitoring Survey of the River Ravi*, Annex A to the main report, Draft Report, TA 2276-PAK, Ministry of Environment, Local Government and Rural Development, Government of Pakistan, Islamabad.

MELGRD (2001) *Environmental Challenges and Responses*, Ministry of Environment, Local Government and Rural Development, Government of Pakistan, Islamabad, www.environment.gov.pk

MHUD (1976) *Comprehensive Urban Housing and Policy Programmes*, Ministry of Housing and Urban Development, Tehran, Iran.

MHUD (1994) *Social and Protected Housing, Some Guidelines for Construction and Allocation*, National Land and Housing Organisation, Ministry of Housing and Urban Development, Tehran, Iran.

Mirzadeh, H. (1995) Housing in the Second NEDP with evaluation of government protection policies, in: *Proceedings of the Second Seminar of Housing Development in Iran*, Ministry of Housing and Urban Development, Tehran, Iran, pp. 517–527.

Mitlin, D. (1993) Funding community level initiatives, *Environment and Urbanization*, 5(1): 148–154.

Mohammadi, M.R.D. (1990) *Policy Impact on Land Use Patterns in Iran*, PhD thesis, University of Wales Cardiff, UK.

Molina, E. (1990) *Repercusiones político-organizativas del acuerdo político firmado entre los frentes de vivienda y el Estado durante la administratión Arias Sánchez*, MSc dissertation, Universidad de Costa Rica, San José, Costa Rica.

Mora, M. and Solano, F. (1994) *Nuevas tendencias del desarrollo urbano en Costa Rica: el caso del Area Metropolitana de San José*, Editorial Alma Mater, San José, Costa Rica.

Moser, C. (1998) The asset vulnerability framework: reassessing urban poverty reduction strategies, *World Development*, 26(1): 1–19.

MOSTE (1981) *Notification of Types and Sizes of Projects or Activities Requiring EIA Reports and Measures for the Prevention of and Remedy for the Adverse Effects on Environmental Quality*, Ministry of Science, Technology and Environment, Bangkok.

MOSTE (1992) *Notification of Types and Sizes of Projects or Activities Requiring EIA Reports and Measures for the Prevention of and Remedy for the Adverse Effects on Environmental Quality*, Ministry of Science, Technology and Environment, Bangkok.

MOSTE (1996) *Notification of Types and Sizes of Projects or Activities Requiring EIA Reports and Measures for the Prevention of and Remedy for the Adverse Effects on Environmental Quality*, Ministry of Science, Technology and Environment, Bangkok.

Mugova, A. and Musandu-Nyamayaro, O. (1997) *Housing Standards Review Processes and Procedures in Zimbabwe*, EHSP Working Paper 1, ITDG, Rugby.

Mugova, A. and Musandu-Nyamayaro, O. (1998) *Housing Urban People in Zimbabwe – A Handbook of Housing Application Procedures and Building Processes*, ITDG Zimbabwe, Harare.

Muhajeri, M. (1982) Housing Foundation, in: *Islamic Revolution: Future Path of the Nation*, Tehran, Iran, pp. 93–94.

Municipio de Medellin (1996) *Medellin, los esfuerzos de una ciudad muestran que la prevencion da resultados*, Mayor's Presentation, Municipio de Medellín, Medellin, Colombia.

Munjee, N. (1992) *Financing Shelter: New Experiments in Formal and Informal Institutional Links in Shelter*, paper presented at the 13th International EAROPH

(Eastern Region Organization for Planning and Housing) Congress, *Planning Towards a Caring Society*, Kuala Lumpur, Malaysia, 14–18 September.

Murphey, R. (1988) Shanghai, in: Dogan, M. and Kasarda, J. (eds), *The Metropolis Era, 1: Mega Cities*, Sage, Newbury Park, CA, USA, pp. 157–184.

Myllyla, S. (1995) Cairo – a mega-city and its water resources, paper presented to the 3rd Nordic conference on Middle Eastern Studies: *Ethnic Encounter and Culture Change*, Joensuu, Finland, 19–22 June 1995, www.hf.uib.no/institutter/smi/paj/Myllyla.html

NSO (1997) *Population and Trends in Thailand*, National Statistical Office, Bangkok.

Nunan, F. and Satterthwaite, D. (1999) *The Urban Environment*, Urban Poverty, Partnership and Poverty WP 6, International Development Department, School of Public Policy, University of Birmingham, UK.

O'Riordan, T. (1995) *Environmental Science for Environmental Management*, Longman, Harlow, UK.

O'Donnell, G.A., Schmitter, P. and Whitehead, L. (1986) Transitions from authoritarian rule: tentative conclusions about uncertain democracies, in: O'Donnell, G.A., Schmitter, P. and Whitehead, L. (eds) *Transitions from Authoritarian Rule: Latin America*, Johns Hopkins University Press, Baltimore, MD, USA.

OECD (1999) *National Climate Policies and the Kyoto Protocol*, Organisation for Economic Cooperation and Development, Paris.

OEPP (1995) *EIA in Thailand: Manual and Guideline for EIA Report Production*, Office of Environmental Policy and Planning, Bangkok.

OEPP (1997) *Statistics on EIA Submission in 1987–1997*, Office of Environmental Policy and Planning, Bangkok.

Okonkwo, O. (1999) *Building Codes and Planning Regulations Review in Malawi*, EHSP Case Study 5, ITDG, Rugby.

Pakistan Environmental Protection Agency (2000) *Policy and Procedures for the Filing, Review and Approval of Environmental Assessments*, www.environment.gov.pk (accessed October 2001).

Parfect, M. and Power, G.(1997) *Planning for Urban Quality – Urban Design in Towns and Cities*, Routledge, London.

Payne, G.K. (1997) *Urban Land Tenure and Property Rights in Developing Countries: A Review*, Intermediate Technology Publications, London.

Payne, G. (ed.) (1999) *Making Common Ground: Public–Private Partnerships in Land for Housing*, Intermediate Technology Publications, London.

Payne, G.K. (2001) Urban land tenure policy options: titles or rights? *Habitat International*, 25(3): 415–429.

Phillips, S. (2002) Social capital, local networks and community development, in: Rakodi, C. with Lloyd-Jones, T. (eds), *Urban Livelihoods: A People-Centred Approach to Reducing Poverty*, Earthscan, London.

Pichardo, A. and Eslava, J. (1995) *Evaluación intermedia: informe final de la misión de evaluación externa. Proyecto COS/91/003/A/01/56 'Fortalecimiento de la Autogestión Comunitaria en el Desarrollo y Operación de los Asentamientos Humanos'*, Ministry of Housing and Human Settlements/PNUD (UNDP), San José, Costa Rica.

Pimcharoen O. (2001) The plan making system and environmental management in Thailand: the role of EIA in the decision-making process. PhD thesis, University of Liverpool, UK.

Planning Commission (1990) *Guidelines of Industries and Investment or Shanghai Pudong New Area*, Shanghai Municipal Government.

PNA (2000) Pudong New Area, www.pudong.shanghaichina.org/news3.htm (6 August 2000).

Potter, R.B. and Lloyd-Evans, S. (1998) *The City in the Developing World*, Longman, Harlow, UK.

Pugh, C. (1994) The idea of enablement in housing sector development, *Cities*, II(6): 357–371.

Qadeer, M. (1983) *Urban Development in the Third World*, Praeger, New York.

Quesada, J.R. (ed.) (1997) *Costa Rica contemporánea: raíces del Estado de la Nación*, Proyecto Estado de la Nación, San José, Costa Rica.

Rafiie, M. (1997) Urban housing in Iran: future outlook and sustainable development, in: *Egtesade-Maskan*, National Land and Housing Organisation, Tehran, Iran, 23: 2–21.

Rakodi, C. (1991) Developing institutional capacity to meet the needs of the urban poor: experience in Kenya, Tanzania and Zambia, *Cities*, 8(3): 228–243.

Rakodi, C. (1995a) Poverty lines or household strategies? A review of conceptual issues in the study of urban poverty, *Habitat International*, 19(4): 407–426.

Rakodi, C. (1995b) The household strategies of the urban poor: coping with poverty and recession in Gweru, Zimbabwe, *Habitat International*, 19(4): 447–471.

Rakodi, C. (1999a) A capital assets framework for analysing household livelihood strategies, *Development Policy Review*, 17(3): 315–342.

Rakodi, C. (1999b) *Poverty in the Peri-urban Interface*, Research Advances No. 5, Natural Resource Systems Research Programme, Department for International Development, London.

Rakodi, C. with Lloyd-Jones, T. (eds) (2002) *Urban Livelihoods: A People-Centred Approach to Reducing Poverty*, Earthscan, London.

Ramirez, R., Fiori, J., Harms, H. and Mathéy, K. (1992) The commodification of self-help housing and state intervention: household experiences in the *Barrios* of Caracas, in: Mathéy, Kosta (ed.), *Beyond Self-Help Housing*, Mansell Publishing, London/New York, pp. 95–144.

Rapoport, A. (1977) *Human Aspects of Urban Form*, Pergamon Press, Oxford, UK.

Rapoport, A. (1986) Culture and built form: a reconsideration, in: Saile, D.G. (ed.), *Architecture in Cultural Change: Essays in Built Form and Culture Research*, University of Kansas, Lawrence, KS, USA, pp. 157–175.

Redclift, M. and Sage, C. (1994) *Strategies for Sustainable Development – Local Agendas for the Southern Hemisphere*, Wiley, Chichester, UK.

Robins, N. and Kumar, R. (1999) Producing, providing, trading: manufacturing industry and sustainable cities, *Environment and Urbanization*, 11(2): 75–93.

Rogers, A. (1993) *The Earth Summit: A Planetary Reckoning*, Global View Press, Los Angeles.

Rogers, R. (1999) *Towards an Urban Renaissance*, E & FN Spon, London.

Rogers, R. and Gumuchdjian, P. (1997) *Cities for a Small Planet*, Faber & Faber, London.

Rogers, R. and Power, A. (2000) *Cities for a Small Country*, Faber & Faber, London.

Romaya, S.M. (1987) A process for quantifiable evaluation of environmental improvement, *The Environmentalist*, 7(4): 253–258.

Rondinelli, D.A. (1993) *Development Projects as Policy Experiments: An Adaptive Approach to Development Administration*, 2nd edn, Routledge, London.

Rothchild, D. and Lawson, L. (1994) The interactions between state and civil society in Africa: from deadlock to new routines, in: Harbeson, J.W., Rothchild, D. and Chazan, N. (eds), *Civil Society and the State in Africa*, Lynne Rienner, Boulder, CO, USA/London, UK, pp. 255–281.

Ruel, M.T., Haddad, L. and Garrett, J.L. (1999) Some urban facts of life: implications for research and policy, *World Development*, 27(11): 1917–1938.

Russell, S. and Vidler, E. (2000) The rise and fall of government–community partnerships for urban development: grassroots testimony from Colombo, *Environment and Urbanization*, 12(1): 73–86.

Rust, K. and Rubenstein S. (eds) (1996) *A Mandate to Build Johannesburg*, Ravan Press, Johannesburg.

Sadler, B. (1995) *Environmental Impact Assessment: Toward Improved Effectiveness,* Interim report and discussion paper prepared for Canadian Environmental Assessment Agency and International Association for Impact Assessment, Ottawa, Canada.

Sahn, D., Dorosh, P. and Younger, S. (1997) *Structural Adjustment Reconsidered,* Oxford University Press, New York.

Satterthwaite, D. (1997a) Sustainable cities or cities that contribute to sustainable development? *Urban Studies,* 34(10): 1667–1691.

Satterthwaite, D. (1997b) Urban poverty: reconsidering its scale and nature, *IDS Bulletin,* 28(2): 7–23.

Satterthwaite, D. (2001) Reducing urban poverty: constraints on the effectiveness of aid agencies and development banks and some suggestions for change, *Environment and Urbanization,* 13(1): 137–158.

Schilderman, T. (1992) Housing standards: can they be made appropriate?, *Appropriate Technology,* 19(1): 5–7.

SMEPB (1997) *Shanghai Environmental Bulletin,* Shanghai Municipal Environmental Protection Bureau, Shanghai.

Sevald, F.J. (1972) *Pre-Investment Survey for Iran Housing Growth Programme,* Department of Housing and Urban Development, Office of International Affairs, Washington, DC.

Shaw, D. and Kidd, S. (1996) Planning sustainable development: principles and implementation, *Journal of Planning Education and Research,* 15(3): 237–241.

Shetty, R. (1990) The impact of kinship systems on the generation of house-types, *Traditional Dwelling Settlements Review,* I(11): 49–60.

Simon, D., van der Spengen, W., Dixon, C. and Narman, A. (eds) (1995) *Structurally Adjusted Africa: Poverty, Debt and Basic Needs,* Pluto Press, London.

Sirivardana, S. (1999) *Sri Lanka Housing Standards Study, Generated with the Urban Poor in Sri Lanka,* EHSP Case Study 9, ITDG, Rugby.

Smith, H. (1999) *Networks and spaces of negotiation in low-income housing: the case of Costa Rica,* PhD thesis, Edinburgh College of Art/Heriot-Watt University, Edinburgh, UK.

Smith, H. and Valverde, J.M. (2001) When community development becomes a political bargaining tool: the case for structural change in low income housing provision in Costa Rica, in: Carley, M., Jenkins, P. and Smith, H. (eds), *Urban Development and Civil Society: The Role of Communities in Sustainable Cities,* Earthscan, London, pp. 121–138.

Songsore, J. and McGranahan, G. (1998) The political economy of household environmental management: gender, environment and epidemiology in the Greater Accra Metropolitan Area, *World Development,* 26(3): 395–412.

Southworth, M. and Ben-Joseph, E. (1997) *Streets and the Shaping of Towns and Cities,* McGraw-Hill, New York.

Souza, C. (2000) Participatory budgeting in Brazilian cities: limits and possibilities in building democratic institutions, *Environment and Urbanization,* 13(1): 159–184.

Spillane, J.J. (1972) *The Housing Process in Iran,* PhD thesis, New York University, Graduate School of Business Administration, New York.

Sriburi, T. (1995) *EIA in Thailand,* Chulalongkorn University, Bangkok.

Steele, J. (1997) *An Architecture for People: The Complete Works of Hassan Fathy,* Whitney, New York.

Stewart, D.J. (1999) Changing Cairo: the political economy of urban form, *International Journal of Urban and Regional Research,* 23(1): 103–121.

Stewart, F. (1995) *Adjustment and Poverty: Options and Choices,* Routledge, London.

Strassmann, W.P. (1987) Home-based enterprises in cities of developing countries, *Economic Development and Cultural Change,* 36(1): 121–144.

Sun, S. (1994) Some thoughts on the development of Shanghai's Pudong District, *China City Planning Review*, 10(4): 21–25.

SWFTZ3UDC (1995) *SWFTZ No. 3 UDC*, Shanghai Waigaoqiao Free Trade Zone No. 3 United Development Company, Shanghai.

SWFTZXDC (2001) www.pudong-xin.com

Tang, S.-Y., Lo, C.W.-H., Cheung, K.-C. and Lo, J.M.-K. (1997) Institutional constraints on environmental management in urban China: environmental impact assessment in Guangzhou and Shanghai, *China Quarterly*, 152: 863–874.

Taylor, S. (1984) Making bureaucracies think: the environmental impact statement strategy of administrative reform, in: Wood, C. (ed.), *Environmental Impact Assessment: A Comparative Review*, Longman, Harlow, UK.

TDRI (1996) *Environmental Strategy for Thailand*, Thailand Development Research Institute, Bangkok.

Thompson, J. (1997) Participatory approaches in government bureaucracies: facilitating institutional change, in: Blackburn, J. with Holland, J. (eds), *Who Changes? Institutionalizing Participation in Development*, IT Publications, London, pp. 108–119.

Tipple, A.G. (2000) *Extending Themselves: User Initiated Transformations of Government Built Housing in Developing Countries*, Liverpool University Press, Liverpool, UK.

Tomlinson, M. (1998) South Africa's new housing policy: an assessment of the first two years 1994–96, *International Journal of Urban and Regional Research*, 22(1): 137–147.

Tremayne, B. (1996) China's Environmental Problem: An Opportunity, *China Review*, Autumn/Winter: 32–33.

Tsao, K.K. (1996) Institutional and Administrative Reform, in: Yeung, Y.-M. and Sung, Y.-W. (eds), *Shanghai: Transformation and Modernisation under China's Open Policy*, Chinese University Press, Hong Kong, pp. 93–121.

Turkstra, J. and Kagawa, A. (2001) Peru: entitled to be titled, in: Payne, G. (ed.), *Land Rites, Innovative Approaches to Secure Tenure for the Urban Poor*, Case Study 10, Geoffrey Payne Associates, London.

UN (1978) *Non-conventional Financing of Housing for Low-income Households*, United Nations, New York.

UN (1990) *EIA: An Enquiry into Operational Aspects*, United Nations, New York.

UNCED (1993) *Earth Summit Agenda 21, The UN Programme of Action from Rio*, United Nations Commission on Environment and Development, United Nations, New York.

UNCHS (1987) *Global Report on Human Settlements 1986*, United Nations Center for Human Settlements, Nairobi.

UNCHS (1993) *Public–Private Partnerships in Enabling Shelter Strategies*, United Nations Centre for Human Settlements, Nairobi.

UNCHS (1996a) *Global Conference on Access to Land and Security of Tenure as a Condition for Sustainable Shelter and Urban Development*, Preparation Document for Habitat Conference, 17–19 January, 1996, New Delhi. United Nations Centre for Human Settlements.

UNCHS (1996b) *The Habitat Agenda: Goals and Principles, Commitments and Global Plan of Action*, UN Conference on Human Settlements (Habitat II), United Nations Centre for Human Settlements, Nairobi.

UNCHS (1997) *The Istanbul Declaration and The Habitat Agenda*, United Nations Centre for Human Settlements, Nairobi.

UNCHS (2001) *Cities in a Globalizing World*, Earthscan, London.

UNDP (1999) *Human Development Report 1999*, United Nations Development Programme, New York.

UNEP (1999) *Global Environmental Outlook 2000*, United Nations Environment Programme, www.grida.no/geo2000

Universidad de Antioquia (1994) *Encuesta Ambiental Urbana*, Concejo de Medellin, Medellin, Colombia.

Valentin, A. and Spangenberg, J.H. (2000) A guide to community sustainability indicators, *Environmental Impact Assessment Review*, 20: 381–392.

Valverde, J.M. and Trejos, M.E. (1993) *Integración o disolución sociocultural: El nuevo rostro de la política social*, Porvenir, San José, Costa Rica.

Vanderschueren, F., Wegelin, E. and Wekwete, K. (1996) *Policy Programme Options for Urban Poverty Reduction: A Framework for Action at the Municipal Level*, World Bank/UNDP/UNCHS Urban Management Program Policy Paper 20, Washington, DC.

Varley, A. (1985) *Ejido Land Development and Regularisation in Mexico City*. PhD thesis, University College London, UK.

Vidal, F.S. (1955) *The Oasis of Al-Hasa*, Arabian American Oil Company, Dhahran.

Wang, X-R., Zha, P. and Lu, J. (1998) Ecological planning and sustainable development: a case study of an urban development zone in Shanghai, China, *International Journal of Sustainable Developing World Ecology*, 5: 204–216.

Ward, P.M. and Chant, S. (1987) Community Leadership and self-help housing. *Progress in Planning*, 27(2): 69–136.

Watson, V., Spiegal, A. and Wilkinson, P. (1996) Devaluing diversity? National housing policy and African household dynamics in Cape Town, *Urban Forum*, 7(1): 1–32.

WCED (1987) *Our Common Future*, World Commission on Environment and Development/Oxford University Press, Oxford, UK.

Weston, J. (ed.) (1997) *Planning and Environmental Impact Assessment in Practice*, Longman, Harlow, UK.

Wheeler, D. (2000) *Racing To The Bottom? Foreign Investment and Air Quality in Developing Countries*, Development Research Group, World Bank, Washington, DC, www.worldbank.org/nipr/work_paper/RaceWP1.pdf

WHO/UNEP (1992) World Health Organization/UN Environment Programme, www.doc.mmu.ac.uk/aric/factsheets

Wilkinson, P. (1998) Housing policy in South Africa, *Habitat International*, 22(3): 215–229.

Willis, K.G. and Tipple, A.G. (1991) Methods of analysis and policy, in: Tipple, A.G. and Willis, K.G. (eds), *Housing the Poor in the Developing World: Methods of Analysis, Case Studies and Policy*, Routledge, London, pp. 258–261.

Wood, C. (1995) *Environmental Impact Assessment: A Comparative Review*, Longman, Harlow, UK.

World Bank (1974) *Thailand ECAT: Appraisal of the Ban Chao Ner Hydroelectic Dam Project*, Document No. 291-TH, World Bank, Washington, DC.

World Bank (1991) *Urban Policy and Economic Development; An Agenda for the 1990s*, World Bank Policy Paper, World Bank, Washington DC.

World Bank (1993) *Housing: Enabling Markets to Work*, World Bank Policy Paper, World Bank, Washington, DC.

World Bank (1999a) *World Development Report 1999*, World Bank, Washington, DC.

World Bank (1999b) News Release No. 2000/032/S, 15 September 1999, World Bank, Washington, DC, www.worldbank.org/html/extdr/extme/032htm

World Bank (2000a) *Greening Industry: New Roles for Communities, Markets and Governments*, Oxford University Press, New York.

World Bank (2000b) *World Development Report 2000*: Oxford University Press, New York, www.worldbank.org/poverty/wdrpoverty/report/index.htm (accessed October 2001).

World Bank (undated) *The World Bank Participation Sourcebook, Chapter IV: Practice Pointers in Enabling the Poor to Participate, Building Community Capacity*, World Bank, Washington, DC, www.worldbank.org/wbi/sourcebook/sb0403t.htm (accessed November 2001).

Wu, V. (1998) The Pudong Development Zone and China's economic reforms, *Planning Perspectives*, 13: 133–165.

Wu, X.-M. (1996) Case Study of Shanghai, in: Stubbs, J. and Clarke, G. (eds), *Megacity Management in the Asian and Pacific Region: Policy Issues and Innovative Approaches*, 2, *City and Country Case Studies*, Asian Development Bank, Manila, pp. 203–226.

Yahya, S., Agevi, E., Lowe, L., Mugova, A., Musandu-Nyamayaro, O. and Schilderman, T. (2001) *Double Standards, Single Purpose – Reforming Housing Regulations to Reduce Poverty*, ITDG Publishing, London.

Yeang, K. (1984) Notes for a critical vernacular in contemporary Malaysian architecture, *UIA International Architect*, 6: 16–18.

Yeung, Y.-M. and Sung, Y.-W. (eds) (1996) *Shanghai: Transformation and Modernisation Under China's Open Policy*, Chinese University Press, Hong Kong.

Younas, M., Afzal, S., Khan, M., Jaffery, I. and Farooq, M. (1997) Forms of Cd, Pb, Zn and Cr in contaminated soils of Raiwand, Lahore, Pakistan, presented at 8th International Chemistry Conference, University of the Punjab, Lahore, Pakistan, cited by Younas, M., Shahzad, F., Afzal, S., Khan, M. and Ali, K. (1998) Assessment of Cd, Ni, Cu, and Pb pollution in Lahore, Pakistan, *Environment International*, 24(7): 761–766.

Young, C. (1991) In search of civil society, in: Harbeson, J.W., Rothchild, D. and Chazan, N. (eds), *Civil Society and the State in Africa*, Lynne Rienner, Boulder, CO, USA/London, UK, pp. 33–50.

Yousry, M. and Atta, T.A.A. (1997) The challenge of urban growth in Cairo, in: Rakodi, C. (ed.), *The Urban Challenge in Africa: Growth and Management of its Large Cities*, UN University Press, Tokyo, pp. 111–149.

Zandi, M.M. (1985) *Preference for Housing Form in a Low Income District of Tehran, Iran*, PhD thesis, University of Pittsburgh, Pittsburgh, PA, USA.

Zetter, R. (2002) Market enablement or sustainable development: The conflicting paradigms of urbanization, in: Zetter, R. (ed.), *Planning in Cities: Sustainability and Growth in the Developing World*, ITDG Publishing, London.

Zhao, Q.-Z. (ed.) (1993) *Shanghai Pudong New Area Handbook*, Shanghai Far East Publishers, Shanghai.

Zheng, J.-C. (1998) Urban Climate and Atmospheric Environmental Quality, in: Foster, H.D., Lai, D.C.-Y. and Zhou, N.-S. (eds), *The Dragon's Head: Shanghai, China's Emerging Megacity*, Canadian Western Geographical Series No. 34, Western Geographical Press, Victoria, BC, pp. 43–64.

Zheng, S.-L. (2000) Shanghai: building its identity, *Villes en developpement*, 49: 2.

Index